U.S. Trade Policy

U.S.
Trade Policy

History, Theory, and the WTO

William A. Lovett,
Alfred E. Eckes Jr.,
and Richard L. Brinkman

M.E. Sharpe
Armonk, New York
London, England

Copyright © 1999 by M. E. Sharpe, Inc.

Library of Congress Cataloging-in-Publication Data

Lovett, William Anthony.
U.S. trade policy : history, theory, and the WTO / William A. Lovett,
Alfred E. Eckes, Jr., and Richard L. Brinkman.
p. cm.
Includes bibliographical references and index.
ISBN 0-7656-0323-3 (alk. paper). — ISBN 0-7656-0324-1 (pbk : alk. paper)
1. World Trade Organization. 2. United States—Commercial policy.
I. Eckes, Alfred E., 1942— . II. Brinkman, Richard L. III. Title.
HF1455.L66 1998
382′.3′0973—dc21 98-26369
CIP

Printed in the United States of America

The paper used in this publication meets the minimum requirements of
American National Standard for Information Sciences—
Permanence of Paper for Printed Library Materials,
ANSI Z 39.48-1984.

∞

BM (c) 10 9 8 7 6 5 4 3 2 1
BM (p) 10 9 8 7 6 5 4 3 2

Contents

List of Tables and Figures

Preface

U.S. trade and industrial policies must engage the global economy more successfully. Some 10 to 12 million jobs have been lost by a failure to enforce reciprocity. Between 1981 and 1997 U.S. trade deficits totaled $2,000 billion; U.S. current account deficits totaled $1,500 billion. The United States switched from being the world's leading creditor to become its largest debtor. U.S. economic growth and industrial competitiveness suffered. Greater structural unemployment, inequality, and social stress followed. America's middle class feels squeezed and uneasy, worried about jobs, income security, and pensions. The U.S. economy has become unbalanced and more vulnerable to economic shocks, speculative disruptions, devaluation pressures, and dislocations. This neglect cannot continue.

This book represents a post–Cold War reassessment of U.S. trade policy. It reviews U.S. trade history, theory, and the evolution of GATT 1947 into GATT 1994 and the World Trade Organization agreement. In Chapter 1 William Lovett provides an introductory overview. Chapter 2 by Alfred Eckes begins U.S. trade history with the new republic emerging from colonialism. The United States had trouble breaking into foreign markets in an era of mercantilism. Like most countries, including Britain between 1650 and the 1840s, the United States used tariffs and industrial development as a nation-building strategy. U.S. trade policy was very successful between 1791 and the 1920s in building up industrial strength, which created the world's most powerful economy.

In Franklin Roosevelt's New Deal era, the United States switched to a freer trade policy—supposedly emphasizing reciprocity. Then World War II and the Cold War led the United States to aid allies and accept trading relations that were not fully reciprocal. Because the United States was stronger in technology, industry, and finance after World War II, it could afford to tolerate asymmetries and unequal access *(at least for a while)*. But by the 1970s, U.S. industry was beginning to suffer competitiveness problems. These difficulties and trade deficits grew worse in the 1980s-90s.

Richard Brinkman traces the evolution of modern trade theory in Chapters 3 and 4. From the freer trade of Adam Smith, through Ricardian Comparative Advantage to Neo-Classical models (often labeled the "pure theory of international trade"), Brinkman clarifies assumptions and explains the shortcomings of the Heckscher–Ohlin model. In Chapter 4 Brinkman offers a revised, more realistic, and dynamic approach to trade, economic growth, and development. It includes more emphasis on asymmetries, imbalances, and non-reciprocity problems. It argues that Adam Smith's "productivity doctrine" serves better than Ricardo's static comparative advantage as the basis for a theory of dynamic comparative advantage.

Finally, in Chapter 5 William Lovett comes back to problems for U.S. trade policy in the late 1990s–early twenty-first century. Alternative solutions for U.S. trade imbalances are dollar devaluation, industrial renewal, and/or reciprocal trade policy. The 1992 election was a mandate, many believe, for a stronger U.S. policy. Yet no significant change occurred. Instead, a flawed GATT 1994 and WTO agreement was implemented without much debate in the United States. But Americans need to get serious about eliminating external deficits and rejuvenating their industrial network. More extensive trade supervision and industrial promotion efforts are essential. The advantages of greater realism, improved teamwork, and sustainable internationalism are explained. If the United States fails to take responsible, corrective action, Americans face weaker economic growth, continued imbalances, growing vulnerability to economic crises, and a blend of stagnation and decline. And U.S. influence in the world will erode along with a weakening economy.

All three coauthors endorse freer trade and the global marketplace. They argue that U.S. policy must now reemphasize greater trade reciprocity. The United States still has an important role as the world's leading democracy. But European unification, increased prosperity elsewhere, and the spread of modern industry and technology to most of the world mean that the United States cannot dominate the global economy. This is a blessing for Americans, though, because we should now focus more realistically on improving the terms of U.S. engagement with the world economy. Americans are only 4 percent of the world's people. We cannot afford to subsidize or support the whole world. We can, with the collaboration of other friendly nations, improve a global economic regime that helps all nations. Yet in the end, while serious problems for many developing nations should not be ignored, most nations must learn to help themselves. The United States, like other countries, must fix its own social and industrial problems. Only the United States can rejuvenate its own industry, eliminate excessive trade deficits, and restore healthy external account discipline and trade reciprocity. This overall economic renewal is a top priority for America as we enter the twenty-first century.

Recent financial crises and trade imbalances from Mexico (1994–95), Southeast Asia, and South Korea (1997–98) highlight the dangers of neglect. Badly informed capital flows, excessive currency speculation, and unsustainable trading and lending relationships are risky. Surging market forces can make serious mistakes. The Great Depression (1929–38) taught this lesson through two generations of economists. Global market euphoria of the mid to late 1990s, however, suggests that a naïve faith in laissez faire may have revived, at least for some countries.

More realistic trading is needed for the twenty-first century. A global marketplace, with better reciprocity and reliable property–contract rights, promotes wider prosperity. Key international institutions, including the International Monetary Fund, Bank for International Settlements, and the World Bank, can facilitate responsible markets. But there are limits to any multilateral governance. There is no substitute for responsible national government as a provider of sound incentives, healthy education, industrial vitality, infrastructure, and policies to promote full employment and social harmony. This requires self-discipline by each country for its engagement with the global marketplace. Excessive trade imbalances, heavy debt burdens, and speculative capital flows are problems for many countries, and they erode the good order and prosperity of the world economy, too. Thus, a healthier global economy requires reasonable efforts by individual nations to live within their means, avoid excessive budget and external deficits, and correct serious imbalance problems. This can often be done by collaborating with other nations. But ultimately every nation bears the main responsibility for making the best of its own resources, trading opportunities, and industrial development.

U.S. Trade Policy

1

WILLIAM A. LOVETT

Introduction

Britain's Free Trade Experiment

During the nineteenth century, Great Britain moved away from mercantilist practices in a freer trade experiment.[1] This had a great impact on subsequent controversies about trading policy. Although many nations (including the United States, Germany, France, Russia, Japan, Austria, and Italy) used more protectionist policies to catch up with "free trade" Britain, economic thought was focused upon these issues and upon the extent to which tariffs and other encouragements to industries were desirable. But throughout the British free trade experiment Britain's colonies were kept largely secure for British investments, companies, and trading activity. Also, Britain could afford to eliminate tariffs in the 1830s and 40s because it enjoyed a substantial lead in technology, industrial scale economies, maritime predominance, and stronger banking–investment resources. Yet by 1900, when the United States, Germany, and others had caught up with British industries, British manufacturers began to seek Imperial Preference tariffs as a means to greater reciprocity. In the 1920s, as Britain suffered adjustment and competitiveness problems, British trade policy became increasingly controversial. The Safeguarding of Industries Act of 1921 was implemented timidly, but finally in 1932 Britain rejoined the great majority of industrial nations by establishing Imperial Preference tariffs.

Despite unequal trade openness, with tariffs and industrial development policies, economic progress flourished in much of Europe, the United States, and other areas. International investments and loans expanded greatly, opening up new markets. Technological progress was dramatic in most fields, including, in particular, armaments, warships, and even aircraft.

Then World War I disrupted things. Casualties and war costs were heavy. A harsh peace was imposed upon Germany, with unsustainable repa-

---

Tables 1.1 to 1.6 have been placed at the end of this chapter.

rations burdens. The Austro-Hungarian Empire disintegrated, and Russia came under Bolshevik rule. Confidence, trade, and capital flows weakened. Britain's exports, steel, and coal slumped. Although the 1920s brought unbalanced economic recovery, a boom in the United States proved fragile. The stock market crash of 1929 brought a world depression. Many defaults occurred on international loans. Hard times brought militaristic governments to Germany, Japan, Italy, and some smaller countries. World War II followed, with heavy casualties and further dislocations (1939–45).

Bretton Woods, GATT 1947, and Trade Asymmetries

But now the Allied Democracies realized that better postwar arrangements were needed. At the 1944 Bretton Woods Conference, Britain, the United States, and other allies agreed upon more collaboration after the war. This led to the International Monetary Fund (IMF), World Bank, and the General Agreement on Tariffs and Trade (GATT 1947).[2] The United States moved away from its long history of protectionist tariff policies (1791–1934); it began to sponsor more open markets, rather like Britain's efforts toward freer trade between the 1840s and 1931. (Like Britain in most of the nineteenth century, the United States now enjoyed a substantial lead in technology, industrial scale economies, maritime leadership, and stronger banking–investment resources. Like Britain, the U.S. could now afford freer trade.) Accordingly, in eight GATT rounds between 1947 and 1994, the United States led the way toward reductions in tariff levels among the industrial nations (more recently labeled the OECD countries). U.S. multinational corporations (MNCs) felt an increasing stake in world trade, and they provided support for the multilateral trade process.

Unfortunately, Stalin's USSR chose not to collaborate with Western-style economic recovery. Instead, Communist governments were imposed in most of Eastern Europe. A rival COMECON was established for the USSR and satellite countries. A Communist government was set up in North Korea, and the Kuomingtang government of China fell to the Red Chinese under Mao Tse-tung. Communist parties and subversion efforts were encouraged elsewhere. In this way, a Cold War threat of aggression and/or subversion developed against the Western democracies and their allies.

Ironically, in response to this Cold War threat, U.S. policies allowed more generous aid (through the Marshall Plan, military assistance, and help to developing countries) than would have been possible otherwise. Under the slogan "trade not aid" the U.S. political establishment was kind to its allies and trading partners. Less than fully reciprocal trade deals were accepted by the United States, especially with developing nations. For less developed countries (LDCs), it was understood that substantial tariffs and other restrictions would promote industrialization and broader prosperity.

However, GATT 1947 allowed safeguard relief under Article XIX, balance of payments relief under Article XII, and antidumping and countervailing duty for subsidy relief under Article VI.[3] In addition, imports could be limited to maintain national security, or to protect agriculture, product standards, consumer safety, and environmental interests. While GATT signatories accepted an obligation to apply these and other regulatory policies in a non-discriminatory manner, and give national treatment to foreign companies, implementation was left up to each importing country. Trade disputes were to be negotiated among the nations involved, largely by mutual conciliation. GATT dispute resolution panels could be constituted, but their function was essentially advisory and for mediation purposes.

Most nations learned from the Great Depression that Keynesian budget deficit policies would be needed to maintain full employment, at least in slumps or recessions.[4] Unemployment compensation, education, and social security measures were popular after World War II in the countries with moderate social democratic governments. Farm price support/subsidy measures were well established, too. Industrial growth and export expansion was desired, but few wanted much import disruption or job losses. Trade unions were more powerful among most industrial countries, so that GATT safeguard, offset, subsidy, or voluntary import restraint measures were used to limit disruptive imports.

Another lesson from the Great Depression and early post-World War II years was the need for balance-of-payments discipline, so as to avoid large and chronic external deficits.[5] Most countries were forced, sooner or later, to live within their means and maintain current account discipline. Countries that failed to discipline themselves suffered recurrent devaluations or became dependent upon foreign aid or loans. Accordingly, GATT safeguard and offset measures, exchange controls (for most NICs [new industrial countries] and LDCs), and/or other industrial–trade policies that encouraged "living within means" became important instruments of macroeconomic policy for the majority of nations.

Dollar Hegemony, Indiscipline, and Euro Challenges

One big exception to this macroeconomic self-discipline, at least since the early 1980s, was the United States.[6] Large U.S. budget deficits became entrenched in the 1980s, caused by political gridlock and a lack of consensus over tax loads and spending. Tighter U.S. monetary policy was used to offset bigger U.S. budget deficits, which meant higher U.S. interest rates.

This attracted heavy borrowing from abroad, and for a while the U.S. dollar became substantially overvalued. By the mid-1980s, the United States had become a net debtor country (for the first time since World War I). By the end of 1997 net U.S. external debt reached at least –$1,250 billion (the biggest debt in the world).[7] Nevertheless, sustained, heavy foreign capital inflows allowed U.S. imports to expand, while U.S. exports slowed (Tables 1.1 and 1.2). Between 1981 and 1997 U.S. merchandise trade deficits totaled $2,000 billion or more, while U.S. current account deficits totaled at least $1,500 billion. (In the period from 1981 to 1997 the U.S. gross federal debt ballooned from $1,000 billion to $5,700 billion, with annual federal debt service burdens increasing from $65 billion to $250 billion (Table 1.3). By 1997, the annual federal debt service for the United States approached its defense spending.) Sadly, in the 1980s the United States lost both its fiscal discipline and balance of payments or external accounts discipline. Large U.S. budget, trade, and current account deficits became entrenched. Increasingly, economists saw this predicament as the "twin deficits problem."

Why was the United States allowed more slack in recent years for excessive budget, trade, and current account deficits? Basically, because the U.S. dollar continued to serve as the primary reserve currency. U.S. capital markets were bigger, wider, more stable and reliable. No other currency (the Japanese yen, the Swiss franc, the British pound, nor the German mark) could offer comparable opportunities as a medium-term, large-scale "parking place," or store of value, than the U.S. dollar, U.S. government securities, and/or U.S. corporate stocks or bonds. Japanese, Swiss, British, and German capital markets simply were not big enough or sufficiently reliable to accommodate large inflows *(and outflows)* of foreign capital. Nor were emerging markets big enough or sufficiently reliable to place large amounts of foreign capital for liquidity or longer-term secure investments.

Only the new European Monetary Union (EMU) and the "euro" offered a possible challenge to the U.S. dollar and its capital markets as a reserve currency and as a major store of value.[8] In the spring of 1998, prospects for the euro and EMS remained uncertain, because of difficulties faced by many countries in Europe in reducing budget deficits, social insurance, and chronic unemployment. Potentially, the EMS and the euro could offer an equal challenge to the United States and the dollar as a currency area and a capital market. However, it might take several years or more for all this to be worked out. In the meantime, the U.S. and the dollar continue to "enjoy" the mixed blessings and "privileges" of primary reserve currency, the "profits" of seigneurage for its investment bankers and financial markets, and a generous "tolerance" for excessive, large-scale U.S. budget, trade, and current account deficits.

But U.S. interest rates were forced up somewhat, and often exceeded Swiss, German, or Japanese rates. Thus, global tolerance for the lack of U.S. self-discipline reflected not only the advantages of the U.S. capital market. Foreign asset holders were compensated for the depreciation risks of holding dollar-denominated assets. And the dollar declined in value substantially over the last twenty-five years, in a saw-tooth pattern, as European and Asian economies increasingly caught up with the United States and its industrial production (Tables 1.3 and 1.4).

MNCs, Integration Economies, and Sharing Benefits

Another big development, although gradual, over the past 15 to 25 years has been the ascendancy of multinational corporations (MNCs) and financial institutions in the global marketplace. U.S. companies led the way in this trend. Marketing outlets, assembly plants, processing centers, basic manufacturing, research and development, financial accounting, and other operations were located for optimal convenience in various countries. Of course, national economic development, industrial, and export promotion policies tried to foster (at least for many OECD and most developing countries) the relocation of plants, operations, and headquarters in their own territories. In this way, countries sought to promote their own employment, economic growth, and national interests.

Interestingly, the U.S. government's policies (especially since the 1980s), have been more generous to MNCs (regardless of national origin) than the policies of most other countries. Why this asymmetry? The explanation is partly ideological. U.S. free market thinking (in both the Republican and Democratic parties) was more inclined to see global markets as "good for us," or at least favorable to U.S. MNC interests. U.S. political processes, lobbying influence, and financial capitalism (at least for the last 15 to 20 years) were more MNC-dominated and less constrained by national policies, labor union pressures, or other concerns than in many nations. Accordingly, U.S. policy favored MNC interests (regardless of national origin), and did not really try to maintain a "fair share" for U.S. MNCs as opposed to companies from foreign nations.

An important consequence of this one-sided "laissez faire" treatment of MNCs by U.S. policy is that the American share of recent economic growth has been less substantial since the mid-1970s (Table 1.5). By contrast, if U.S. trade policy had been tougher and more reciprocity oriented, U.S. MNCs and national growth could have retained a larger share of global markets.

Because of trade asymmetries and lack of U.S. concern for reciprocity for American companies, industries, and workers, U.S. per capita income grew less rapidly than the per capita income in many other countries (Table 1.5). Real wages (adjusted for inflation) stagnated in the United States since 1973, with families able to keep up only by putting women more fully to work (Table 1.6). Single-earner families lost ground in the United States, and the poor and low-middle class were hit hard. By the mid-1990s a number of countries had forged ahead of the United States in terms of their per capita incomes. Many Western European countries caught up to U.S. living standards. Singapore, Taiwan, South Korea, and Southeast Asian countries were moving up fast, while China and India enjoyed rapid growth since the late 1970s.

Strictly speaking, it is good for more countries to enjoy prosperity. But U.S. industrial–trade policies need not concede more than Japanese, European, or other NIC trade policies. A growing majority of Americans came to believe in the mid- to late 1990s that U.S. policy could have enforced more effective reciprocity in its trading relationships. U.S. tolerance of entrenched trade deficits and asymmetries (see Table 1.2) was simply weak policy. This does not mean, of course, that growing world trade was wrong. No—*fairly shared, mutual* growth in the benefits from global economic integration, expanding trade, and increased productivity is desirable for most countries.

GATT 1994 and the World Trade Organization

In the early 1980s, the United States suggested a broader GATT round to include services and agriculture, and to open more NIC and LDC markets. But few other countries supported another trade negotiation at that stage. Yet when the LDC debt overload–debt rescheduling crisis threatened insolvency for leading international banks (from 1982 to 1985), and protectionist interests gained ground in many countries, a consensus developed for a broad Uruguay GATT Round trade negotiation effort. Initial U.S. goals were ambitious; they included greatly reduced subsidies, more open markets in agriculture, access to developing countries, stronger intellectual property and investment protection, and hopefully, stronger remedies for unfair trade practices. Many Americans felt a more level playing field was essential. From the standpoint of MNC interests, however, the goals of the Uruguay Round negotiation (1985 to 1993) were defensive, that is, to "save" the global trading system from breakdown. The Great Depression's financial collapse and reductions in trade in the early to mid-1930s were recalled as warnings. Meanwhile, Gorbachev's reform efforts for the USSR—*perestroika* (restructuring) and *glasnost* (openness)—could revitalize economic competition from the Russians. But most developing countries resisted any significant market opening, while the European Union (EU) resisted any great liberalization for agriculture. Soon it became apparent that "progress" for the Uruguay Round would be slow and difficult, and that U.S. hopes for major changes in the world trading system were probably unrealistic.

The mid- to late 1980s were controversial for U.S. trade policy.[9] Democrats and some Republicans in Congress pushed for greater use of U.S. trade law remedies (e.g., countervailing duties for subsidies, antidumping remedies, and stronger Section 301 unfair trade practice enforcement efforts) to level the playing field. An Omnibus Trade Act was proposed between 1984 and 1988 for these purposes, but was greatly weakened; it was finally enacted in 1988 with a "Super 301" provision that mainly amounted to a reporting requirement for foreign trade barriers. Unfortunately, the U.S. Trade Representative (USTR) made a crucial concession at the outset of the Uruguay Round in pledging the United States to a "standstill" in use of trade restrictions. From the MNCs' viewpoint, this pledge was important for their interests in allowing MNCs to rely on existing openness to major U.S., and to a lesser extent, European, markets, so that more plants could be relocated to lower-wage countries. But from the standpoint of trade asymmetries and efforts to level the playing field, this was a blunder. U.S. negotiating leverage to open markets, equalize tariffs downward, and eliminate foreign restrictions would have been substantially greater without the "standstill" concession.

In the late 1980s, Mexico made a historic shift toward greater trade openness—realizing that excessive subsidies, restrictions, and protectionism had become counterproductive. Thus, Mexico proposed to expand the recent U.S.–Canada Free Trade Area (negotiated from 1985 to 1988) into a North American Free Trade Agreement (NAFTA). The Bush administration welcomed NAFTA and mainly sought to protect U.S. investment and MNC interests. U.S. labor and environmental interests opposed NAFTA, fearing more relocation of manufacturing jobs and lowered levels of environmental protection. Meanwhile, the Gorbachev reform efforts in the USSR worked out badly for the Communists. Pressures for a free press and for democracy boiled up quickly, but Russian restructuring efforts were timid, inadequate, and only made the economy weaker. Between 1989 and 1991 communism collapsed as a political system in the USSR and Eastern Europe. But China's economy-oriented liberalization gained momentum, unleashing expanded production, and attracting foreign investment that accelerated China's success. Finally, the European Community moved to deepen integration with its Single Europe Act, Maastricht Treaty, and efforts toward a

European Monetary Union (EMU) and common currency (later named the "euro"). All these developments created greater world confidence in freer markets in many developing countries. By the early 1990s an investment boom (from the United States, Europe, Japan, and elsewhere) began to shift more capital into "emerging markets"—broadly speaking, many NICs and LDCs.

Between 1991 and 1993, final negotiations for the Uruguay GATT Round were completed. Results were controversial.[10] Tariffs were already low among most OECD nations, but NICs and LDCs only lowered tariffs modestly (from levels previously averaging 30–50 percent down to 20–35 percent). Thus, manufacturing markets in developing countries remained substantially protected. Meanwhile, safeguard, antisubsidy, and antidumping remedies for the United States were made more difficult to use. Agreements on services (GATS) and intellectual property (TRIPs) were reached, but remained largely aspirational. Reservations were used by most developing countries to limit market opening in services. MNC lobbies, however, were pleased overall, because U.S. and European markets became more securely open, and a trend toward greater investment opportunities in many NICs and LDCs seemed to be under way. But labor and environmental interests, especially in the United States, were greatly disappointed. More jobs would move now to low-wage countries, and the playing field had not been leveled. Structural asymmetries, leading to chronic U.S. trade and current account deficits, were, in fact, entrenched by the GATT 1994 (Uruguay Round) agreement.

An important element of the final Uruguay GATT Round deal was the new World Trade Organization Agreement (WTO).[11] This expanded the GATT's secretariat into a continuing multilateral agency. The most controversial features, from the U.S. viewpoint, were voting arrangements and the dispute resolution process. Voting for most purposes in the WTO is by majority, with one country/one vote (like the United Nations General Assembly). Accession of new members (China, Cuba, or Russia) or Amendments merely requires a two-thirds majority, while Interpretations require a three-fourths majority. But the EU gets 15 votes directly, with another 10 to 15 candidates for EU membership, and sixty Lomé Convention states (mostly former European colonies) likely to vote with Europe for many purposes. From another perspective, developing countries have about three-fourths of the votes in the WTO. In dramatic contrast, the International Monetary Fund (IMF) has weighted voting—according to financial quotas and economic strength. Super majority requirements are higher (85 percent) for key issues, with the United States having 17 percent of the quotas, that is, a blocking vote power.

In addition, WTO dispute resolution panels come close to mandatory arbitration. Thus, if the U.S. invokes Section 301 unfair trade practice proceedings (the strongest weapon in U.S. trade law), countries that feel disfavored can challenge this process and convene a WTO dispute settlement panel. Panel decisions upheld by the WTO's Appellate Body (a seven-member court) cannot be overturned except by consensus (a *unanimous* vote by *all* WTO members). Ordinarily, any country or group of countries that wins a decision adverse to the U.S. would not support its overturn. Thus, *negative consensus* makes it almost impossible to overturn adverse WTO panel decisions.

Goals for U.S. Trade Policy

U.S. trade policy for the twenty-first century should promote the overall interests of Americans in the global economy. Fortunately, the U.S. no longer needs to "subsidize" economic development abroad with one-sided trade concessions. The Communist challenge ended in collapse and transformation to market-oriented economies, with more mutual tolerance and respect among most nations. Now most countries accept the logic of market-oriented, decentralized enterprise, and self-sustaining development. The United States, along with other OECD nations, should be reasonably kind to a larger number of poor, unstable countries that have not yet established strong, fully secure governments and institutions. Some multilateral aid, IMF support, foreign investment, and export opportunities need to be extended to these troubled countries. But the post–World War II experience demonstrates, with many economic success stories in Europe, Asia, and Latin America, that self-sustaining, healthy development and progress require sound and responsible governments in each country. Foreign aid, investment, and export opportunities can build upon and reinforce domestic progress, but they cannot substitute for a basic lack of security and respect for property, or inadequate incentives provided by local governments.

Accordingly, U.S. trade and external policies must engage the global economy more successfully. By not enforcing sufficient reciprocity in trade relations, the United States "gave up" some of its industrial markets, technology base, and growth potential. We estimate that 10 to 12 million U.S. jobs were lost by a failure to enforce trade reciprocity.[12] By not enforcing reciprocity, the United States lost economic growth. With stronger U.S. trade policies, especially since the 1980s, the United States would have enjoyed fuller employment, less social stress, and more cohesion. While some interests did all right (especially the MNCs), overall U.S. prosperity would have been greater if its industrial–trade interests had not been neglected.

Now the time has come to correct this accumulated neglect of U.S. industrial–trade interests. Between 1981 and 1997 U.S. trade deficits totaled $2,000 billion; U.S. current account (or net balance of payments) deficits totaled $1,500 billion. The United States switched from being the world's leading creditor to become its largest debtor. The United States gave up a strong lead in many areas of manufacturing. U.S. industrial competitiveness declined; this neglect cannot continue.

Consequently, U.S. policy should focus upon restoring its own good health, broader prosperity, and full employment.[13] Gradually Americans have come to understand that their excessive budget deficits have to be disciplined, and both political parties are moving in that direction. But U.S. trade, current account, and external deficits must be eliminated also. This requires four changes: (1) U.S. trade/investment flows need more careful supervision; (2) the U.S. must enforce more effective reciprocity in trading relationships; (3) unconditional most-favored nation (MFN) status needs to be replaced by "conditional" MFN for those countries not allowing comparable trade openness or those countries well out of reasonable balance in longer term trade flows; (4) U.S. industries need substantial renewal, with more efforts devoted to offsetting foreign trade restrictions, subsidies, and marginal cost discounting activity. How to achieve these objectives raises many important and interesting technical issues.

Tables 1.1–1.6

Table 1.1A   U.S. GNP, Debt, and External Accounts 1961–1998 (in billions of $U.S.)

Year	GNP	Gross Fed'l Debt	Merchand. Imports [1]	Merchand. Exports [2]	Merch. Trade Balance	Current Acc't Bal. [3]	U.S. Gov't Pub. Merch. Trade Bal. [4]	U.S. Gov't Pub. Current Acc't Bal. [5]
1961	520.1	292.6	14.8	20.2	5.5	3.8	5.5	3.8
1962	560.3	302.9	16.5	21.0	4.5	3.4	4.5	3.4
1963	590.5	310.3	17.2	22.5	5.3	4.4	5.3	4.4
1964	632.4	316.1	18.7	25.8	7.1	6.8	7.1	6.8
1965	684.9	322.3	21.4	26.7	5.3	5.4	5.3	5.4
1966	749.9	328.5	25.6	29.5	3.9	3.0	3.9	3.0
1967	793.9	340.4	28.7	30.0	1.3	-0.3	4.1	2.6
1968	865.0	368.7	35.3	34.1	-1.3	-1.5	0.8	0.6
1969	930.3	365.8	38.2	37.3	-0.9	-1.8	1.3	0.4
1970	977.1	380.9	42.4	42.7	0.2	-0.1	2.7	2.3
1971	1,054.9	408.2	48.3	43.5	-4.8	-4.2	-2.0	-1.4
1972	1,158.0	435.9	58.9	49.2	-9.7	-9.8	-5.7	-5.8
1973	1,294.9	466.3	73.6	71.9	-1.7	3.1	2.4	7.1
1974	1,397.4	483.9	110.9	99.4	-11.5	-5.6	-3.9	2.0
1975	1,528.8	541.9	105.9	108.9	3.0	11.5	9.6	18.1
1976	1,700.1	629.0	132.5	116.8	-15.7	-3.6	-7.8	4.3
1977	1,887.2	706.4	160.4	123.2	-37.2	-23.1	-28.4	-14.3
1978	2,156.1	776.6	186.0	145.8	-40.2	-25.1	-30.2	-15.1
1979	2,413.9	829.5	222.2	186.4	-35.8	-12.2	-23.9	-0.3
1980	2,626.1	909.1	257.0	225.7	-31.3	-9.2	-19.7	2.3
1981	2,957.8	994.8	273.4	238.7	-34.7	-7.3	-22.3	5.0
1982	3,069.3	1,137.3	254.9	216.4	-38.4	-22.4	-27.5	-11.4
1983	3,304.8	1,371.7	269.9	205.6	-64.2	-54.0	-54.2	-44.0

Table 1.1A *(continued)*

1984	3,772.2	1,564.7	346.4	224.0	-122.4	-114.6	-106.7	-98.9
1985	4,010.3	1,817.5	352.5	218.8	-133.6	-139.9	-117.7	-124.0
1986	4,235.0	2,120.6	382.3	227.2	-155.1	-170.0	-138.3	-153.2
1987	4,545.6	2,346.1	424.4	254.1	-170.3	-186.3	-152.1	-168.1
1988	5,062.6	2,601.3	460.2	321.8	-138.4	-148.1	-118.5	-128.2
1989	5,452.8	2,868.0	487.6	363.8	-123.7	-118.6	-109.4	-104.2
1990	5,764.9	3,026.6	512.5	393.6	-119.0	-109.1	-101.7	-91.9
1991	5,932.4	3,598.5	504.4	421.7	-82.6	-14.2	-74.1	-5.7
1992	6,255.5	4,002.1	546.0	448.2	-97.8	-58.1	-96.1	-56.4
1993	6,576.8	4,351.4	597.4	465.1	-132.3	-90.5	-132.6	-90.8
1994	6,955.2	4,643.7	689.2	512.6	-176.6	-143.9	-166.2	-133.5
1995	7,270.6	4,920.9	770.9	582.1	-188.8	-144.3	-173.6	-129.1
1996	7,637.7	5,181.9	817.8	622.8	-195.0	-152.0	-191.2	-148.2
1997	8,060.10	5,369.70	898.3	687.6	-210.7	-178.1	-199.0	-166.4
1998	----	5,543.6 (e)	----	----	----	----	----	----

Source: U.S. Dept. of Commerce, Econ. & Stat. Admin., Bur. of Econ. Analysis, *National Accounts Data* (Dec. 9, 1997). <http://www.fedstats.gov/index20.html>; Bur. of Econ. Analysis, *Survey of Current Business*, July 1997; Bur. of Econ. Analysis, U.S. Council of Economic Advisors, *Economic Indicators*, various issues 1965–1998; *Economic Report of the President*, 1982, 1984, 1986, 1993, 1996, 1997, and 1998.

[1]Merchandise imports are based on CIF (cost-insurance-freight) values. However, CIF figures are not available for 1961–1966: those imports are based on Customs values. CIF figures for 1967–1998 are based on estimates.

[2]Exports are based on FAS (free-along-side) value.

[3]Current account balance reflects the net balance on merchandise trade, services trade, investment income, and other unilateral transfers. However, the years 1961–1964 show only the results of merchandise imports, exports, services, and income from investments.

[4]The U.S. Government publishes its merchandise trade figures using Customs values for imports and FAS values for exports.

[5]The discrepancy between the estimated and U.S. government published current account balances is due to the difference in the merchandise trade balance arising from valuing imports using CIF values versus valuing imports using Customs values.

Table 1.1B   Composition of U.S. Current Accounts, 1980–1997
1980–1984

Year	1980	1981	1982	1983	1984
Merchandise Trade Balance [a]	-31.3	-34.7	-38.4	-64.2	-122.4
Services Trade Balance					
~Imports	-41.5	-45.5	-51.7	-55.0	-67.7
~Exports	47.6	57.4	64.1	64.3	71.2
Net Services Trade Balance	6.1	11.9	12.3	9.3	3.4
Investment Income Balance					
~ Income Receipts on U.S. Assets Abroad					
* Direct Investment Receipts	37.1	32.5	23.9	27.0	31.3
* Other Private Receipts	32.9	50.3	58.2	53.4	68.3
* U.S. Government Receipts	2.6	3.7	4.1	4.8	5.2
~ Income Payments on Foreign Assets in U.S.					
* Direct Investment Payments	-8.6	-6.9	-1.9	-4.2	-8.7
* Other Private Payments	-21.2	-29.4	-35.2	-30.5	-44.2
* U.S. Government Payments	-12.7	-17.3	-19.3	-19.0	-21.2
Net Investment Income Balance	30.1	32.9	29.8	31.5	30.7
Net Unilateral Transfers	-8.3	-11.7	-17.1	-17.7	-20.6
Current Account Balance	-3.4	-1.6	-13.4	-41.1	-108.8

Table 1.1B *(continued)*
1985–1989

Year	1985	1986	1987	1988	1989
Merchandise Trade Balance [a]	-133.6	-155.1	-170.3	-138.4	-123.7
Services Trade Balance					
~Imports	-72.9	-81.8	-92.3	-100.0	-104.2
~Exports	73.2	86.3	98.6	111.0	127.1
Net Services Trade Balance	0.3	4.5	6.2	11.1	23.0
Investment Income Balance					
~ Income Receipts on U.S. Assets Abroad					
* Direct Investment Receipts	30.5	32.0	39.6	52.1	55.4
* Other Private Receipts	57.6	52.8	55.6	70.6	92.6
* U.S. Government Receipts	5.5	6.4	5.3	6.7	5.7
~ Income Payments on Foreign Assets in U.S.					
* Direct Investment Payments	-7.2	-7.1	-7.4	-11.7	-6.5
* Other Private Payments	-42.7	-47.4	-57.7	-72.3	-93.8
* U.S. Government Payments	-23.1	-24.6	-26.2	-31.7	-38.4
Net Investment Income Balance	20.6	12.1	9.2	13.6	15.0
Net Unilateral Transfers	-22.7	-24.7	-23.9	-26.0	-27.0
Current Account Balance	-135.5	-163.2	-178.8	-139.7	-112.7

Table 1.1B *(continued)*
1990–1993

Year	1990	1991	1992	1993
Merchandise Trade Balance [a]	-119.0	-82.6	-97.9	-132.3
Services Trade Balance				
~Imports	-120.0	-121.2	-120.3	-126.4
~Exports	147.8	164.2	177.2	186.7
Net Services Trade Balance	27.8	43.0	56.9	60.3
Investment Income Balance				
~ Income Receipts on U.S. Assets Abroad				
* Direct Investment Receipts	58.7	52.2	51.9	61.2
* Other Private Receipts	94.1	81.2	66.8	63.5
* U.S. Government Receipts	10.5	8.0	7.1	5.1
~ Income Payments on Foreign Assets in U.S.				
* Direct Investment Payments	-2.9	3.4	-0.3	-5.6
* Other Private Payments	-95.5	-83.1	-67.1	-63.0
* U.S. Government Payments	-41.0	-41.5	-40.5	-41.6
Net Investment Income Balance	23.9	20.2	18.0	19.7
Net Unilateral Transfers	-34.6	5.1	-35.2	-38.1
Current Account Balance	-101.8	-14.2	-58.1	-90.5

Table 1.1B *(continued)*
1994–1997

Year	1994	1995	1996	1997
Merchandise Trade Balance [a]	-176.6	-188.8	-195.0	-210.7
Services Trade Balance				
~Imports	-135.5	-147.0	-156.6	-167.9
~Exports	197.2	218.7	236.8	253.2
Net Services Trade Balance	61.8	71.7	80.1	85.3
Investment Income Balance				
~ Income Receipts on U.S. Assets Abroad				
* Direct Investment Receipts	70.9	90.3	98.9	109.2
* Other Private Receipts	79.5	101.8	102.9	123.3
* U.S. Government Receipts	4.1	4.7	4.6	3.5
~ Income Payments on Foreign Assets in U.S.				
* Direct Investment Payments	-20.2	-30.3	-32.1	-41.5
* Other Private Payments	-77.6	-98.4	-100.1	-117.7
* U.S. Government Payments	-47.0	-61.3	-71.3	-91.1
Net Investment Income Balance	9.7	6.8	2.8	-14.3
Net Unilateral Transfers	-38.8	-34.0	-40.0	-38.5
Current Account Balance	-143.9	-144.4	-152.0	-178.1

Source: Table 1, "U.S. International Transactions,"*Survey of Current Business* (July 1997 and March 1998).

[a]Imports based on CIF value; exports based on FAS value. See Table 1.2 for detailed presentation.

Table 1.2 U.S. Merchandise Trade Balances, 1980–1997 (in Billions of $U.S.)
(Imports based on CIF value, exports based on FAS value)
1980–1982

	1980				1981				1982			
	Imports	Exports	Balance	Ratio	Imports	Exports	Balance	Ratio	Imports	Exports	Balance	Ratio
World	256.984	225.722	-31.26	1.14	273.352	238.686	-34.67	1.15	254.884	216.442	-38.44	1.18
North America												
~ Canada	41.995	40.331	-1.66	1.04	46.827	44.602	-2.23	1.05	46.792	37.887	-8.91	1.24
~ Mexico	12.774	15.145	2.37	0.84	14.013	17.789	3.78	0.79	15.770	11.817	-3.95	1.33
Europe												
~ Western Europe - Non-E.U. [a]	9.067	8.819	-0.25	1.03	8.799	8.532	-0.27	1.03	8.393	7.826	-0.57	1.07
Norway	2.734	0.843	-1.89	3.24	2.559	0.892	-1.67	2.87	2.047	0.950	-1.10	2.15
Switzerland	2.851	3.781	0.93	0.75	2.504	3.022	0.52	0.83	2.394	2.707	0.31	0.88
Turkey	0.187	0.540	0.35	0.35	0.276	0.789	0.51	0.35	0.290	0.868	0.58	0.33
~ Western Europe - E.U. [b]	39.941	58.855	18.91	0.68	45.582	57.011	11.43	0.80	46.414	52.361	5.95	0.89
Austria	0.407	0.448	0.04	0.91	0.400	0.484	0.08	0.83	0.515	0.371	-0.14	1.39
Denmark	0.767	0.863	0.10	0.89	0.898	0.887	-0.01	1.01	0.956	0.732	-0.22	1.31
Finland	0.480	0.505	0.03	0.95	0.565	0.613	0.05	0.92	0.447	0.489	0.04	0.91
France	5.532	7.485	1.95	0.74	6.139	7.341	1.20	0.84	5.815	7.110	1.30	0.82
Germany	12.370	10.960	-1.41	1.13	11.918	10.277	-1.64	1.16	12.503	9.291	-3.21	1.35
Greece	0.320	0.922	0.60	0.35	0.383	0.676	0.29	0.57	0.260	0.721	0.46	0.36
Ireland	0.433	0.836	0.40	0.52	0.522	1.025	0.50	0.51	0.582	0.983	0.40	0.59
Italy	4.676	5.511	0.84	0.85	5.549	5.360	-0.19	1.04	5.656	4.616	-1.04	1.23
Netherlands	2.041	8.669	6.63	0.24	2.520	8.595	6.08	0.29	2.652	8.604	5.95	0.31
Portugal	0.283	0.914	0.63	0.31	0.264	1.084	0.82	0.24	0.308	0.840	0.53	0.37
Spain	1.329	3.340	2.01	0.40	1.665	3.563	1.90	0.47	1.639	3.590	1.95	0.46
Sweden	1.705	1.767	0.06	0.96	1.799	1.842	0.04	0.98	2.092	1.689	-0.40	1.24
United Kingdom	10.184	12.694	2.51	0.80	13.315	12.439	-0.88	1.07	13.541	10.645	-2.90	1.27

Table 1.2 (continued), 1980–1982

~ Eastern Europe[c]	1.562	3.861	2.30	0.40	1.697	4.246	2.55	0.40	1.162	3.610	2.45	0.32
Czechoslovakia (former)[d]	0.072	0.185	0.11	0.39	0.073	0.083	0.01	0.88	0.068	0.084	0.02	0.81
USSR (former)[e]	0.485	1.513	1.03	0.32	0.377	2.340	1.96	0.16	0.247	2.593	2.35	0.10
Russia	n/a	n/a	n/a	n/a	n/a	n/a	n/a	n/a	n/a	n/a	n/a	n/a
Central America[f]	2.431	2.709	0.28	0.90	2.100	2.686	0.59	0.78	1.970	2.308	0.34	0.85
Costa Rica	0.405	0.498	0.09	0.81	0.426	0.373	-0.05	1.14	0.421	0.330	-0.09	1.28
El Salvador	0.444	0.272	-0.17	1.63	0.270	0.308	0.04	0.88	0.333	0.292	-0.04	1.14
Guatemala	0.465	0.553	0.09	0.84	0.384	0.559	0.18	0.69	0.364	0.390	0.03	0.93
Honduras	0.475	0.379	-0.10	1.25	0.493	0.349	-0.14	1.41	0.426	0.275	-0.15	1.55
Nicaragua	0.226	0.250	0.02	0.90	0.152	0.184	0.03	0.83	0.098	0.118	0.02	0.83
Panama	0.353	0.699	0.35	0.51	0.329	0.844	0.52	0.39	0.289	0.839	0.55	0.34
South America[g]	14.982	17.131	2.15	0.87	16.210	17.471	1.26	0.93	15.230	15.063	-0.17	1.01
Argentina	0.792	2.625	1.83	0.30	1.215	2.192	0.98	0.55	1.222	1.294	0.07	0.94
Bolivia	0.189	0.172	-0.02	1.10	0.184	0.189	0.01	0.97	0.113	0.099	-0.01	1.14
Brazil	4.000	4.344	0.34	0.92	4.852	3.798	-1.05	1.28	4.643	3.423	-1.22	1.36
Chile	0.559	1.354	0.80	0.41	0.661	1.465	0.80	0.45	0.729	0.925	0.20	0.79
Colombia	1.326	1.736	0.41	0.76	0.900	1.771	0.87	0.51	0.883	1.903	1.02	0.46
Ecuador	0.938	0.864	-0.07	1.09	1.104	0.854	-0.25	1.29	1.227	0.828	-0.40	1.48
Paraguay	0.085	0.109	0.02	0.78	0.052	0.108	0.06	0.48	0.041	0.078	0.04	0.53
Venezuela	5.547	4.573	-0.97	1.21	5.800	5.445	-0.36	1.07	4.957	5.206	0.25	0.95

Footnotes and sources located at end of table.

Table 1.2 (continued), 1980–1982

	1980				1981				1982			
	Imports	Exports	Balance	Ratio	Imports	Exports	Balance	Ratio	Imports	Exports	Balance	Ratio
Other W. Hemisphere												
~ Caribbean Basin [h]	10.905	6.223	-4.68	1.75	10.496	6.605	-3.89	1.59	8.531	6.477	-2.05	1.32
Bahamas	1.433	0.396	-1.04	3.62	1.306	0.441	-0.87	2.96	1.086	0.590	-0.50	1.84
Dominican Republic	0.827	0.795	-0.03	1.04	0.977	0.772	-0.21	1.27	0.669	0.664	-0.01	1.01
Jamaica	0.418	0.305	-0.11	1.37	0.399	0.479	0.08	0.83	0.323	0.468	0.15	0.69
Netherland Antilles	2.680	0.448	-2.23	5.98	2.715	0.499	-2.22	5.44	2.186	0.660	-1.53	3.31
Trinidad & Tobago	2.449	0.680	-1.77	3.60	2.269	0.688	-1.58	3.30	1.667	0.894	-0.77	1.86
Asia [i]	65.926	48.270	-17.66	1.37	78.218	48.884	-29.33	1.60	78.047	48.872	-29.18	1.60
China	1.161	3.755	2.59	0.31	2.062	3.603	1.54	0.57	2.502	2.912	0.41	0.86
Japan	32.961	20.790	-12.17	1.59	39.904	21.823	-18.08	1.83	39.932	20.966	-18.97	1.90
~ E. Asia NICs [j]	18.804	14.741	-4.06	1.28	22.057	15.059	-7.00	1.46	23.767	15.563	-8.20	1.53
Hong Kong	5.026	2.686	-2.34	1.87	5.757	2.635	-3.12	2.18	5.895	2.453	-3.44	2.40
South Korea	4.432	4.685	0.25	0.95	5.474	5.116	-0.36	1.07	6.011	5.529	-0.48	1.09
Singapore	1.984	3.033	1.05	0.65	2.195	3.003	0.81	0.73	2.274	3.214	0.94	0.71
Taiwan	7.362	4.337	-3.03	1.70	8.631	4.305	-4.33	2.00	9.587	4.367	-5.22	2.20
~ Other Asia [k]	13.000	8.984	-4.02	1.45	14.195	8.399	-5.80	1.69	11.846	9.431	-2.42	1.26
Burma	0.009	0.029	0.020	0.310	0.016	0.034	0.018	0.471	0.018	0.034	0.016	0.529
Cambodia	0.000	0.026	0.026	0.000	0.001	0.011	0.010	0.091	0.000	0.002	0.002	0.000
India	1.209	1.689	0.48	0.72	1.325	1.748	0.42	0.76	1.522	1.598	0.08	0.95
Indonesia	5.503	1.545	-3.96	3.56	6.413	1.302	-5.11	4.93	4.509	2.025	-2.48	2.23
Malaysia	2.688	1.337	-1.35	2.01	2.272	1.537	-0.74	1.48	1.959	1.736	-0.22	1.13
Pakistan	0.140	0.642	0.50	0.22	0.189	0.492	0.30	0.38	0.181	0.700	0.52	0.26
Philippines	1.913	1.999	0.09	0.96	2.161	1.787	-0.37	1.21	1.956	1.854	-0.10	1.06
Sri Lanka	0.140	0.062	-0.08	2.26	0.172	0.091	-0.08	1.89	0.194	0.198	0.00	0.98
Thailand	0.866	1.263	0.40	0.69	1.007	1.170	0.16	0.86	0.956	0.915	-0.04	1.04
Viet Nam	0.000	0.001	0.001	0.000	0.000	0.010	0.010	0.000	0.000	0.031	0.031	0.000

Table 1.2 (continued), 1980–1982

Middle East[1]	18.345	11.900	-6.45	1.54	19.579	14.964	-4.62	1.31	12.440	15.951	3.51	0.78
Israel[m]	0.972	2.046	1.07	0.48	1.280	2.521	1.24	0.51	1.209	2.271	1.06	0.53
Kuwait	0.498	0.886	0.39	0.56	0.091	0.976	0.89	0.09	0.043	0.941	0.90	0.05
Saudi Arabia	13.323	5.769	-7.55	2.31	15.237	7.327	-7.91	2.08	7.860	9.026	1.17	0.87
United Arab Emirates	2.115	0.998	-1.12	2.12	2.102	1.077	-1.03	1.95	2.139	1.101	-1.04	1.94
Africa[n]	33.590	8.858	-24.73	3.79	28.113	10.902	-17.21	2.58	18.546	10.105	-8.44	1.84
Algeria	6.881	0.542	-6.34	12.70	5.208	0.717	-4.49	7.26	2.792	0.909	-1.88	3.07
Angola	0.559	0.111	-0.45	5.04	0.938	0.268	-0.67	3.50	0.724	0.159	-0.57	4.55
Egypt	0.487	1.874	1.39	0.26	0.412	2.159	1.75	0.19	0.569	2.875	2.31	0.20
Gabon	0.293	0.048	-0.25	6.10	0.455	0.128	-0.33	3.55	0.635	0.110	-0.53	5.77
Ivory Coast	0.303	0.185	-0.12	1.64	0.372	0.130	-0.24	2.86	0.326	0.097	-0.23	3.36
Morocco	0.041	0.344	0.30	0.12	0.041	0.429	0.39	0.10	0.051	0.396	0.35	0.13
Nigeria	11.316	1.150	-10.17	9.84	9.554	1.523	-8.03	6.27	7.274	1.295	-5.98	5.62
South Africa	3.428	2.463	-0.97	1.39	2.553	2.912	0.36	0.88	2.048	2.368	0.32	0.86
Zaire	0.370	0.155	-0.22	2.39	0.440	0.141	-0.30	3.12	0.424	0.091	-0.33	4.66
Oceania												
Australia	2.782	4.093	1.31	0.68	2.707	5.242	2.54	0.52	2.552	4.535	1.98	0.56
New Zealand	0.793	0.595	-0.20	1.33	0.820	0.922	0.10	0.89	0.870	0.897	0.03	0.97

Footnotes and sources located at end of table.

Table 1.2 (continued), 1983–1985

	1983 Imports	Exports	Balance	Ratio	1984 Imports	Exports	Balance	Ratio	1985 Imports	Exports	Balance	Ratio
World	269.878	205.639	-64.24	1.31	346.364	223.999	-122.37	1.55	352.463	218.828	-133.64	1.61
North America												
~ Canada	52.546	43.345	-9.20	1.21	66.911	51.777	-15.13	1.29	69.427	53.287	-16.14	1.30
~ Mexico	17.019	9.082	-7.94	1.87	18.267	11.992	-6.28	1.52	19.392	13.635	-5.76	1.42
Europe												
~ Western Europe - Non-E.U. [a]	8.566	7.693	-0.87	1.11	11.508	7.521	-3.99	1.53	12.593	7.770	-4.82	1.62
Norway	1.432	0.813	-0.62	1.76	2.004	0.859	-1.15	2.33	1.249	0.666	-0.58	1.88
Switzerland	2.552	2.960	0.41	0.86	3.199	2.562	-0.64	1.25	3.579	2.288	-1.29	1.56
Turkey	0.337	0.783	0.45	0.43	0.464	1.249	0.79	0.37	0.645	1.295	0.65	0.50
~ Western Europe - E.U. [b]	47.876	48.439	0.56	0.99	63.411	50.498	-12.91	1.26	71.616	48.996	-22.62	1.46
Austria	0.468	0.371	-0.10	1.26	0.760	0.375	-0.39	2.03	0.889	0.441	-0.45	2.02
Denmark	1.126	0.649	-0.48	1.73	1.518	0.605	-0.91	2.51	1.796	0.706	-1.09	2.54
Finland	0.544	0.413	-0.13	1.32	0.857	0.350	-0.51	2.45	0.976	0.438	-0.54	2.23
France	6.308	5.961	-0.35	1.06	8.516	6.037	-2.48	1.41	9.959	6.096	-3.86	1.63
Germany	13.229	8.737	-4.49	1.51	17.810	9.084	-8.73	1.96	21.232	9.050	-12.18	2.35
Greece	0.256	0.503	0.25	0.51	0.383	0.456	0.07	0.84	0.427	0.498	0.07	0.86
Ireland	0.582	1.115	0.53	0.52	0.874	1.354	0.48	0.65	0.942	1.342	0.40	0.70
Italy	5.819	3.908	-1.91	1.49	8.504	4.375	-4.13	1.94	10.381	4.625	-5.76	2.24
Netherlands	3.149	7.767	4.62	0.41	4.329	7.554	3.23	0.57	4.368	7.269	2.90	0.60
Portugal	0.308	1.214	0.91	0.25	0.519	0.961	0.44	0.54	0.598	0.695	0.10	0.86
Spain	1.689	2.915	1.23	0.58	2.627	2.561	-0.07	1.03	2.773	2.524	-0.25	1.10
Sweden	2.549	1.581	-0.97	1.61	3.426	1.542	-1.88	2.22	4.339	1.925	-2.41	2.25
United Kingdom	12.900	10.621	-2.28	1.21	15.044	12.210	-2.83	1.23	15.573	11.273	-4.30	1.38

22

Table 1.2 *(continued)*, 1983–1985

~ **Eastern Europe** [c]	1.475	2.891	1.42	0.51	2.352	4.187	1.84	0.56	2.114	3.215	1.10	0.66
Czechoslovakia (former) [d]	0.068	0.059	-0.01	1.15	0.096	0.058	-0.04	1.66	0.085	0.063	-0.02	1.35
USSR (former) [e]	0.375	2.003	1.63	0.19	0.600	3.284	2.68	0.18	0.443	2.423	1.98	0.18
Russia	n/a	n/a	n/a	n/a	n/a	n/a	n/a	n/a	n/a	n/a	n/a	n/a
Central America [f]	2.170	2.278	0.11	0.95	2.361	2.470	0.11	0.96	2.429	2.353	-0.08	1.03
Costa Rica	0.453	0.382	-0.07	1.19	0.544	0.423	-0.12	1.29	0.570	0.422	-0.15	1.35
El Salvador	0.362	0.365	0.00	0.99	0.406	0.426	0.02	0.95	0.413	0.445	0.03	0.93
Guatemala	0.404	0.316	-0.09	1.28	0.479	0.377	-0.10	1.27	0.448	0.405	-0.04	1.11
Honduras	0.435	0.299	-0.14	1.45	0.450	0.322	-0.13	1.40	0.432	0.308	-0.12	1.40
Nicaragua	0.109	0.132	0.02	0.83	0.069	0.112	0.04	0.62	0.050	0.042	-0.01	1.19
Panama	0.378	0.748	0.37	0.51	0.365	0.757	0.39	0.48	0.467	0.675	0.21	0.69
South America [g]	17.374	10.297	-7.08	1.69	22.242	10.828	-11.41	2.05	22.282	10.780	-11.50	2.07
Argentina	0.939	0.965	0.03	0.97	1.041	0.900	-0.14	1.16	1.167	0.721	-0.45	1.62
Bolivia	0.172	0.102	-0.07	1.69	0.159	0.106	-0.05	1.50	0.101	0.120	0.02	0.84
Brazil	5.381	2.557	-2.82	2.10	8.273	2.640	-5.63	3.13	8.147	3.140	-5.01	2.59
Chile	1.053	0.729	-0.32	1.44	0.871	0.805	-0.07	1.08	0.857	0.682	-0.18	1.26
Colombia	1.058	1.514	0.46	0.70	1.253	1.450	0.20	0.86	1.456	1.468	0.01	0.99
Ecuador	1.520	0.597	-0.92	2.55	1.803	0.655	-1.15	2.75	1.976	0.591	-1.39	3.34
Paraguay	0.034	0.036	0.00	0.94	0.044	0.064	0.02	-0.69	0.025	0.099	0.07	0.25
Venezuela	5.173	2.811	-2.36	1.84	6.820	3.377	-3.44	2.02	6.830	3.399	-3.43	2.01

Footnotes and sources located at end of table.

Table 1.2 *(continued)*, 1983–1985

	1983				1984				1985			
	Imports	Exports	Balance	Ratio	Imports	Exports	Balance	Ratio	Imports	Exports	Balance	Ratio
Other W. Hemisphere												
~ Caribbean Basin [h]	9.557	6.054	-3.50	1.58	9.491	6.529	-2.96	1.45	7.387	6.200	-1.19	1.19
Bahamas	1.746	0.452	-1.29	3.86	1.218	0.555	-0.66	2.19	0.652	0.786	0.13	0.83
Dominican Republic	0.855	0.632	-0.22	1.35	1.067	0.646	-0.42	1.65	1.031	0.742	-0.29	1.39
Jamaica	0.307	0.452	0.15	0.68	0.415	0.495	0.08	0.84	0.292	0.404	0.11	0.72
Netherland Antilles	2.367	0.553	-1.81	4.28	2.112	0.648	-1.46	3.26	0.836	0.427	-0.41	1.96
Trinidad & Tobago	1.357	0.728	-0.63	1.86	1.411	0.601	-0.81	2.35	1.304	0.504	-0.80	2.59
Asia [i]	89.789	50.019	-39.77	1.80	119.493	53.399	-66.09	2.24	133.466	51.037	-82.43	2.62
China	2.477	2.173	-0.30	1.14	3.381	3.004	-0.38	1.13	4.224	3.856	-0.37	1.10
Japan	43.559	21.894	-21.67	1.99	60.371	23.575	-36.80	2.56	72.380	22.631	-49.75	3.20
~ E. Asia NICs [j]	29.561	16.915	-12.65	1.75	39.135	17.723	-21.41	2.21	41.880	16.918	-24.96	2.48
Hong Kong	6.825	2.564	-4.26	2.66	8.899	3.062	-5.84	2.91	8.994	2.786	-6.21	3.23
South Korea	7.657	5.925	-1.73	1.29	10.027	5.983	-4.04	1.68	10.713	5.956	-4.76	1.80
Singapore	2.969	3.759	0.79	0.79	4.121	3.675	-0.45	1.12	4.412	3.476	-0.94	1.27
Taiwan	12.110	4.667	-7.44	2.59	16.088	5.003	-11.09	3.22	17.761	4.700	-13.06	3.78
~ Other Asia [k]	14.192	9.037	-5.16	1.57	16.606	9.097	-7.51	1.83	14.982	7.632	-7.35	1.96
Burma	0.012	0.016	0.004	0.750	0.015	0.016	0.001	0.938	0.015	0.010	-0.005	1.50
Cambodia	0.000	0.002	0.002	0.000	0.000	0.001	0.001	0.000	0.000	0.000	0.00	0.00
India	2.334	1.828	-0.51	1.28	2.737	1.570	-1.17	1.74	2.478	1.642	-0.84	1.51
Indonesia	5.657	1.466	-4.19	3.86	5.867	1.216	-4.65	4.82	4.933	0.795	-4.14	6.21
Malaysia	2.205	1.684	-0.52	1.31	2.825	1.856	-0.97	1.52	2.399	1.539	-0.86	1.56
Pakistan	0.183	0.812	0.63	0.23	0.268	1.092	0.82	0.25	0.299	1.042	0.74	0.29
Philippines	2.159	1.807	-0.35	1.19	2.622	1.766	-0.86	1.48	2.334	1.379	-0.96	1.69
Sri Lanka	0.206	0.075	-0.13	2.75	0.302	0.092	-0.21	3.28	0.313	0.073	-0.24	4.29
Thailand	1.035	1.063	0.03	0.97	1.426	1.113	-0.31	1.28	1.543	0.849	-0.69	1.82
Viet Nam	0.000	0.021	0.021	0.000	0.000	0.022	0.022	0.000	0.000	0.020	0.02	0.00

Table 1.2 (continued), 1983–1985

Middle East[l]	7.492	13.796	6.30	0.54	8.554	11.131	2.58	0.77	6.600	9.708	3.11	0.68
Israel[m]	1.300	2.020	0.72	0.64	1.810	2.194	0.38	0.82	2.201	2.580	0.38	0.85
Kuwait	0.139	0.741	0.60	0.19	0.280	0.635	0.36	0.44	0.198	0.551	0.35	0.36
Saudi Arabia	3.840	7.903	4.06	0.49	4.009	5.564	1.56	0.72	2.027	4.474	2.45	0.45
United Arab Emirates	0.542	0.864	0.32	0.63	1.278	0.695	-0.58	1.84	0.721	0.596	-0.13	1.21
Africa[n]	15.194	8.591	-6.60	1.77	14.984	8.799	-6.19	1.70	12.533	7.362	-5.17	1.70
Algeria	3.815	0.594	-3.22	6.42	3.771	0.520	-3.25	7.25	2.426	0.430	-2.00	5.64
Angola	0.948	0.091	-0.86	10.42	1.053	0.103	-0.95	10.22	1.094	0.137	-0.96	7.99
Egypt	0.325	2.813	2.49	0.12	0.182	2.704	2.52	0.07	0.084	2.323	2.24	0.04
Gabon	0.685	0.063	-0.62	10.87	0.707	0.036	-0.67	19.64	0.523	0.091	-0.43	5.75
Ivory Coast	0.371	0.061	-0.31	6.08	0.499	0.064	-0.44	7.80	0.558	0.070	-0.49	7.97
Morocco	0.034	0.440	0.41	0.08	0.039	0.526	0.49	0.07	0.044	0.279	0.24	0.16
Nigeria	3.883	0.864	-3.02	4.49	2.606	0.577	-2.03	4.52	3.108	0.676	-2.43	4.60
South Africa	2.099	2.129	0.03	0.99	2.577	2.265	-0.31	1.14	2.180	1.205	-0.98	1.81
Zaire	0.378	0.083	-0.30	4.55	0.518	0.082	-0.44	6.32	0.415	0.105	-0.31	3.95
Oceania												
Australia	2.422	3.954	1.53	0.61	2.898	4.793	1.90	0.60	3.068	5.441	2.37	0.56
New Zealand	0.828	0.620	-0.21	1.34	0.879	0.708	-0.17	1.24	0.965	0.727	-0.24	1.33

Footnotes and sources located at end of table.

Table 1.2 *(continued)*, 1986–1988

	1986 Imports	Exports	Balance	Ratio	1987 Imports	Exports	Balance	Ratio	1988 Imports	Exports	Balance	Ratio
World	382.295	227.159	-155.14	1.68	424.442	254.122	-170.32	1.67	460.209	321.813	-138.40	1.43
North America												
~ Canada	68.662	55.512	-13.15	1.24	71.510	59.814	-11.70	1.20	82.009	70.862	-11.15	1.16
~ Mexico	17.558	12.392	-5.17	1.42	20.520	14.582	-5.94	1.41	23.545	20.643	-2.90	1.14
Europe												
~ Western Europe - Non-E.U. [a]	14.776	8.487	-6.29	1.74	15.057	9.143	-5.91	1.65	16.339	12.121	-4.22	1.35
Norway	1.170	0.937	-0.23	1.25	1.514	0.842	-0.67	1.80	1.561	0.932	-0.63	1.67
Switzerland	5.367	2.976	-2.39	1.80	4.363	3.151	-1.21	1.38	4.745	4.207	-0.54	1.13
Turkey	0.690	1.160	0.47	0.59	0.897	1.482	0.59	0.61	1.071	1.843	0.77	0.58
~ Western Europe - E.U. [b]	79.521	53.154	-26.37	1.50	84.876	60.575	-24.30	1.40	88.698	75.872	-12.83	1.17
Austria	0.912	0.464	-0.45	1.97	0.979	0.549	-0.43	1.78	1.137	0.745	-0.39	1.53
Denmark	1.869	0.758	-1.11	2.47	1.882	0.893	-0.99	2.11	1.756	0.970	-0.79	1.81
Finland	0.986	0.381	-0.61	2.59	1.085	0.514	-0.57	2.11	1.297	0.763	-0.53	1.70
France	10.586	7.216	-3.37	1.47	11.177	7.943	-3.23	1.41	12.689	10.085	-2.60	1.26
Germany	26.128	10.561	-15.57	2.47	28.028	11.748	-16.28	2.39	27.421	14.331	-13.09	1.91
Greece	0.437	0.430	-0.01	1.02	0.529	0.402	-0.13	1.32	0.589	0.649	0.06	0.91
Ireland	1.046	1.434	0.39	0.73	1.155	1.810	0.66	0.64	1.425	2.182	0.76	0.65
Italy	11.312	4.838	-6.47	2.34	11.698	5.530	-6.17	2.12	12.277	6.782	-5.50	1.81
Netherlands	4.363	7.847	3.48	0.56	4.236	8.217	3.98	0.52	4.874	10.095	5.22	0.48
Portugal	0.600	0.638	0.04	0.94	0.713	0.581	-0.13	1.23	0.738	0.752	0.01	0.98
Spain	2.956	2.615	-0.34	1.13	3.101	3.148	0.05	0.99	3.470	4.217	0.75	0.82
Sweden	4.637	1.871	-2.77	2.48	4.981	1.894	-3.09	2.63	5.217	2.705	-2.51	1.93
United Kingdom	16.033	11.418	-4.62	1.40	17.998	14.114	-3.88	1.28	18.740	18.404	-0.34	1.02

Table 1.2 (continued), 1986–1988

~ Eastern Europe [c]	2.204	1.990	-0.21	1.11	2.119	2.200	0.08	0.96	2.385	3.653	1.27	0.65
Czechoslovakia (former) [d]	0.093	0.072	-0.02	1.29	0.086	0.047	-0.04	1.83	0.096	0.055	-0.04	1.75
USSR (former) [e]	0.605	1.248	0.64	0.48	0.470	1.480	1.01	0.32	0.649	2.768	2.12	0.23
Russia	n/a	n/a	n/a	n/a	n/a	n/a	n/a	n/a	n/a	n/a	n/a	n/a
Central America [f]	2.732	2.537	-0.20	1.08	2.605	2.687	0.08	0.97	2.505	2.990	0.49	0.84
Costa Rica	0.730	0.483	-0.25	1.51	0.750	0.582	-0.17	1.29	0.861	0.696	-0.17	1.24
El Salvador	0.401	0.518	0.12	0.77	0.300	0.390	0.09	0.77	0.299	0.483	0.18	0.62
Guatemala	0.647	0.400	-0.25	1.62	0.542	0.480	-0.06	1.13	0.477	0.591	0.11	0.81
Honduras	0.487	0.363	-0.12	1.34	0.565	0.418	-0.15	1.35	0.516	0.478	-0.04	1.08
Nicaragua	0.001	0.003	0.002	0.33	0.001	0.003	0.002	0.33	0.001	0.006	0.005	0.17
Panama	0.412	0.711	0.299	0.58	0.402	0.742	0.340	0.54	0.297	0.633	0.336	0.47
South America [g]	19.803	11.789	-8.01	1.68	21.720	12.774	-8.95	1.70	23.317	14.703	-8.61	1.59
Argentina	0.938	0.944	0.01	0.99	1.176	1.090	-0.09	1.08	1.568	1.056	-0.51	1.48
Bolivia	0.127	0.112	-0.02	1.13	0.113	0.140	0.03	0.81	0.121	0.148	0.03	0.82
Brazil	7.340	3.885	-3.46	1.89	8.433	4.040	-4.39	2.09	9.977	4.289	-5.69	2.33
Chile	0.935	0.823	-0.11	1.14	1.105	0.796	-0.31	1.39	1.325	1.065	-0.26	1.24
Colombia	2.039	1.319	-0.72	1.55	2.414	1.412	-1.00	1.71	2.349	1.758	-0.59	1.34
Ecuador	1.603	0.601	-1.00	2.67	1.390	0.621	-0.77	2.24	1.368	0.684	-0.68	2.00
Paraguay	0.031	0.171	0.14	0.18	0.024	0.183	0.16	0.13	0.040	0.194	0.15	0.21
Venezuela	5.446	3.141	-2.31	1.73	5.881	3.586	-2.30	1.64	5.578	4.611	-0.97	1.21

Footnotes and sources located at end of table.

Table 1.2 (continued), 1986–1988

	1986				1987				1988			
	Imports	Exports	Balance	Ratio	Imports	Exports	Balance	Ratio	Imports	Exports	Balance	Ratio
Other W. Hemisphere												
~ Caribbean Basin [h]	6.720	6.594	-0.13	1.02	6.827	7.183	0.36	0.95	6.814	7.946	1.13	0.86
Bahamas	0.463	0.761	0.30	0.61	0.450	0.782	0.33	0.58	0.426	0.741	0.32	0.57
Dominican Republic	1.138	0.921	-0.22	1.24	1.217	1.142	-0.08	1.07	1.479	1.362	-0.12	1.09
Jamaica	0.322	0.457	0.14	0.70	0.422	0.601	0.18	0.70	0.473	0.758	0.29	0.62
Netherland Antilles	0.501	0.398	-0.10	1.26	0.557	0.507	-0.05	1.10	0.442	0.530	0.09	0.83
Trinidad & Tobago	0.840	0.532	-0.31	1.58	0.859	0.361	-0.50	2.38	0.773	0.328	-0.45	2.36
Asia [i]	154.072	56.119	-97.95	2.75	172.503	63.765	-108.74	2.71	187.877	88.848	-99.03	2.11
China	5.241	3.106	-2.14	1.69	6.911	3.497	-3.41	1.98	9.270	5.039	-4.23	1.84
Japan	85.457	26.882	-58.58	3.18	88.074	28.249	-59.83	3.12	93.168	37.732	-55.44	2.47
~ E. Asia NICs [j]	49.106	18.289	-30.82	2.69	61.282	23.548	-37.73	2.60	66.501	34.882	-31.62	1.91
Hong Kong	9.474	3.030	-6.44	3.13	10.490	3.983	-6.51	2.63	10.810	5.691	-5.12	1.90
South Korea	13.497	6.355	-7.14	2.12	17.991	8.099	-9.89	2.22	21.209	11.290	-9.92	1.88
Singapore	4.884	3.380	-1.50	1.44	6.395	4.053	-2.34	1.58	8.226	5.770	-2.46	1.43
Taiwan	21.251	5.524	-15.73	3.85	26.406	7.413	-18.99	3.56	26.256	12.131	-14.13	2.16
~ Other Asia [k]	14.268	7.842	-6.43	1.82	16.236	8.471	-7.77	1.92	18.938	11.195	-7.74	1.69
Burma	0.015	0.016	0.001	0.938	0.013	0.008	-0.005	1.625	0.013	0.011	-0.002	1.18
Cambodia	0.001	0.000	-0.001	0.000	0.000	0.000	0.00	0.00	0.001	0.000	0.00	0.00
India	2.465	1.536	-0.93	1.60	2.725	1.463	-1.26	1.86	3.167	2.498	-0.67	1.27
Indonesia	3.675	0.946	-2.73	3.88	3.719	0.767	-2.95	4.85	3.494	1.056	-2.44	3.31
Malaysia	2.534	1.730	-0.80	1.46	3.053	1.897	-1.16	1.61	3.853	2.139	-1.71	1.80
Pakistan	0.353	0.830	0.48	0.43	0.438	0.733	0.30	0.60	0.498	1.093	0.60	0.46
Philippines	2.150	1.363	-0.79	1.58	2.481	1.599	-0.88	1.55	2.906	1.880	-1.03	1.55
Sri Lanka	0.376	0.066	-0.31	5.70	0.464	0.077	-0.39	6.03	0.463	0.124	-0.34	3.73
Thailand	1.873	0.936	-0.94	2.00	2.387	1.544	-0.84	1.55	3.423	1.964	-1.46	1.74
Viet Nam	0.000	0.030	0.03	0.00	0.000	0.023	0.02	0.00	0.000	0.016	0.02	0.00

Table 1.2 *(continued)*, 1986–1988

Middle East [1]	8.594	8.413	-0.18	1.02	11.601	9.501	-2.10	1.22	12.482	10.858	-1.62	1.15
Israel [m]	2.505	2.239	-0.27	1.12	2.724	3.130	0.41	0.87	3.068	3.248	0.18	0.94
Kuwait	0.307	0.657	0.35	0.47	0.569	0.505	-0.06	1.13	0.507	0.690	0.18	0.73
Saudi Arabia	4.054	3.449	-0.61	1.18	4.886	3.373	-1.51	1.45	6.237	3.799	-2.44	1.64
United Arab Emirates	0.390	0.493	0.10	0.79	0.723	0.619	-0.10	1.17	0.616	0.711	0.10	0.87
Africa [n]	11.043	5.951	-5.09	1.86	12.668	6.254	-6.41	2.03	11.695	7.414	-4.28	1.58
Algeria	1.980	0.453	-1.53	4.37	2.144	0.426	-1.72	5.03	1.972	0.732	-1.24	2.69
Angola	0.729	0.086	-0.64	8.48	1.372	0.095	-1.28	14.44	1.343	0.101	-1.24	13.30
Egypt	0.123	1.982	1.86	0.06	0.498	2.210	1.71	0.23	0.243	2.340	2.10	0.10
Gabon	0.225	0.025	-0.20	9.00	0.379	0.052	-0.33	7.29	0.199	0.056	-0.14	3.55
Ivory Coast	0.454	0.060	-0.39	7.57	0.404	0.082	-0.32	4.93	0.313	0.075	-0.24	4.17
Morocco	0.047	0.486	0.44	0.10	0.054	0.383	0.33	0.14	0.102	0.428	0.33	0.24
Nigeria	2.681	0.409	-2.27	6.56	3.767	0.295	-3.47	12.77	3.535	0.356	-3.18	9.93
South Africa	2.476	1.158	-1.32	2.14	1.399	1.281	-0.12	1.09	1.589	1.690	0.10	0.94
Zaire	0.239	0.104	-0.14	2.30	0.321	0.103	-0.22	3.12	0.384	0.125	-0.26	3.07
Oceania												
Australia	2.868	5.551	2.68	0.52	3.285	5.495	2.21	0.60	3.856	6.981	3.13	0.55
New Zealand	1.090	0.881	-0.21	1.24	1.174	0.819	-0.36	1.43	1.303	0.942	-0.36	1.38

Footnotes and sources located at end of table.

Table 1.2 *(continued)*, 1989–1991

	1989				1990				1991			
	Imports	Exports	Balance	Ratio	Imports	Exports	Balance	Ratio	Imports	Exports	Balance	Ratio
World	487.558	363.812	-123.75	1.34	512.542	393.592	-118.95	1.30	504.366	421.730	-82.64	1.20
North America												
~Canada	89.323	78.809	-10.51	1.13	93.601	83.674	-9.93	1.12	93.514	85.150	-8.36	1.10
~Mexico	26.947	24.982	-1.97	1.08	30.127	28.279	-1.85	1.07	31.087	33.277	2.19	0.93
Europe												
~Western Europe - Non-E.U. [a]	17.131	13.835	-3.30	1.24	17.446	14.939	-2.51	1.17	16.374	15.560	-0.81	1.05
Norway	2.124	1.037	-1.09	2.05	1.959	1.281	-0.68	1.53	1.707	1.489	-0.22	1.15
Switzerland	4.767	4.911	0.14	0.97	5.365	4.943	-0.42	1.09	5.536	5.557	0.02	1.00
Turkey	1.399	2.003	0.60	0.70	1.266	2.243	0.98	0.56	0.981	2.467	1.49	0.40
~Western Europe - E.U. [b]	87.653	86.425	-1.23	1.01	95.349	98.128	2.78	0.97	88.052	103.123	15.07	0.85
Austria	1.177	0.873	-0.30	1.35	1.364	0.875	-0.49	1.56	1.325	1.056	-0.27	1.25
Denmark	1.602	1.051	-0.55	1.52	1.746	1.311	-0.44	1.33	1.724	1.574	-0.15	1.10
Finland	1.454	0.969	-0.49	1.50	1.346	1.126	-0.22	1.20	1.171	0.952	-0.22	1.23
France	13.125	11.579	-1.55	1.13	13.252	13.664	0.41	0.97	13.644	15.345	1.70	0.89
Germany	25.608	16.956	-8.65	1.51	28.908	18.760	-10.15	1.54	26.363	21.302	-5.06	1.24
Greece	0.525	0.697	0.17	0.75	0.522	0.763	0.24	0.68	0.429	1.039	0.61	0.41
Ireland	1.605	2.483	0.88	0.65	1.783	2.540	0.76	0.70	2.015	2.681	0.67	0.75
Italy	12.557	7.215	-5.34	1.74	13.240	7.992	-5.25	1.66	12.162	8.570	-3.59	1.42
Netherlands	5.012	11.364	6.35	0.44	5.219	13.022	7.80	0.40	5.066	13.511	8.45	0.37
Portugal	0.836	0.925	0.09	0.90	0.875	0.922	0.05	0.95	0.743	0.792	0.05	0.94
Spain	3.505	4.796	1.29	0.73	4.493	5.213	0.72	0.86	2.993	5.474	2.48	0.55
Sweden	5.051	3.138	-1.91	1.61	5.085	3.405	-1.68	1.49	4.640	3.287	-1.35	1.41
United Kingdom	18.550	20.837	2.29	0.89	20.559	23.490	2.93	0.88	18.675	22.046	3.37	0.85

Table 1.2 *(continued)*, 1989–1991

~ Eastern Europe [c]	2.071	5.307	3.24	0.39	2.321	4.203	1.88	0.55	1.953	4.786	2.83	0.41
Czechoslovakia (former) [d]	0.091	0.053	-0.038	1.717	0.087	0.091	0.004	0.956	0.156	0.123	-0.033	1.268
USSR (former) [e]	0.772	4.284	3.51	0.18	1.132	3.087	1.96	0.37	0.894	3.579	2.69	0.25
Russia	n/a	n/a	n/a	n/a	n/a	n/a	n/a	n/a	n/a	n/a	n/a	n/a
Central America [f]	2.848	3.405	0.56	0.84	3.089	3.908	0.82	0.79	3.525	4.380	0.86	0.80
Costa Rica	1.064	0.882	-0.18	1.21	1.103	0.986	-0.12	1.12	1.252	1.034	-0.22	1.21
El Salvador	0.257	0.520	0.26	0.49	0.255	0.554	0.30	0.46	0.322	0.534	0.21	0.60
Guatemala	0.667	0.662	-0.01	1.01	0.869	0.763	-0.11	1.14	0.976	0.945	-0.03	1.03
Honduras	0.532	0.515	-0.02	1.03	0.555	0.564	0.01	0.98	0.612	0.625	0.01	0.98
Nicaragua	0.000	0.002	0.002	0.000	0.017	0.067	0.050	0.254	0.066	0.150	0.084	0.440
Panama	0.283	0.723	0.440	0.391	0.244	0.869	0.625	0.281	0.260	0.978	0.718	0.266
South America [g]	24.484	13.990	-10.49	1.75	27.197	15.067	-12.13	1.81	24.127	19.210	-4.92	1.26
Argentina	1.509	1.039	-0.47	1.45	1.626	1.179	-0.45	1.38	1.368	2.045	0.68	0.67
Bolivia	0.122	0.145	0.02	0.84	0.205	0.138	-0.07	1.49	0.212	0.192	-0.02	1.10
Brazil	9.095	4.804	-4.29	1.89	8.362	5.048	-3.31	1.66	7.268	6.148	-1.12	1.18
Chile	1.410	1.414	0.00	1.00	1.429	1.664	0.24	0.86	1.466	1.839	0.37	0.80
Colombia	2.742	1.924	-0.82	1.43	3.387	2.029	-1.36	1.67	2.958	1.952	-1.01	1.52
Ecuador	1.638	0.643	-1.00	2.55	1.526	0.678	-0.85	2.25	1.503	0.948	-0.56	1.59
Paraguay	0.046	0.167	0.12	0.28	0.056	0.307	0.25	0.18	0.047	0.374	0.33	0.13
Venezuela	6.873	3.025	-3.85	2.27	9.613	3.108	-6.51	3.09	8.287	4.656	-3.63	1.78

Footnotes and sources located at end of table.

Table 1.2 *(continued)*, 1989–1991

	1989				1990				1991			
	Imports	Exports	Balance	Ratio	Imports	Exports	Balance	Ratio	Imports	Exports	Balance	Ratio
Other W. Hemisphere												
~ Caribbean Basin [h]	7.437	9.422	1.99	0.79	8.064	9.963	1.90	0.81	8.705	10.450	1.75	0.83
Bahamas	0.477	0.772	0.30	0.62	0.524	0.800	0.28	0.66	0.483	0.721	0.24	0.67
Dominican Republic	1.709	1.645	-0.06	1.04	1.803	1.656	-0.15	1.09	2.051	1.743	-0.31	1.18
Jamaica	0.563	1.006	0.44	0.56	0.605	0.943	0.34	0.64	0.600	0.961	0.36	0.62
Netherland Antilles	0.401	0.539	0.14	0.74	0.454	0.745	0.29	0.61	0.669	0.861	0.19	0.78
Trinidad & Tobago	0.817	0.563	-0.25	1.45	1.062	0.428	-0.63	2.48	0.882	0.468	-0.41	1.88
Asia [i]	195.530	101.409	-94.12	1.93	196.134	109.050	-87.08	1.80	202.099	115.311	-86.79	1.75
China	12.762	5.755	-7.01	2.22	16.186	4.806	-11.38	3.37	20.176	6.278	-13.90	3.21
Japan	95.108	44.494	-50.61	2.14	92.701	48.580	-44.12	1.91	94.156	48.125	-46.03	1.96
~ E. Asia NICs [j]	65.190	38.429	-26.76	1.70	62.744	40.735	-22.01	1.54	61.481	45.628	-15.85	1.35
Hong Kong	10.165	6.291	-3.87	1.62	9.859	6.817	-3.04	1.45	9.643	8.137	-1.51	1.19
South Korea	20.410	13.459	-6.95	1.52	19.123	14.404	-4.72	1.33	17.571	15.505	-2.07	1.13
Singapore	9.116	7.344	-1.77	1.24	10.039	8.023	-2.02	1.25	10.139	8.804	-1.34	1.15
Taiwan	25.499	11.335	-14.16	2.25	23.723	11.491	-12.23	2.06	24.128	13.182	-10.95	1.83
~ Other Asia [k]	22.470	12.731	-9.74	1.76	24.503	14.929	-9.57	1.64	26.286	15.280	-11.01	1.72
Burma	0.018	0.005	-0.013	3.600	0.024	0.020	-0.004	1.200	0.029	0.023	-0.006	1.261
Cambodia	0.000	0.000	0.000	0.000	0.000	0.000	-0.0001	0.000	0.000	0.000	0.000	0.000
India	3.516	2.458	-1.06	1.43	3.429	2.486	-0.94	1.38	3.432	1.999	-1.43	1.72
Indonesia	3.813	1.247	-2.57	3.06	3.677	1.897	-1.78	1.94	3.809	1.891	-1.92	2.01
Malaysia	4.853	2.870	-1.98	1.69	5.451	3.425	-2.03	1.59	6.321	3.900	-2.42	1.62
Pakistan	0.567	1.134	0.57	0.50	0.645	1.143	0.50	0.56	0.704	0.950	0.25	0.74
Philippines	3.295	2.202	-1.09	1.50	3.596	2.471	-1.13	1.46	3.664	2.265	-1.40	1.62
Sri Lanka	0.487	0.143	-0.34	3.41	0.574	0.137	-0.44	4.19	0.652	0.121	-0.53	5.39
Thailand	4.620	2.288	-2.33	2.02	5.575	2.995	-2.58	1.86	6.393	3.753	-2.64	1.70
Viet Nam	0.000	0.011	0.011	0.000	0.000	0.007	0.007	0.000	0.000	0.003	0.003	0.000

Table 1.2 *(continued)*, 1989–1991

Middle East [l]	16.001	11.126	-4.88	1.44	19.952	11.220	-8.73	1.78	17.183	15.311	-1.872	1.12
Israel [m]	3.322	2.828	-0.49	1.17	3.396	3.203	-0.19	1.06	3.583	3.911	0.33	0.92
Kuwait	1.066	0.853	-0.21	1.25	0.622	0.403	-0.22	1.54	0.039	1.228	1.19	0.03
Saudi Arabia	7.706	3.574	-4.13	2.16	10.721	4.049	-6.67	2.65	12.132	6.557	-5.58	1.85
United Arab Emirates	0.735	1.238	0.50	0.59	0.967	1.004	0.04	0.96	0.769	1.455	0.69	0.53
Africa [n]	14.951	7.691	-7.26	1.94	16.956	7.930	-9.03	2.14	15.093	8.805	-6.29	1.71
Algeria	1.986	0.756	-1.23	2.63	2.854	0.951	-1.90	3.00	2.245	0.727	-1.52	3.09
Angola	1.972	0.097	-1.88	20.33	2.090	0.152	-1.94	13.75	1.925	0.186	-1.74	10.35
Egypt	0.246	2.612	2.37	0.09	0.431	2.249	1.82	0.19	0.222	2.720	2.50	0.08
Gabon	0.442	0.046	-0.40	9.61	0.812	0.049	-0.76	16.57	0.766	0.085	-0.68	9.01
Ivory Coast	0.254	0.079	-0.18	3.22	0.224	0.079	-0.15	2.84	0.239	0.081	-0.16	2.95
Morocco	0.107	0.394	0.29	0.27	0.117	0.495	0.38	0.24	0.163	0.404	0.24	0.40
Nigeria	5.615	0.490	-5.13	11.46	6.397	0.553	-5.84	11.57	5.699	0.831	-4.87	6.86
South Africa	1.581	1.659	0.08	0.95	1.749	1.732	-0.02	1.01	1.775	2.113	0.34	0.84
Zaire	0.356	0.122	-0.23	2.92	0.332	0.138	-0.19	2.41	0.317	0.062	-0.26	5.11
Oceania												
Australia	4.149	8.331	4.18	0.50	4.690	8.538	3.85	0.55	4.353	8.404	4.05	0.52
New Zealand	1.341	1.117	-0.22	1.20	1.313	1.135	-0.18	1.16	1.338	1.007	-0.33	1.33

Footnotes and sources located at end of table.

Table 1.2 (continued), 1992–1994

	1992				1993				1994			
	Imports	Exports	Balance	Ratio	Imports	Exports	Balance	Ratio	Imports	Exports	Balance	Ratio
World	546.016	448.164	-97.85	1.22	597.394	465.091	-132.30	1.28	689.213	512.627	-176.59	1.34
North America												
~ Canada	101.032	90.594	-10.44	1.12	113.148	100.444	-12.70	1.13	131.956	114.439	-17.52	1.15
~ Mexico	34.592	40.592	6.00	0.85	39.433	41.581	2.15	0.95	50.356	50.844	0.49	0.99
Europe												
~ Western Europe - Non-E.U. [a]	17.275	14.142	-3.13	1.22	17.492	16.708	-0.78	1.05	20.070	15.359	-4.71	1.31
Norway	2.078	1.279	-0.80	1.62	2.037	1.212	-0.83	1.68	2.500	1.267	-1.23	1.97
Switzerland	5.628	4.540	-1.09	1.24	5.997	6.806	0.81	0.88	6.504	5.624	-0.88	1.16
Turkey	1.607	2.735	1.13	0.59	1.318	3.429	2.11	0.38	1.692	2.752	1.06	0.61
~ Western Europe - E.U. [b]	94.800	102.960	8.16	0.92	99.837	96.974	-2.86	1.03	114.924	102.820	-12.10	1.12
Austria	1.343	1.256	-0.09	1.07	1.452	1.326	-0.13	1.10	1.818	1.372	-0.45	1.33
Denmark	1.730	1.473	-0.26	1.17	1.731	1.092	-0.64	1.59	2.212	1.215	-1.00	1.82
Finland	1.262	0.785	-0.48	1.61	1.715	0.848	-0.87	2.02	1.928	1.068	-0.86	1.81
France	15.161	14.593	-0.57	1.04	15.381	13.267	-2.11	1.16	17.300	13.619	-3.68	1.27
Germany	28.316	21.249	-7.07	1.33	28.924	18.932	-9.99	1.53	32.690	19.229	-13.46	1.70
Greece	0.391	0.901	0.51	0.43	0.437	0.880	0.44	0.50	0.494	0.829	0.34	0.60
Ireland	2.312	2.862	0.55	0.81	2.530	2.728	0.20	0.93	2.953	3.419	0.47	0.86
Italy	12.625	8.721	-3.90	1.45	13.649	6.464	-7.19	2.11	15.438	7.183	-8.26	2.15
Netherlands	5.510	13.752	8.24	0.40	5.676	12.839	7.16	0.44	6.358	13.582	7.22	0.47
Portugal	0.698	1.025	0.33	0.68	0.825	0.727	-0.10	1.13	0.949	1.054	0.11	0.90
Spain	3.086	5.537	2.45	0.56	3.170	4.168	1.00	0.76	3.810	4.622	0.81	0.82
Sweden	4.848	2.845	-2.00	1.70	4.601	2.354	-2.25	1.95	5.243	2.518	-2.73	2.08
United Kingdom	20.149	22.800	2.65	0.88	21.945	26.438	4.49	0.83	25.858	26.900	1.04	0.96

Table 1.2 *(continued)*, 1992–1994

~ Eastern Europe[c]	2.126	5.517	3.39	0.39	3.722	6.105	2.38	0.61	6.261	5.302	-0.96	1.18
Czechoslovakia (former)[d]	0.251	0.413	0.162	0.608	0.367	0.301	-0.07	1.22	0.472	0.340	-0.13	1.39
USSR (former)[e]	0.873	3.799	2.93	0.23	2.188	3.984	1.80	0.55	4.126	3.562	-0.56	1.16
Russia	0.500	2.112	1.61	0.24	1.834	2.970	1.14	0.62	3.437	2.578	-0.86	1.33
Central America[f]	4.339	5.520	1.18	0.79	4.888	6.099	1.21	0.80	5.558	6.743	1.19	0.82
Costa Rica	1.531	1.357	-0.17	1.13	1.673	1.542	-0.13	1.08	1.775	1.870	0.10	0.95
El Salvador	0.408	0.742	0.33	0.55	0.506	0.873	0.37	0.58	0.635	0.931	0.30	0.68
Guatemala	1.179	1.205	0.03	0.98	1.282	1.312	0.03	0.98	1.386	1.352	-0.03	1.03
Honduras	0.849	0.811	-0.04	1.05	0.985	0.899	-0.09	1.10	1.175	1.012	-0.16	1.16
Nicaragua	0.075	0.185	0.110	0.41	0.134	0.150	0.02	0.89	0.179	0.186	0.01	0.96
Panama	0.235	1.103	0.868	0.21	0.255	1.187	0.93	0.21	0.354	1.277	0.92	0.28
South America[g]	24.813	23.042	-1.77	1.08	25.680	23.422	-2.26	1.10	28.971	27.328	-1.64	1.06
Argentina	1.338	3.223	1.89	0.42	1.280	3.776	2.50	0.34	1.834	4.462	2.63	0.41
Bolivia	0.167	0.222	0.06	0.75	0.190	0.218	0.03	0.87	0.268	0.185	-0.08	1.45
Brazil	8.110	5.751	-2.36	1.41	8.325	6.058	-2.27	1.37	9.307	8.102	-1.21	1.15
Chile	1.556	2.466	0.91	0.63	1.687	2.599	0.91	0.65	2.072	2.774	0.70	0.75
Colombia	3.105	3.286	0.18	0.94	3.245	3.235	-0.01	1.00	3.407	4.064	0.66	0.84
Ecuador	1.473	0.999	-0.47	1.47	1.553	1.100	-0.45	1.41	1.937	1.195	-0.74	1.62
Paraguay	0.038	0.415	0.38	0.09	0.054	0.521	0.47	0.10	0.085	0.788	0.70	0.11
Venezuela	8.020	5.444	-2.58	1.47	8.325	4.590	-3.74	1.81	8.989	4.039	-4.95	2.23

Footnotes and sources located at end of table.

Table 1.2 (continued), 1992–1994

	1992				1993				1994			
	Imports	Exports	Balance	Ratio	Imports	Exports	Balance	Ratio	Imports	Exports	Balance	Ratio
Other W. Hemisphere												
~ Caribbean Basin [h]	9.845	11.743	1.90	0.84	10.419	12.746	2.33	0.82	11.731	13.802	2.07	0.85
Bahamas	0.602	0.712	0.11	0.85	0.360	0.704	0.34	0.51	0.220	0.685	0.47	0.32
Dominican Republic	2.446	2.100	-0.35	1.16	2.753	2.350	-0.40	1.17	3.188	2.799	-0.39	1.14
Jamaica	0.638	0.938	0.30	0.68	0.755	1.116	0.36	0.68	0.790	1.066	0.28	0.74
Netherland Antilles	0.606	0.766	0.16	0.79	0.409	0.785	0.38	0.52	0.455	0.795	0.34	0.57
Trinidad & Tobago	0.899	0.448	-0.45	2.01	0.852	0.529	-0.32	1.61	1.199	0.541	-0.66	2.22
Asia [i]	223.494	121.389	-102.11	1.84	248.927	129.902	-119.03	1.92	287.479	144.950	-142.53	1.98
China	27.241	7.418	-19.82	3.67	33.577	8.763	-24.81	3.83	41.362	9.282	-32.08	4.46
Japan	98.364	47.813	-50.55	2.06	109.154	47.891	-61.26	2.28	122.469	53.488	-68.98	2.29
~ E. Asia NICs [j]	64.533	48.592	-15.94	1.33	66.660	52.502	-14.16	1.27	75.114	59.595	-15.52	1.26
Hong Kong	10.145	9.077	-1.07	1.12	9.854	9.874	0.02	1.00	10.142	11.441	1.30	0.89
South Korea	17.186	14.639	-2.55	1.17	17.640	14.782	-2.86	1.19	20.374	18.025	-2.35	1.13
Singapore	11.472	9.626	-1.85	1.19	12.996	11.678	-1.32	1.11	16.656	13.020	-3.64	1.28
Taiwan	25.730	15.250	-10.48	1.69	26.170	16.168	-10.00	1.62	27.942	17.109	-10.83	1.63
~ Other Asia [k]	33.356	17.566	-15.79	1.90	39.536	20.746	-18.79	1.91	48.534	22.585	-25.95	2.15
Burma	0.041	0.004	-0.037	10.250	0.050	0.012	-0.04	4.17	0.073	0.011	-0.06	6.64
Cambodia	0.000	0.016	0.016	0.006	0.001	0.016	0.015	0.06	0.001	0.008	0.007	0.13
India	4.035	1.917	-2.12	2.10	4.866	2.778	-2.09	1.75	5.663	2.294	-3.37	2.47
Indonesia	4.807	2.779	-2.03	1.73	5.783	2.770	-3.01	2.09	7.020	2.809	-4.21	2.50
Malaysia	8.472	4.363	-4.11	1.94	10.835	6.064	-4.77	1.79	14.419	6.969	-7.45	2.07
Pakistan	0.911	0.881	-0.03	1.03	0.955	0.811	-0.14	1.18	1.085	0.718	-0.37	1.51
Philippines	4.576	2.759	-1.82	1.66	5.141	3.529	-1.61	1.46	6.025	3.886	-2.14	1.55
Sri Lanka	0.853	0.178	-0.68	4.79	1.075	0.203	-0.87	5.30	1.173	0.198	-0.98	5.92
Thailand	7.884	3.989	-3.90	1.98	8.979	3.766	-5.21	2.38	10.799	4.865	-5.93	2.22
Viet Nam	0.000	0.004	0.004	0.000	0.000	0.007	0.01	0.00	0.055	0.173	0.12	0.32

Table 1.2 (continued), 1992–1994

	1992				1993				1994			
Middle East [1]	16.772	16.872	0.10	0.99	16.662	16.819	0.16	0.99	16.799	16.045	-0.75	1.05
Israel [m]	3.903	4.077	0.17	0.96	4.525	4.429	-0.10	1.02	5.337	4.997	-0.34	1.07
Kuwait	0.310	1.337	1.03	0.23	1.993	0.999	-0.99	1.99	1.598	1.176	-0.42	1.36
Saudi Arabia	11.206	7.167	-4.04	1.56	8.552	6.661	-1.89	1.28	8.307	6.013	-2.29	1.38
United Arab Emirates	0.870	1.553	0.68	0.56	0.780	1.811	1.03	0.43	0.479	1.599	1.12	0.30
Africa [n]	15.109	9.896	-5.21	1.53	15.815	9.412	-6.40	1.68	15.098	9.190	-5.91	1.64
Algeria	1.684	0.688	-1.00	2.45	1.718	0.938	-0.78	1.83	1.664	1.192	-0.47	1.40
Angola	2.407	0.158	-2.25	15.23	2.250	0.174	-2.08	12.93	2.209	0.197	-2.01	11.21
Egypt	0.463	3.088	2.63	0.15	0.649	2.768	2.12	0.23	0.594	2.855	2.26	0.21
Gabon	0.983	0.055	-0.93	17.87	0.989	0.048	-0.94	20.60	1.238	0.040	-1.20	30.95
Ivory Coast	0.206	0.087	-0.12	2.37	0.200	0.089	-0.11	2.25	0.205	0.111	-0.09	1.85
Morocco	0.194	0.496	0.30	0.39	0.201	0.600	0.40	0.34	0.211	0.409	0.20	0.52
Nigeria	5.297	1.001	-4.30	5.29	5.619	0.895	-4.72	6.28	4.706	0.509	-4.20	9.25
South Africa	1.791	2.434	0.64	0.74	1.933	2.188	0.26	0.88	2.131	2.172	0.04	0.98
Zaire	0.259	0.033	-0.23	7.85	0.254	0.035	-0.22	7.26	0.198	0.040	-0.16	4.95
Oceania												
Australia	3.874	8.876	5.00	0.44	3.510	8.276	4.77	0.42	3.447	9.781	6.33	0.35
New Zealand	1.304	1.307	0.00	1.00	1.315	1.249	-0.07	1.05	1.545	1.508	-0.04	1.02

Footnotes and sources located at end of table.

Table 1.2 (continued), 1995–1997

	1995				1996				1997			
	Imports	Exports	Balance	Ratio	Imports	Exports	Balance	Ratio	Imports	Exports	Balance	Ratio
World	770.943	582.120	-188.82	1.32	817.819	622.827	-194.99	1.31	898.324	687.598	-210.73	1.31
North America												
~ Canada	148.303	126.024	-22.28	1.18	159.746	132.584	-27.16	1.20	171.440	150.124	-21.32	1.14
~ Mexico	62.756	45.401	-17.36	1.38	74.111	56.761	-17.35	1.31	87.125	71.378	-15.75	1.22
Europe												
~ Western Europe - Non-E.U. [a]	13.324	11.192	-2.13	1.19	14.373	13.510	-0.86	1.06	15.749	14.555	-1.19	1.08
Norway	3.251	1.293	-1.96	2.51	4.057	1.557	-2.50	2.61	3.925	1.720	-2.21	2.28
Switzerland	7.746	6.227	-1.52	1.24	7.935	8.370	0.44	0.95	8.536	8.306	-0.23	1.03
Turkey	1.926	2.768	0.84	0.70	1.883	2.886	1.00	0.65	2.245	3.539	1.29	0.63
~ Western Europe - E.U. [b]	136.852	123.673	-13.18	1.11	147.650	127.268	-20.38	1.16	162.579	140.803	-21.78	1.15
Austria	2.040	2.017	-0.02	1.01	2.281	2.009	-0.27	1.14	2.452	2.073	-0.38	0.69
Denmark	2.033	1.518	-0.52	1.34	2.223	1.730	-0.49	1.28	2.225	1.758	-0.47	1.27
Finland	2.392	1.250	-1.14	1.91	2.464	2.438	-0.03	1.01	2.528	1.741	-0.79	1.45
France	17.756	14.245	-3.51	1.25	19.180	14.428	-4.75	1.33	21.317	15.982	-5.34	1.33
Germany	38.043	22.394	-15.65	1.70	39.990	23.474	-16.52	1.70	44.193	24.467	-19.73	1.81
Greece	0.438	1.519	1.08	0.29	0.536	0.820	0.28	0.65	0.498	0.954	0.46	0.52
Ireland	4.149	4.109	-0.04	1.01	4.870	3.660	-1.21	1.33	5.959	4.641	-1.32	1.28
Italy	17.298	8.862	-8.44	1.95	19.001	8.784	-10.22	2.16	20.183	8.973	-11.21	2.25
Netherlands	6.769	16.558	9.79	0.41	7.012	16.614	9.60	0.42	7.683	19.822	12.14	0.39
Portugal	1.117	0.898	-0.22	1.24	1.067	0.960	-0.11	1.11	1.194	0.955	-0.24	1.25
Spain	4.161	5.526	1.37	0.75	4.563	5.486	0.92	0.83	4.911	5.544	0.63	0.89
Sweden	6.468	3.080	-3.39	2.10	7.575	3.429	-4.15	2.21	7.533	3.316	-4.22	2.27
United Kingdom	27.709	28.857	1.15	0.96	29.700	30.916	1.22	0.96	33.531	36.435	2.90	0.92

Table 1.2 (continued), 1995–1997

~ Eastern Europe [c]	7.506	5.700	-1.81	1.32	7.264	7.254	-0.01	1.00	8.944	7.722	-1.22	1.16
Czechoslovakia (former) [d]	0.519	0.424	-0.10	1.22	0.520	0.472	-0.05	1.10	0.815	0.674	-0.14	1.21
USSR (former) [e]	5.247	3.806	-1.44	1.38	4.958	5.068	0.11	0.98	5.650	5.030	-0.62	1.12
Russia	4.270	2.823	-1.45	1.51	3.745	3.340	-0.41	1.12	4.524	3.289	-1.24	1.38
Central America [f]	6.658	7.513	0.86	0.89	7.746	7.838	0.09	0.99	9.365	9.105	-0.26	1.03
Costa Rica	1.998	1.736	-0.26	1.15	2.121	1.814	-0.31	1.17	2.489	2.023	-0.47	1.23
El Salvador	0.843	1.111	0.27	0.76	1.111	1.072	-0.04	1.04	1.385	1.398	0.01	0.99
Guatemala	1.632	1.647	0.02	0.99	1.785	1.564	-0.22	1.14	2.105	1.728	-0.38	1.22
Honduras	1.542	1.279	-0.26	1.21	1.900	1.641	-0.26	1.16	2.439	2.014	-0.43	1.21
Nicaragua	0.252	0.250	0.00	1.01	0.368	0.262	-0.11	1.40	0.459	0.289	-0.17	1.59
Panama	0.335	1.391	1.06	0.24	0.388	1.378	0.99	0.28	0.406	1.538	1.13	0.26
South America [g]	31.686	33.422	1.74	0.95	36.632	35.470	-1.16	1.03	39.240	43.140	3.90	0.91
Argentina	1.881	4.189	2.31	0.45	2.451	4.516	2.07	0.54	2.380	5.808	3.43	0.41
Bolivia	0.271	0.214	-0.06	1.27	0.284	0.269	-0.02	1.06	0.232	0.295	0.06	0.79
Brazil	9.428	11.439	2.01	0.82	9.296	12.699	3.40	0.73	10.149	15.912	5.76	0.64
Chile	2.197	3.615	1.42	0.61	2.580	4.131	1.55	0.62	2.627	4.375	1.75	0.60
Colombia	3.992	4.624	0.63	0.86	4.525	4.709	0.18	0.96	5.034	5.199	0.17	0.97
Ecuador	2.158	1.538	-0.62	1.40	2.121	1.257	-0.86	1.69	2.280	1.523	-0.76	1.50
Paraguay	0.060	0.992	0.93	0.06	0.046	0.897	0.85	0.05	0.045	0.913	0.87	0.05
Venezuela	10.428	4.640	-5.79	2.25	13.719	4.741	-8.98	2.89	14.389	6.607	-7.78	2.18

Footnotes and sources located at end of table.

Table 1.2 (continued), 1995–1997

	1995				1996				1997			
	Imports	Exports	Balance	Ratio	Imports	Exports	Balance	Ratio	Imports	Exports	Balance	Ratio
Other W. Hemisphere												
~ **Caribbean Basin** [h]	13.035	15.673	2.64	0.83	14.740	15.937	1.20	0.92	16.490	17.802	1.31	0.93
Bahamas	0.171	0.661	0.49	0.26	0.178	0.725	0.55	0.25	0.179	0.810	0.63	0.22
Dominican Republic	3.511	3.015	-0.50	1.16	3.677	3.183	-0.49	1.16	4.445	3.928	-0.52	1.13
Jamaica	0.895	1.420	0.53	0.63	0.890	1.491	0.60	0.60	0.779	1.417	0.64	0.55
Netherland Antilles	0.310	0.751	0.44	0.41	0.696	0.729	0.03	0.95	n/a	n/a	n/a	n/a
Trinidad & Tobago	1.055	0.689	-0.37	1.53	1.106	0.665	-0.44	1.66	1.227	1.106	-0.12	1.11
Asia [i]	317.052	179.829	-137.22	1.76	317.356	187.095	-130.26	1.70	345.464	192.822	-152.64	1.79
China	48.521	11.748	-36.77	4.13	54.409	11.978	-42.43	4.54	65.832	12.805	-53.03	5.14
Japan	127.195	64.298	-62.90	1.98	117.963	67.535	-50.43	1.75	124.266	65.673	-58.59	1.89
~ **E. Asia NICs** [j]	84.690	74.246	-10.44	1.14	85.230	75.637	-9.59	1.13	88.560	78.297	-10.26	1.13
Hong Kong	10.745	14.220	3.48	0.76	10.262	13.956	3.69	0.74	10.675	15.115	4.44	0.71
South Korea	24.890	25.413	0.52	0.98	23.297	26.583	3.29	0.88	23.798	25.067	1.27	0.95
Singapore	18.897	15.318	-3.58	1.23	20.648	16.685	-3.96	1.24	20.368	17.727	-2.64	1.15
Taiwan	30.158	19.295	-10.86	1.56	31.023	18.413	-12.61	1.68	33.718	20.388	-13.33	1.65
~ **Other Asia** [k]	56.646	29.537	-27.11	1.92	59.754	31.945	-27.81	1.87	66.807	36.047	-30.76	1.85
Burma	0.087	0.016	-0.07	5.44	0.116	0.032	-0.08	3.63	0.123	0.020	-0.10	6.15
Cambodia	0.006	0.027	0.021	0.22	0.005	0.021	0.016	0.24	0.010	0.018	0.01	0.56
India	6.091	3.296	-2.80	1.85	6.529	3.318	-3.21	1.97	7.712	3.616	-4.10	2.13
Indonesia	7.955	3.360	-4.60	2.37	8.743	3.965	-4.78	2.21	9.738	4.532	-5.21	2.15
Malaysia	17.981	8.816	-9.17	2.04	18.331	8.521	-9.81	2.15	18.523	10.828	-7.70	1.71
Pakistan	1.278	0.941	-0.34	1.36	1.349	1.277	-0.07	1.06	1.526	1.234	-0.29	1.24
Philippines	7.364	5.295	-2.07	1.39	8.496	6.125	-2.37	1.39	10.797	7.427	-3.37	1.45
Sri Lanka	1.343	0.279	-1.06	4.81	1.477	0.211	-1.27	7.00	1.711	0.155	-1.56	11.04
Thailand	11.854	6.665	-5.19	1.78	11.798	7.211	-4.59	1.64	13.056	7.357	-5.70	1.77
Viet Nam	0.210	0.253	0.04	0.83	0.342	0.616	0.27	0.56	0.413	0.278	-0.14	1.49

Table 1.2 *(continued)*, 1995–1997

Middle East [l]	17.434	17.535	0.10	0.99	19.159	19.930	0.77	0.96	21.597	20.922	-0.68	1.03
Israel [m]	5.841	5.621	-0.22	1.04	6.546	6.009	-0.54	1.09	7.459	5.992	-1.47	1.24
Kuwait	1.469	1.437	-0.03	1.02	1.782	1.979	0.20	0.90	1.998	1.394	-0.60	1.43
Saudi Arabia	8.898	6.155	-2.74	1.45	9.443	7.295	-2.15	1.29	10.148	8.451	-1.70	1.20
United Arab Emirates	0.485	2.006	1.52	0.24	0.538	2.527	1.99	0.21	0.965	2.606	1.64	0.37
Africa [n]	16.237	9.888	-6.35	1.64	19.450	10.503	-8.95	1.85	21.102	11.356	-9.75	1.86
Algeria	1.807	0.774	-1.03	2.33	2.270	0.632	-1.64	3.59	2.646	0.695	-1.95	3.81
Angola	2.390	0.260	-2.13	9.19	2.855	0.268	-2.59	10.65	2.937	0.280	-2.66	10.49
Egypt	0.655	2.985	2.33	0.22	0.714	3.146	2.43	0.23	0.695	3.840	3.15	0.18
Gabon	1.558	0.054	-1.50	28.85	2.067	0.056	-2.01	36.91	2.348	0.084	-2.26	27.95
Ivory Coast	0.230	0.173	-0.06	1.33	0.431	0.141	-0.29	3.06	0.314	0.151	-0.16	2.08
Morocco	0.255	0.517	0.26	0.49	0.272	0.476	0.20	0.57	0.346	0.435	0.09	0.80
Nigeria	5.055	0.603	-4.45	8.38	6.171	0.816	-5.36	7.56	6.705	0.814	-5.89	8.24
South Africa	2.311	2.751	0.44	0.84	2.436	3.106	0.67	0.78	2.616	3.000	0.38	0.87
Zaire	0.273	0.077	-0.20	3.55	0.260	0.073	-0.19	3.56	0.295	0.038	-0.26	7.76
Oceania												
Australia	3.565	10.788	7.22	0.33	4.127	11.992	7.87	0.34	4.911	12.041	7.13	0.41
New Zealand	1.596	1.693	0.10	0.94	1.608	1.727	0.12	0.93	1.734	1.957	0.22	0.89

Footnotes and sources located at end of table.

Table 1.2 *(continued)*

Source: U.S. Foreign Trade Highlights (1988, 1989, 1994). U.S. Dept. of Commerce, Intl. Trade Admin.; *National Trade Data Bank* (May 1997, Jan. 1997, Jan. 1996, March 1995, March 1994, March 1993), U.S. Dept. of Commerce, Econ. and Statistics Admin., Office of Business Analysis.

[a]**Non-European Union (Non-E.U.) Europe** includes:

- From 1980 to December 31, 1994: Austria, Cyprus, Finland, Gibraltar, Iceland, Malta, Norway, Sweden, Switzerland, Turkey, and Yugoslavia.
- From 1995 forward: Cyprus, Gibraltar, Iceland, Malta, Norway, Switzerland, Turkey, and (former) Yugoslavia (as of 1992; former Yugoslavia includes Bosnia-Herzegovina, Croatia, Macedonia, Serbia and Montenegro, and Slovenia).

[b]**E.U. Europe** includes:

- From 1980 to December 31, 1994: Belgium, Denmark, France, Germany, Greece, Ireland, Italy, Luxembourg, Netherlands, Portugal, Spain, and the United Kingdom.
- From 1995 forward: Austria, Belgium, Denmark, Finland, France, Germany, Greece, Ireland, Italy, Luxembourg, Netherlands, Portugal, Spain, Sweden, and the United Kingdom.

[c]**Eastern Europe** includes: Albania, Bulgaria, (former) Czechoslovakia (see footnote d), East Germany (until 1989, at which time it is counted as part of Germany), Hungary, Poland, Romania, and the (former) Soviet Union (see footnote e).

[d]**Czechoslovakia** existed until the end of 1992. As of 1993, former Czechoslovakia includes the Czech Republic and Slovakia.

[e]The **Soviet Union** existed until the end of 1991. As of 1992, the former Soviet Union includes: Armenia, Azerbaijan, Belarus, Estonia, Georgia, Kazakhstan, Kyrgyzstan, Latvia, Lithuania, Moldova, Russia, Tajikistan, Turkmenistan, Ukraine, and Uzbekistan.

[f]**Central America** includes: Belize, Costa Rica, El Salvador, Guatemala, Honduras, Nicaragua, and Panama.

[g]**South America** includes: Argentina, Bolivia, Brazil, Chile, Colombia, Ecuador, Paraguay, Peru, Uruguay, Venezuela.

Table 1.2 *(continued)*

[h]**Caribbean Basin** includes: Bahamas, Barbados, Belize, Cayman Islands, Costa Rica, Dominican Republic, El Salvador, Guatemala, Guyana, Haiti, Honduras, Jamaica, Leeward and Windward Islands, Netherland Antilles, Nicaragua, Panama, Suriname, Trinidad and Tobago, Turks and Caicos Islands.

[i]**Asia** includes: China, Japan, the East Asia NICs (see footnote j), and Other Asia (see footnote k).

[j]**East Asia NICs** includes: Hong Kong, South Korea, Singapore, and Taiwan.

[k]**Other Asia** includes: Afghanistan, Bangladesh, Brunei, Burma, Cambodia, India, Indonesia, North Korea, Laos, Macao, Malaysia, Mongolia, Nepal, Pakistan, Philippines, South Asia NEC, Sri Lanka, Thailand, and Vietnam.

[l]**Middle East** includes: Bahrain, Iran, Iraq, Israel (including Gaza) Jordan, Kuwait, Lebanon, Neutral Zone, Oman, Qatar, Saudi Arabia, Syria, United Arab Emirates, Yemen.

[m]**Israel** includes the Gaza Strip.

[n]**Africa** includes: Algeria, Angola, Benin, Botswana, Burkina Faso, Burundi, Cameroon, Central African Republic, Chad, Comoros Islands, Congo, Djibouti, Egypt, Equatorial Guinea, Ethiopia, Gabon, The Gambia, Ghana, Guinea, Guinea Bissau, Ivory Coast, Kenya, Lesotho, Liberia, Madagascar, Malawi, Mali, Mauritania, Mauritius, Morocco, Mozambique, Namibia, Niger, Nigeria, Reunion, Rwanda, Senegal, Seychelles, Sierra Leone, Somalia, South Africa, Sudan, Swaziland, Tanzania, Togo, Tunisia, Uganda, Western Sahara, Zaire, Zambia, Zimbabwe.

Table 1.3 U.S. GNP and Federal Government Expenditures, Selected Years, 1980–1997 (in billions of $U.S.)

Year	1980	1984	1988	1990	1991	1992	1993	1994	1995	1996	1997
GNP[a]	2,819.5	3,933.5	5,062.6	5,764.9	5,932.4	6,255.5	6,563.5	6,931.9	7,246.7	7,567.1	8,060.1
Gross Federal Debt[b]	908.5	1,564.1	2,600.8	3,206.3	3,599.0	4,002.1	4,351.4	4,643.7	4,921.0	5,181.9	5,369.70
Total Federal Expenditures[c]	613.1	892.7	1,109.0	1,273.6	1,332.7	1,479.4	1,530.9	1,567.3	1,637.6	1,698.1	1,752.2
Federal Receipts	553.0	725.8	972.3	1,107.4	1,122.2	1,198.5	1,275.3	1,377.0	1,463.2	1,587.6	---
Federal Deficits	-60.1	-166.9	-136.7	-166.2	-210.5	-280.9	-255.6	-190.3	-174.4	-110.5	---
Interest Paid on Federal Debt[d]	64.5	137.7	175.5	209.2	220.9	217.9	214.4	224.1	250.0	253.1	254.5
National Defense Outlays (total)[e]	134.0	227.4	290.4	299.3	273.3	298.4	291.1	281.6	272.1	265.7	270.5
Military Retirement & Disability[f]	11.9	16.5	19.0	21.5	23.1	24.5	25.7	26.7	27.8	28.8	30.1
Veterans' Benefits[g]	11.0	12.8	14.8	13.4	14.4	15.7	18.0	18.0	20.8	21.6	22.4
Social Security[h]	118.5	178.2	219.3	248.6	269.0	287.6	304.6	319.6	335.8	349.7	365.3
Medicare[i]	34.0	61.0	85.7	107.4	114.2	129.4	143.2	159.6	177.1	174.2	190.0
Welfare (means-tested programs)[j]	45.9	61.3	80.5	99.9	122.3	146.4	162.4	177.1	190.6	186.9 (e)	200.2 (e)
- Student Loans[k]	1.4	3.2	2.8	4.4	4.8	1.7	2.2	2.8	4.4	n/a	n/a
- Medicaid	14.0	20.1	30.5	41.1	52.5	67.8	75.8	82.0	89.1	92.0	95.6
- Food Stamps	9.1	12.4	13.1	15.9	19.6	22.8	24.6	25.4	25.6	25.4	22.3
- Child Nutrition	3.4	3.5	4.3	5.0	5.5	6.1	6.6	7.0	7.5	7.9	8.3
- Earned Income Tax Credit	1.3	1.2	2.7	4.4	4.9	8.2	9.4	11.7	15.2	19.2	21.9
- Supplemental Security Income	5.7	7.6	11.4	11.5	14.8	17.9	21.2	24.5	24.5	22.9	25.4
- Family Support	7.3	8.9	10.8	12.2	14.1	15.7	16.4	17.3	18.1	16.7	15.1
- Veterans' Pensions	3.6	3.9	3.9	3.6	4.0	3.7	3.5	3.4	3.0	2.8	3.1
- Other	0.1	0.5	1.0	1.8	2.1	2.5	2.7	3.0	3.2	n/a	n/a

Sources:

[a]Table 1, "Gross Domestic Product (1929–1996)," *Survey of Current Business* (May 1997, U.S. Dept. of Commerce, Econ. and Statistics Admin., Bur. of Econ. Analysis. 1997 data from Table 1.9, "Relation of Gross Domestic Product, Gross National Product, Net National Product & Personal Income," *Survey of Current Business* (Sept. 1997).

[b]Table 1-15, "Federal Finances and the Federal Debt, 1995–1996)," *1996 Green Book*, U.S. House of Representatives Ways and Means Committee.

[c]Data for: 1980–1988 taken from Table 3.2, "Federal Government Receipts and Expenditures," *National Income and Product Accounts of the United States, Volume 2, 1959–1988*, U.S. Dept. of Commerce, Econ. and Statistics Admin., Bureau of Econ. Analysis; 1989–1990 from Table 3.2, "Federal Government Receipts and Expenditures," *Survey of Current Business* (Dec. 1991); 1991 from Table 3.2, "Federal Government Receipts and Expenditures" (Dec. 1992); 1992–1994 from Table 3.2, "Federal Government Receipts and Current Expenditures," *Survey of Current Business* (Aug. 1996); 1995–1997 from Table 3.2, "Federal Government Receipts and Current Expenditures," *Survey of Current Business* (Sept. 1997).

[d]Ibid.

[e]Table B-78, "Federal Receipts and Outlays, by Major Category, and Surplus or Deficit (Fiscal Years 1940–1998)," *Economic Report of the President* (1997).

[f]Table 1-5, "Historical Outlays for Entitlements and Other Mandatory Spending, Sel. Fiscal Years 1975–95)," *1996 Green Book*.

[g](Incl. veterans' comp., readj. benefits, life ins., and housing programs.) 1980–1994 from Table 1-5, "Historical Outlays for Entitlements and Other Mandatory Spending, Sel. Years, 1975–95," *1996 Green Book*. 1995–1997 from Table 2.1, "Personal Income and its Disposition," *Survey of Current Business* (Sept. 1997).

[h]Table B-78, "Federal Receipts and Outlays, by Major Category, and Surplus or Deficit (Fiscal Years 1940–1998)," *Economic Report of the President* (1997).

[i]Table 1-5, "Historical Outlays for Entitlements and Other Mandatory Spending, Sel. Fiscal years 1975–95," *1996 Green Book*.

[j]Ibid.

[k]Formerly known as guaranteed student loans.

[l]Data for 1997 taken from Historical Tables 1.1, 2.1, 3.1, 6.1, 7.1, 11.3, and 16.1, *Budget of the United States Government Fiscal Year 1999*; *Economic Report of the President* (1998); and *Survey of Current Business* (March 1998).

Table 1.4   **Foreign Exchange Rates, Selected Years, 1971–1998**
(in currency units per $U.S.)

Country/currency:	Jan. 1971	Sep. 1973	Dec. 1976
U.S./dollar [1]	120.4000	95.1100	105.3300
Japan/yen	358.0100	265.4800	294.7000
Germany/deutsche mark	3.6369	2.4245	2.3829
Switzerland/franc	4.3053	3.1070	2.4496
Taiwan/dollar	n/a	n/a	n/a
South Korea/won	n/a	n/a	n/a
United Kingdom/pound [2]	240.5800	241.8300	167.8400
Country/currency:	May 1995	May 1996	Jan. 1997
U.S./dollar [1]	82.7300	88.2800	91.0100
Japan/yen	85.1100	106.3400	117.9100
Germany/deutsche mark	1.4096	1.5324	1.6047
Switzerland/franc	1.1693	1.2539	1.3913
Taiwan/dollar	25.5370	27.3520	27.4770
South Korea/won	764.4300	780.8600	854.0700
United Kingdom/pound [2]	158.7400	151.5200	165.8500

Source: (unless otherwise noted) *Federal Reserve Bulletin,* Board of Governors of the Federal Reserve System (various issues).

[1] Index of weighted-average exchange value of U.S. dollar against the currencies of ten industrial countries. The weight for each of the ten countries is the 1972–76 average world trade of that country divided by the average world trade of all ten countries combined. Series revised as of August 1978.

[2] Value in U.S. cents per pound.

Dec. 1980	Jan. 1985	Dec. 1987	Dec. 1991	Dec. 1994
90.9900	152.8300	88.7000	85.6500	89.6400
209.4400	254.1800	128.2400	128.0400	100.1800
1.9697	3.1706	1.6335	1.5630	1.5716
1.7850	2.6590	1.3304	1.3855	1.3289
n/a	39.2090	29.0040	25.7590	26.2860
n/a	832.1600	798.3400	761.6800	794.8100
234.5900	112.7100	182.8800	182.7200	155.8700
Apr. 1997[3]	Sep. 1997[4]	Dec. 1997[5]	Jan. 1998[6]	Apr. 1998[7]
97.4000	97.4700	98.4900	101.0800	101.8700
127.0300	120.7100	129.1500	133.9900	133.7600
1.7330	1.7671	1.7770	1.8223	1.8542
1.4745	1.4548	1.4330	1.4803	1.5335
27.6800	28.6600	32.4500	33.6000	32.9000
894.0000	917.0000	1,188.0000	1,790.0000	1,392.0000
162.0000	161.1700	168.2500	163.3000	167.4000

[3]Rates as of April 30, 1997; *Foreign Exchange Rates (weekly)*. Board of Governors of the Federal Reserve System (rel. date May 27, 1997)
<http://www.bog.frb.fed.us/releases/H10/19970527/>.

[4]Rates as of Sept. 30, 1997; *Foreign Exchange Rates (weekly)*, Board of Governors of the Federal Reserve System (rel. date Oct 24, 1997)
<http://www.bog.frb.fed.us/releases/H10/19971027/>.

[5]Rates as of Dec. 1, 1997; *Foreign Exchange Rates (weekly)*, Board of Governors of the Federal Reserve System (rel. date Dec. 5, 1997)
<http://www.bog.frb.fed.us/releases/H10/>.

[6]Rates as of January 9, 1998; *Foreign Exchange Rates (weekly)*, Board of Governors of the Federal Reserve System (rel. date Jan. 5, 1998)
<http:/www.bog.frb.fed.us/releases/H10/19980112/>.

[7]Rates as of April 3, 1998; *Foreign Exchange Rates (weekly)*, Board of Governors of the Federal Reserve System (rel. date April 1, 1998)
<http://www.bog.frb.fed.us/releases/H10/Current/>.

Table 1.5   Per Capita Gross National Product by Nation, Selected Years, 1953–1995 (in current $U.S.)

Country: / Year	1953	1960	1965	1970	1975	1980	1985	1991	1994	1995
U.S.	2,310	2,830	3,580	4,826	7,141	11,446	16,693	22,240	25,860	26,980
USSR (Russia)	----	1,600	1,900	2,300	2,700	5,730	5,749	3,220	2,650	2,240
Japan	230	460	900	1,964	4,481	9,069	11,024	26,930	34,630	39,640
West Germany	740	1,310	1,950	3,042	6,751	13,216	10,123	23,650	25,580	27,510
France	1,010	1,350	2,050	2,775	6,430	12,163	9,270	20,380	23,470	24,990
U.K.	940	1,380	1,640	2,213	4,162	9,470	8,039	16,550	18,410	18,700
Belgium	940	1,250	1,610	2,616	6,304	11,927	8,068	18,950	22,920	24,710
Italy	430	700	1,120	1,875	3,464	7,011	6,278	18,520	19,270	19,020
Sweden	1,120	1,740	2,660	4,139	8,843	14,938	11,975	25,110	23,630	23,750
Switzerland	1,150	1,600	2,330	3,308	8,477	15,920	14,194	33,610	37,180	40,630
Spain	----	340	680	1,086	2,952	5,665	4,340	12,490	13,280	13,580
Netherlands	610	990	1,570	2,567	6,364	11,970	8,525	18,780	21,970	24,000
Norway	870	1,240	1,890	2,883	7,100	14,121	13,953	24,220	26,480	31,250
Hungary	----	1,500	1,800	2,000	2,400	4,180	1,956	2,720	3,840	4,120
Yugoslavia	----	590	520	714	1,557	2,470	1,878	----	----	----
Poland	----	1,500	1,800	2,100	2,800	----	2,241	1,790	2,470	2,790
China	93	117	134	167	209	240	333	370	530	620
South Korea	----	152	115	266	583	1,620	1,986	6,350	8,220	9,700
Taiwan	100	150	199	227	910	2,260	3,140	7,190	11,597	12,439
India	62	74	103	100	147	210	255	330	310	340
Canada	1,710	2,090	2,460	3,870	7,213	10,800	13,096	20,440	19,570	19,380
Mexico	232	334	455	701	1,463	1,950	2,260	3,030	4,010	3,320
Brazil	----	208	236	505	1,219	2,060	1,623	2,940	3,370	3,640

Source: National Accounts of OECD Countries, 1950–1968, p. 10; *National Accounts of OECD Countries, 1960–1984,* "Comparative Table 21," OECD, Dept. of Econ. and Statistics. *Yearbook of National Account Statistics, 1969,* Vol. II, Table 1C and *1972,* Vol. III, Table 1A, United Nations, Dept. of Econ. and Social Affairs, Statistics Office. *Geographical Distribution of Financial Flows, 1981–84,* Section C, pp. 274–75, OECD (Paris 1986). *Worldmark Encyclopedia of the Nations, Vol. V; Hungary, Poland, and USSR,* Worldmark Press Ltd. Paul S. Shoup, *The East European and Soviet Data Handbook: Political and Development Indicators, 1965–75,* Table 11-4, Columbia Univ. Press (New York 1991). Willy Kraus, *Economic Development and Social Change in the People's Republic of China,* Table A1, Springer-Verlag (New York 1979). *Morgan International Data,* Table A-1, Morgan Guaranty Trust Co., Intl., Econ. Dept (June 1986). *World Financial Markets,* Morgan Guaranty Trust Co. (Oct./Nov. 1986). *OECD Economic Outlook* (Dec. 1986). "Korea Business Brief," *Asia Wall Street Journal* (Jan. 5, 1987), p. 4. *The World Bank Atlas, 1990; The World Development Report, 1992–94,* The World Bank, 1990; *The World Bank Atlas, 1996,* The World Bank; *The World Bank Atlas, 1997,* The World Bank. *World Information Country Outlooks,* Bank of America, Taiwan (Nov. 1990). *Taiwan Statistical Data Book, 1996,* Council for Econ. Planning and Devt., Rep. of China.

Note: The fluctuations in relative GNPs in 1980, 1985, 1991, 1994, and 1995 reflect a "low" dollar in 1980, a "high" dollar in 1985, a "declining" dollar in 1991, a somewhat "lower" dollar in 1994, and a "low" dollar in 1995.

Table 1.6   **Average Weekly Earnings of U.S. Production or Nonsupervisory Workers on Nonagricultural Payrolls, Selected Years, 1940–1997 (in $U.S.)**

Year	Total Private		Manufacturing	
	Current Dollars	Constant Dollars [a]	Current Dollars	Constant Dollars [a]
1940	n.a.	n.a.	24.96	n.a.
1947	45.58	196.47	49.13	211.77
1955	67.72	243.60	75.30	270.87
1965	95.45	291.90	107.53	328.84
1972	136.90	315.44	154.71	356.48
1978	203.70	300.89	249.27	368.20
1980	235.10	274.65	288.62	337.17
1981	255.20	270.63	318.00	337.23
1982	267.26	267.26	330.26	330.26
1983	280.70	272.52	354.08	343.76
1984	292.86	274.73	374.03	350.88
1985	299.09	271.16	386.37	350.29
1986	304.85	271.94	396.01	353.26
1987	312.50	269.16	406.31	349.96
1988	322.02	266.79	418.81	346.98
1989	334.24	264.22	429.68	339.67
1990	345.35	259.47	441.86	331.98
1991	353.98	255.40	455.03	328.31
1992	363.61	254.99	469.86	329.50
1993	373.64	254.87	486.04	331.54
1994	385.86	256.73	506.94	337.29
1995	394.34	255.07	514.59	332.85
1996	406.26	255.51	531.65	334.37
1997 [b]	421.40	259.19	548.02	337.07

Source: National Employment, Hours and Earnings, Series EEU00500004, EEU30000004, and EEU00500051, U.S. Dept. of Labor, Bureau of Labor Statistics.
Note: n.a. = not available.
[a]Constant dollars in 1982 base year.
[b]As of October 1, 1997.

2

ALFRED E. ECKES JR.

U.S. Trade History

Products and Partners

To survive and prosper in the New World, the courageous settlers of British
North America relied on trade. Beginning in the seventeenth century, the
colonists shipped large quantities of foodstuffs and raw materials across the
Atlantic to England—particularly furs, tobacco, rice, indigo, rum, grain, pot-
ash, coal, fish, timber, and naval stores. This external trade contributed 20
percent of total income during colonial times and established a pattern that
would endure for many years. Until the 1960s the majority of U.S. exports
(by value) consisted of food products and industrial materials, although para-
doxically the United States became the world's leading manufacturing power
before World War I. Early American settlers also built ships, and U.S. shipping soon played a big role in the Atlantic carrying trade. But, it was in
primary and semi-processed products, not finished goods and services, that
colonial America prospered and penetrated world markets.[1]

Europe soon developed an insatiable appetite for American commodities—especially tobacco, cotton, wheat, and petroleum. Tobacco brought
prosperity to the Chesapeake region and it quickly emerged as the leading
export crop, amounting to one-third to one-half of total exports. Despite the
health hazards of smoking, American tobacco remains an important export.
In 1995, this country sold abroad $6.6 billion in tobacco and tobacco prod-
ucts. But, early in the nineteenth century cotton displaced tobacco as the
leading export. American grown long-staple cotton quickly became an essential raw material for the spindles of Lancashire. In the generation before
the American Civil War cotton was considered king. It constituted more
than half of total U.S. exports, and during the war the South hoped that
English dependence on American cotton would bring favorable intervention. As late as the 1920s raw cotton still accounted for more than 20
percent of U.S. exports, and in 1995 it earned a respectable $3.7 billion
from foreign sales.

By the middle of the nineteenth century, an industrializing Europe developed an appetite for other American raw-materials and farm products, such as wheat, lard, pork, and petroleum. Wheat and flour exports soared as improved railroad transportation integrated the American Midwest into the international economy. Wheat would remain a sizable export, amounting to $5.5 billion in 1995. Petroleum never became America's leading export, but late in the nineteenth century the United States emerged for a while as the world's leading oil exporter. American oil proved critical to Allied victory in World War I, supplying 80 percent of petroleum needs. Lord Curzon observed how "the Allied cause had floated to victory upon a wave of [American] oil." As late as 1929 the United States produced 68 percent of the world's oil.[2]

American imports exhibited a more complex pattern. From colonial times until the Civil War finished manufactures and consumer goods composed the majority of imports. These included clothing, tools, equipment, and home furnishings. A different pattern emerged after the Civil War and continued for more than a century—until the 1980s. During this period a majority of American imports were food (particularly coffee and sugar) and industrial supplies (rubber and petroleum). This shift reflected the requirements of the American protective system, which imposed higher duties on manufactures and encouraged the importation of tropical foods and raw materials. As tariff levels declined to minimal levels, and as a global economy took shape in the 1980s, the composition of American imports changed again. With large quantities of foreign-made cars, machine tools, apparel, footwear, and other consumer goods entering the open American market, it is not surprising that finished goods again came to dominate the import trade (see Table 2.1).

This second shift in import composition coincided with the emergence of major new trading partners in Asia (see Table 2.2). At the beginning of the twentieth century Europe accounted for the majority of total U.S. trade. Indeed, until the 1890s Britain had purchased more than half of exports—a statistic that reflected the importance of American cotton for the English textile industry—and the United Kingdom would remain the largest export market until World War I, when Canada took the lead. In 1900, 75 percent of U.S. exports crossed the Atlantic to Europe. As a market for U.S. products Germany ranked second to Britain; France held fourth place behind Canada. In the early twentieth century the Asian market was small but rising. Asia bought about 5 percent of exports, while Latin America purchased another 10 percent. In 1900 Great Britain remained the leading supplier of U.S. imports—and would remain so until the 1920s when Canada moved to the front.

Table 2.1 Percentage of Exports and Imports by Broad End-Use Class, 1925–1997

Year	Food, Feed & Beverages		Industrial Supplies		Capital Goods (excluding auto)		Automotive (including parts)		Consumer Goods	
	Imports	Exports	Imports	Exports	Imports	Exports	Imports	Exports	Imports	Exports
1925	21.7%	18.1%	67.5%	58.1%	0.3%	8.5%	-----	6.6%	9.3%	5.8%
1929	21.7%	14.4%	64.5%	54.0%	0.8%	12.5%	-----	10.4%	11.7%	6.5%
1930	22.3%	14.1%	63.5%	54.9%	0.9%	14.2%	-----	7.4%	11.3%	6.6%
1935	31.0%	9.5%	57.8%	60.0%	0.7%	11.6%	-----	10.2%	8.9%	6.4%
1939	25.9%	10.1%	61.8%	52.6%	0.6%	18.4%	-----	8.2%	8.5%	6.9%
1946	26.5%	22.6%	61.3%	39.5%	0.6%	17.0%	-----	5.7%	9.8%	11.1%
1950	29.5%	14.4%	61.3%	42.4%	1.2%	20.8%	0.3%	7.3%	6.0%	8.3%
1955	26.9%	13.6%	59.2%	39.0%	2.2%	19.7%	0.7%	8.2%	8.6%	7.3%
1960	21.8%	15.4%	52.3%	38.5%	3.7%	26.7%	4.2%	6.1%	12.6%	6.7%
1965	18.3%	17.9%	51.2%	32.4%	6.8%	29.2%	4.4%	7.0%	15.4%	6.5%
1970	15.4%	13.5%	37.8%	31.9%	9.5%	33.2%	14.9%	8.4%	18.9%	6.3%
1975	9.8%	18.5%	52.0%	27.9%	10.4%	34.2%	11.9%	9.9%	13.5%	6.2%
1980	7.4%	16.2%	53.0%	32.1%	12.6%	34.0%	11.3%	7.8%	13.7%	7.9%
1985	6.5%	11.4%	33.7%	28.3%	18.1%	36.7%	19.2%	11.6%	19.6%	6.8%
1990	5.3%	9.0%	29.1%	27.1%	23.3%	39.2%	17.8%	9.4%	21.1%	11.2%
1997	4.6%	7.5%	24.6%	22.9%	29.2%	42.7%	16.2%	10.7%	22.2%	11.2%

Source: Survey of Current Business (June 1993, June 1995, June 1997, April 1998), U.S. Department of Commerce, Economics & Statistical Administration, Bureau of Economic Analysis: *Historical Statistics of the United States,* Bicentennial Edition, II:895, U.S. Bureau of the Census (1975).

Table 2.2   Geography of American Trade as a Percentage of U.S. Exports and Imports by Country or Region, 1850–1997

Country/Region	1850		1900		1929		1960		1997	
	Imports	Exports	Imports	Exports	Imports	Exports	Imports	Exports	Imports	Exports
Canada	2.9%	6.9%	4.6%	6.8%	11.4%	18.1%	19.8%	18.5%	19.2%	22.3%
Mexico	0.5%	1.4%	3.4%	2.5%	2.7%	2.6%	3.0%	4.0%	9.8%	10.5%
Latin America	19.0%	13.9%	21.8%	9.5%	25.4%	18.9%	27.0%	18.8%	15.9%	19.8%
Great Britain	43.1%	49.3%	18.8%	38.3%	7.5%	16.2%	6.8%	7.2%	3.7%	5.4%
Germany	5.2%	3.4%	11.4%	13.4%	5.8%	7.8%	6.1%	6.2%	4.9%	3.6%
Europe	71.3%	75.7%	51.9%	74.6%	30.3%	44.7%	29.1%	40.0%	19.7%	22.9%
Japan	----	----	3.9%	2.1%	9.8%	4.9%	7.8%	7.0%	13.8%	9.7%
China	----	----	3.2%	1.1%	3.8%	2.4%	----	----	7.1%	1.9%
Asia	6.3%	2.1%	17.2%	4.9%	29.1%	12.3%	18.6%	20.3%	35.9%	32.9%

Source: Historical Statistics of the United States, Bicentennial Edition, II:895, U.S. Bureau of the Census (1975); *Statistical Abstract of the United States* (various issues); and *Survey of Current Business* (June 1993, June 1995, June 1997, April 1998), U.S. Department of Commerce, Economics & Statistics Administration, Bureau of Economic Analysis.

A century later Europe no longer dominates U.S. trade. During the last thirty years, Asian suppliers and markets rose rapidly in significance. In 1974 imports from that region surpassed imports from Europe, and in 1986 exports to Asia exceeded those to Europe (including Eastern Europe). By 1997, only 23 percent of U.S. merchandise exports crossed the Atlantic Ocean to Europe, while 29 percent went to Pacific Rim markets. This figure included Japan, 9.7 percent, and China, 1.9 percent. By comparison, Canada took 22 percent of U.S. exports and Latin America took 20 percent. On the import side the rise of Asia was even more pronounced. In 1997 the Pacific Rim supplied 36 percent of all imports (Japan, 13.8 percent, and China, 7.1 percent), compared to 20 percent for all of Western Europe. Canada held another 19.2 percent of the U.S. import market, and Latin America 15.9 percent.[3]

Colonial Antecedents

Colonial experiences and the lessons of the Revolutionary War both left an imprint on American trade policy after independence. On the one hand, many colonists prospered from participating in the eighteenth-century Atlantic economy, trading raw materials for import manufactures; they had a stake in trade expansion. But, if commercial interdependence produced prosperity, it also brought vulnerability. When the great colonial powers of Europe fought, as Britain and France did for much of the period from 1689 to 1815, their wars disrupted commerce in the North Atlantic and dislocated colonial life. Britain's effort to finance the costs of empire led to higher taxes and commercial regulations intended to sustain the mercantile system. These aggravations (taxation without representation) radicalized colonial merchants and encouraged colonial leaders, like Benjamin Franklin, to think of establishing a new nation that would protect American commerce, develop American industry, promote American agriculture, and encourage settlement of the frontier. Noting how America's population grew more rapidly than England's, Franklin conceived a time when America would lead the Atlantic economy.[4]

From these experiences, America's founders drew several conclusions that shaped public policy for 150 years. To maintain its political independence in an unstable international environment, America needed to focus on balanced internal development—to include industry as well as agriculture and commerce. This meant a national government prepared to focus on developing the nation's resources and on securing respect for American rights. Leaders like Benjamin Franklin and Thomas Jefferson did not contemplate self-sufficiency. They thought an expanding but agricultural America could pay its way in the Atlantic economy if it had access to foreign markets for its agricultural products and raw materials. This strategy hinged on developing a navy and a merchant marine, and using diplomacy to obtain respect for neutral rights, particularly for the principle, "Free ships make free goods."

In commercial treaties, intended to provide access to major European markets, Americans desired reciprocity and non-discrimination. They construed the latter as national treatment, meaning equality of treatment with foreign nations, not simply equality with the treatment accorded lesser third countries. Ideally, they wanted the benefits of unconditional most-favored-nation treatment, that is, trade conditions equal to those accorded most-favored parties.

Some merchants like Benjamin Franklin, planters like Thomas Jefferson, and New England lawyers like John Adams who shaped early commercial policy had an initial predisposition toward free trade. Franklin knew the famous Scottish economist Adam Smith, author of the *Wealth of Nations* (1776), a book that later generations have interpreted as a manifesto for free markets and freer trade. Jefferson, a young cosmopolitan, instinctively sympathized with such arguments. Indeed, in 1774 he boldly asserted that "free trade with all parts of the world" was a "natural right" that no law could abridge. Yet both Jefferson and his friend John Adams, who spoke publicly about removing the "shackles upon trade" and letting market forces dictate, worried about the conflict between economic prosperity and political independence. Said Adams in 1786:

> [I]f the United States would adopt the principle of the French economists, and allow the ships and merchants of all nations equal privileges with their own citizens, they need not give themselves any further trouble about treaties or ambassadors. The consequence nevertheless would be the sudden annihilation of all their manufactures and navigation. We should have the most luxurious set of farmers that ever existed, and should not be able to defend our sea coast against the insults of a pirate.[5]

These concerns about a lack of reciprocity were evident during the American Revolution when the Continental Congress sent Benjamin Franklin and several colleagues to Europe in pursuit of diplomatic recognition, assistance, and commercial agreements. With Britain's archenemy France, they succeeded in negotiating America's first trade treaty, the Franco-American Treaty of Amity and Commerce of February 1778. But, that agreement represented only a modest beginning. It failed to secure either *equality* (national treatment) or *unconditional* most-favored-nation treatment. Indeed, the commercial treaty contained only a *conditional* form of the most-favored-nation clause that gave each party the right to purchase concessions either provided to third countries. Probably the negotiators adopted this approach in order to keep Britain from gaining reciprocal access to either the French or the American states. The King of France was wary of a reconciliation between England and its former colonies. The Americans later wanted a commercial agreement with England that provided reciprocal access to Britain's market. Resorting to the unconditional most-favored-nation clause might have jeopardized those objectives. Despite its imperfections, and departure from principles, the 1778 agreement proved an important trade-policy document. The preamble committed America to the pursuit of "the most perfect equality and reciprocity." Secretary of State John Quincy Adams would later claim that the preamble was "the foundation of our commercial intercourse with the rest of mankind." He asserted it "should be the political manual for every negotiator of the United States, in every quarter of the globe." It placed "the true principles of all fair commercial negotiation between independent states" on the "diplomatic record of nations" for the first time.[6]

As it turned out, this first generation of American trade negotiators had little other success in promoting commercial reciprocity and equality. Although the Netherlands and Sweden signed similar agreements before independence, and Prussia did later, the Americans could not pry open access to European colonies in the Western Hemisphere, or obtain a commercial agreement with Great Britain. London excluded American ships from the British Isles and the West Indies, and sought to dominate the Atlantic trade. Most monarchs of continental Europe regarded the American revolutionaries with suspicion. Even the agreement with France proved difficult to implement, despite the efforts of officials in Paris. French merchants refused credit and ports openly discriminated against the Americans.[7]

Frustrated in Europe, the American traders had better luck accessing Asian markets. In February 1784 a group of New York merchants dispatched a 360–ton merchant ship, the *Empress of China,* to Canton with a cargo of ginseng. Exchanging it for tea, they returned in May 1785 having opened commercial relations with "the Eastern Extreme of the Globe." Their return on capital was 25 percent, a strong inducement to further trade expansion.[8]

Confederation to Constitution

During the first years of American independence, Europeans also had commercial grievances, as American debtors sought to escape their obligations and as individual states indulged in various forms of trade discrimination. Under the Articles of Confederation the thirteen states ceded only limited powers to the confederation government and retained power to levy taxes and regulate commerce. The thirteen pursued separate and discriminatory policies intended to raise revenues and protect local manufactures. Given the weakness of the central government in collecting taxes and regulating commerce, it is perhaps understandable that European powers adopted a wait-and-see attitude and discriminated against American shipping. Frustrated in his efforts to negotiate a commercial treaty with true reciprocity, John Adams could only lobby for a stronger central government, one having the power to regulate commerce and conduct foreign affairs. "[N]othing but retaliation, reciprocal prohibitions, and imposts, and putting ourselves in a posture of defense will have any effect," he wrote.[9]

It is important to remember that the commercial chaos of the Confederation period produced a consensus in favor of a strong central government. Chief Justice John Marshall observed later, "the deep and general conviction that commerce ought to be regulated by Congress" contributed significantly to the governmental revolution brought about by the Constitution. That text, adopted by delegates to the Constitutional Convention and approved by individual states, established what economists now call a customs union with internal free trade and a common external tariff. Previously, under the Articles of Confederation, individual states had imposed both import tariffs and export tariffs on trade with sister states. Moreover, the weak national government had no authority to raise revenue, and it lacked the resources to promote internal development and to support a merchant marine and a navy.[10]

The Constitution of 1787 specified a separation of powers between the Legislative and Executive branches. The former acquired specific authority to regulate commerce and levy taxes (Article I: Section 8); the latter gained the responsibility to conduct diplomatic negotiations and to negotiate treaties subject to the approval of Congress (Article II: Section 2). In effect, this arrangement provided the legal basis for a bifurcated trade policy. Only Congress could fix tariffs and regulate commerce; only the Executive could negotiate with foreign powers.

The first Act of the Congress in 1789 indicated the overriding importance that the new government attached to commercial policy. On July 4, 1789, the anniversary of independence, Congress enacted a revenue tariff—averaging about 8.5 percent ad valorem—to raise revenue for President George Washington's new national government. Although some in Congress favored higher protective duties, Secretary of the Treasury Alexander Hamilton urged moderation. To fund the national debt he wanted a dependable source of revenue, and a moderate tariff would meet the new government's needs by taxing commerce, but not prohibiting it. In enacting the tariff Congress opted for a single schedule, one that applied the same duties to imports from all countries. While this was consistent with the American desire for equal treatment and nondiscrimination, it left the Executive Branch without leverage to bargain down or retaliate against foreign trade barriers. In effect, the United States had chosen to treat its old friend France the same as its old adversary, Great Britain.[11]

America First

President George Washington's administration pursued a nationalistic course, one that reflected the general's own experiences and desire to promote development. He sought to strengthen the nation's economic base and reduce dependence on Europe, to develop internal transportation and communications, and to protect military security. Determined to promote domestic manufactures, the first president ordered an American-made suit for his inauguration in 1789 and pledged to give preference to domestic fabrics and produce.

Perhaps the most significant initiative to promote domestic industry was Treasury Secretary Hamilton's famous Report on Manufactures. In it Hamilton made the case for active government. If laissez faire were the prevailing practice of nations, he argued, the United States and other developing countries might forego the production of manufactures. But he noted that manufacturing nations, like Great Britain, sought to preserve "a monopoly of the domestic market to its own manufacturers." In such circumstances the United States needed to pursue a "similar policy" to secure for its citizens a "reciprocity of advantages." Hamilton was not worried about the short-run impact of trade barriers on domestic consumers. He argued that in a developing country the establishment of new manufactures would expand competition and with new suppliers prices would inevitably fall.[12]

Congress, diverted by more immediate problems such as Indian unrest on the frontier, took no immediate action on the report, but Hamilton's basic recommendations reverberated for generations. Describing Hamilton as "the greatest American," Arthur H. Vandenberg, later a U.S. senator from Michigan, concluded: "His whole 'Report on Manufactures' remains . . . the most lucid and convincing and complete defense of a protective tariff system which has ever been given to the American people. . . ." Even the Jeffersonians, who feared a strong central government, came to espouse industrial policy as the French Revolution destabilized Europe and brought Napoleon Bonaparte to power. In 1810, President James Madison's treasury secretary, Albert Gallatin, an enthusiastic supporter of free trade, issued his own statement on manufactures. It recommended import duties, export subsidies, and government loans to promote manufactures.[13]

The relatively low-revenue tariff approved in the act of 1789 continued until conflict between Britain and France during the Napoleonic Wars led to widespread disregard for American neutral rights, to the impressment of American sailors, and to property losses. To cope with this challenge, Jefferson espoused unilateral retaliation. Indeed, use of trade sanctions to obtain respect for American commercial rights had origin in Secretary of State Jefferson's policy statements during the French Revolution. Later, as President, Jefferson experimented with sanctions—including non-intercourse and the embargo. Under pressure from war hawks in Congress to stand up for American rights and commerce, Jefferson's successor President James Madison made the fateful decision to seek a war declaration in 1812. This second conflict with Britain exposed America's vulnerabilities, as British troops burned the White House and the Capitol. Afterward, British merchants indulged in discount pricing to move accumulated inventories. This dumping was intended, as a member of Parliament said, to "stifle in the cradle, those rising manufactures in the United States, which the war had forced into existence. . . ."[14]

American System

After the War of 1812, a more nationalistic Congress responded to the public desire for economic security and industry requests for protection. It enacted substantially higher duties on imports. This nationalistic trade policy, associated with House Speaker Henry Clay from Kentucky, became known as the American System, and it endured for more than a century. From the War of 1812 to World War II, American import duties averaged over 25 percent ad valorem on all dutiable goods in all but six years. In sixty of those years the average rate was 40 percent or higher.[15]

Today many economists and pundits associate free trade with rapid economic growth. This assertion, frankly, is incompatible with American economic history. The most rapid growth occurred during periods of high protectionism, not free trade. From 1889 to 1929, a forty-year period ending in the Great Depression, U.S. growth averaged 3.6 percent, significantly above the 3 percentage point average real growth for the twentieth century. And, for all but two of those years the United States enjoyed a merchandise trade surplus. Can protectionism spur economic growth? Paul Bairoch, a prominent Swiss economic historian, concluded that in the late nineteenth century countries pursuing protective policies (Germany and America) experienced higher growth rates than Great Britain, a country that unilaterally adopted free trade. Of course, it is arguable that developing countries typically have higher growth rates than mature economies. Nonetheless, the history of economic development suggests that protectionism is frequently one aspect of a successful development strategy. None of the world's present industrial nations achieved economic success without experiencing a sustained protectionist phase.[16] Of course, not every nation that practiced protectionism pursued successful development policies. And in the case of the United States and Germany the establishment of large national markets (internal free trade areas) clearly gave stimulus to economic growth as business expanded to serve larger markets.

In the nineteenth century many leaders, and most Republicans, considered protectionism indispensable to American development. Indeed, from the Civil War to World War II Republicans regularly celebrated the success of their protectionist policies. Said the GOP platform in 1896: "We renew and emphasize our allegiance to the policy of protection, as the bulwark of American industrial independence, and the foundation of American development and prosperity. This true American policy taxes foreign products and encourages home industry." Four years later in 1900 Republicans renewed their faith in protectionism. "In that policy our industries have been established, diversified and maintained. By protecting the home market competition has been stimulated and production cheapened." As a result, American working people enjoyed "better conditions of life from those of any competing country."[17] In nineteenth-century America substantial tariffs were not simply trade barriers imposed to advance the narrow interests of favored manufacturers. They served a larger national purpose, one intended to secure American independence from foreign interference and to promote national prosperity. Economic data show that the United States achieved high levels of economic growth after the American Civil War, and declining prices for many protected goods suggest that in the context of a large continental market protectionism was not inconsistent with rapid economic development.

If America's industrial policy—the protective tariff—promoted national economic development, it complicated efforts of export-oriented businesses and emerging industries to gain improved access to foreign markets. Because Congress legislated tariffs and subjected all imports to a uniform schedule, the Executive Branch had no leverage to effect preferential bilateral agreements with foreign powers. The State Department, which handled trade negotiations from 1789 to 1962, when Congress established the White House position of special trade representative, found several opportunities to test congressional resolve on this issue, but was unable to effect a modification.

One such episode occurred in the early 1840s after tobacco growers pressured the State Department to promote tobacco exports. The U.S. minister to Prussia, Henry Wheaton, a fervent free-trader, opened negotiations with the Zollverein. He signed a treaty that opened the German market for agricultural exports while lowering American duties on manufactures. This had broader significance, because the Convention of 1815 with Britain appeared to contain an unconditional most-favored-nation clause. London thus argued that approval of the Zollverein Treaty entitled British exporters to identical low-tariff treatment in the American market. The matter became moot after the Senate tabled the proposed treaty in June 1844. The Senate construed the agreement as an effort to undercut the authority of Congress to regulate commerce. Like many trade-policy disputes, this one had partisan elements, but fundamentally it involved a test of wills between Congress and the Executive over which branch was to control trade policy. Eager to satisfy the tobacco industry and its many congressional supporters, a U.S. diplomatic representative tried to trade off domestic manufacturing interests to benefit agricultural exporters and promote foreign policy objectives. In the 1840s Congress had no disposition to accept a one-sided agreement that opened the American market without obtaining significant export opportunities.[18]

Cobden's Challenge

The Senate had good reason to worry about the efforts of doctrinaire free-traders to subvert the American system. Across the Atlantic in Great Britain doctrinaire free-traders had effected a major change in British commercial policy when Parliament repealed the corn laws. Cotton manufacturer Richard Cobden and other reformers touted free trade as the "grand panacea" for promoting peace and prosperity. In 1843 they started a magazine called *The Economist* "solely for the purpose of advocating these principles." Said the magazine's founders: "we seriously believe that *free trade,* free intercourse, will do more than any other visible agent to extend civilization and morality throughout the world." Later, Cobden and his corn-law reformers persuaded Sir Robert Peel and Parliament to repeal Britain's tariff structure and adopt unilateral free trade, generally.[19]

They were less successful in exporting the free trade doctrine to America. Robert J. Walker, President James K. Polk's Secretary of the Treasury, fancied himself a Democratic free-trader, and he proposed major tariff reforms in the United States. As adopted, the Walker Tariff, the Tariff Act of 1846, lowered average duties on all imports from about 29 percent in 1845 to 23 percent. It also converted many duties from a specific to an ad valorem basis. Until the Civil War, Democrats flirted with tariff liberalization, including an 1854 reciprocity treaty with Canada lowering duties on raw materials. The Pierce administration wanted to move faster toward free trade, but Congress and the domestic business community remained skeptical and resisted fundamental change. Even so, "tariff-for-revenue-only" Democrats succeeded in whittling down the average ad valorem equivalent tariff on dutiable imports from 61.7 percent in 1830 to under 20 percent by 1860. Even these moderate tariffs had very substantial effects in fostering domestic manufacturing industries.[20]

Protectionists in Charge

From the Civil War to the Great Depression of 1930, protection was predominant. No Southern Democrat would chair the Senate Finance Committee from the outbreak of the Civil War to the election of Woodrow Wilson. Instead, strong committee chairmen defended the American System against tariff liberalizers and do-gooders in the Executive Branch. The three most influential chairmen were Republicans Justin Morrill of Vermont, Nelson Aldrich of Rhode Island, and Reed Smoot of Utah, three senators who dominated the Senate Finance Committee for some sixty-five years. They had strong allies in the House Ways and Means Committee, particularly chairmen William "Pig Iron" Kelley and William McKinley, supporters of the protective system. Morrill, who moved to the Senate in 1867 after chairing the Ways and Means Committee as a Whig, served on the Finance Committee for thirty-one years (1867–98) and chaired it for twenty-two. He consistently opposed the "humbug" of reciprocity treaties, thinking them unconstitutional in law and one-sided in effect. He regularly lambasted free trade theorists. "There is a transcendental philosophy of free trade, with devotees as ardent as any of those who preach the millennium. . . . Free trade abjures patriotism and boasts of cosmopolitism. It regards the labor of our own people with no more favor than that of the barbarian on the Danube or the cooly on the Ganges." Concerned about balancing the federal budget, Morrill considered tariff reductions a threat to the nation's fiscal health. Aldrich apprenticed under Chairman Morrill, and Smoot learned from Aldrich. All three battled to protect congressional prerogatives and the American protective system.[21]

From 1860 to World War II every Republican presidential candidate ran on platforms supporting the protective tariff. They preached class harmony and warned that removal of the protective tariff would "bring widespread discontent." As McKinley put it, "Free trade results in giving our money, our manufactures, and our markets to other nations." Protection, the policy of the Republican Party, "has made the lives of the masses of our countrymen sweeter and brighter, and has entered the homes of America carrying comfort and cheer and courage." Republicans during the Gilded Age embraced protection as the key component of industrial policy, which they favored. Said McKinley: "In the mind of every American workingman is the thought that this great American doctrine of protection is associated with wages and work, and linked with home, family, country, and prosperity. . . . [T]he people of this country want an industrial policy that is for America and Americans."[22]

In American political history the tariff issue has usually ignited partisan debate. Until the Great Depression, Republicans generally favored the protective tariff, while Democrats backed a tariff for revenue only. With a strong base of support in the rural and non-industrial South, it is not surprising that Democrats eagerly promoted export expansion and favored tariffs for revenue. In 1850, cotton and tobacco, the two most important southern export crops, accounted for 61 percent of all U.S. exports. Sixty-two years later, in 1912, when the Democrats elected Woodrow Wilson president, those two products still accounted for 28 percent of U.S. exports.[23] Eager to cut tariffs, Democrats proposed the income tax as an alternative revenue source.

As the Democratic Party revived in the generation after the Civil War, it offered a different interpretation of the tariff than Republican economic nationalists who backed import-sensitive industries. Democrats argued that the tariff exploited consumers for the benefit of rich monopolists. In Ida Minerva Tarbell, the muckraking journalist, they found a popular communicator to champion these antimonopoly, antitariff ideas. Tarbell's assault on the tariff so impressed Woodrow Wilson that he lobbied hard to place her on his Tariff Commission in 1917.[24]

In 1884, Democrat Grover Cleveland, the governor of New York, won the presidential election and attempted to pursue a low-tariff Democratic agenda. Complaining that existing tariffs generated far more revenue that the government could spend prudently, Cleveland urged downward revision. Republican critics lampooned Cleveland as a dupe of John Bull, the symbol of Great Britain, and suggested that unilateral tariff reductions, such as Cleveland proposed, benefited English monopolists eager to exploit the American market. But, absence of a Democratic majority in Congress and the 1893 depression defeated Cleveland's plans to reduce the tariff and substitute an income tax. The Supreme Court also held the income tax unconstitutional.[25]

During the McKinley, Roosevelt, and Taft administrations, some public pressure for downward tariff revision continued. Whereas American industry long defended high tariffs, export-competing industries increasingly sought access to foreign markets. The National Association of Manufacturers (NAM), founded in 1895, declared that one of its main purposes was "the discussion of ways and means whereby trade relations between the United States and foreign countries may be developed and extended." While favoring the principle of protection, the NAM favored making duties "as low as possible consistent with the fair protection of our industries and the labor they employ." Concerned about discrimination against America's export industries, the NAM urged adoption of a dual schedule tariff, with maximum and minimum rates. Such a provision would give the Executive discretion to negotiate reciprocal access to foreign markets. But, early in the twentieth century most U.S. business opposed free trade. Said the NAM in 1907: "The National Association of Manufacturers is unalterably opposed to free trade in any particular. It stands first, last and always for the protection of American industries and American manufacturers, and . . . protection in liberal measure, not in scant measure. . . ."[26]

But some big business also endorsed reforms to take the tariff out of politics. The congressional tariff-writing process had proven costly and cumbersome. Campaign contributions from special interests and legislative logrolling compounded business uncertainty. In 1907 the NAM urged establishment of a non-partisan Tariff Commission "with semi-judicial powers . . . to investigate thoroughly and scientifically the various schedules. . . ." Elements of the business community embraced progressive tariff reforms before the major political parties. Not until 1912 would one of the major political parties, the Progressives, endorse a "non-partisan scientific tariff commission."

While Presidents McKinley and Roosevelt later embraced reciprocity, they were reluctant to undertake sweeping tariff revision knowing that it would divide the Republican Party. For them reciprocity must be treated as the handmaiden of protection. It must come without injury to domestic workers and to producers of import-competing products. They did make exceptions, however, for territory acquired in the Spanish-American War. In order to assist Cuba, President Roosevelt persuaded Congress to adopt a Cuban reciprocity agreement in 1903. It provided a 20 percent uniform reduction in tariffs on dutiable imports from Cuba. In effect, it gave Cuban sugar producers a price premium, and represented backdoor aid to the Cuban economy. Security concerns also led the Republicans to provide duty-free access for Philippine sugar.

In 1909, however, President William Howard Taft yielded to the public mood and summoned a special session of Congress to revise the tariff. The new Payne–Aldrich Tariff embodied for the first time the concept of a maximum and minimum tariff. In writing the bill, Republicans in Congress bowed to business desires for a more flexible tariff mechanism, one that the Executive could use to improve market access abroad. As it turned out,

President Taft and the State Department, fearful of foreign reactions, chose not to apply the maximum schedule, claiming that it was not flexible enough to permit the selective imposition of penalty duties.

But Payne–Aldrich did facilitate reciprocal negotiations with Canada. Taft, who spent his summers at a home along the St. Lawrence River, wanted to make improved Canadian relations a hallmark of his administration. After brief secret negotiations, the Taft administration signed a bilateral agreement placing more than 40 percent of U.S. imports from Canada on the free list and about 10 percent of Canadian imports from the United States. Canadians would gain access to the U.S. market for agricultural produce, fish, and raw materials but retain duties on manufactured imports. Despite the asymmetries benefiting Canada, Congress approved the agreement; the Canadian Parliament did not. In a general election Canadian voters soundly rejected the Liberal Party and reciprocity.[27]

Wilson's Low-Tariff Revolution

An important turning point in U.S. trade policy came after the election of 1912. In that presidential election, Democrat Woodrow Wilson, a former Princeton University professor of history and government, triumphed over a divided Republican Party. Gaining control of the presidency and both houses of Congress for the first time since 1892, the Democrats moved promptly to reduce protective rates. The Underwood–Simmons Act of 1913 sharply lowered American tariffs from an average of 19.3 percent on dutiable and free imports under the Payne–Aldrich Tariff of 1895 to 9.1 percent in 1916. Unfortunately, the Democrats ignored the opportunity to bargain down foreign trade barriers. Instead, eager to redeem domestic campaign pledges to cut duties and aid consumers, Wilson and the Democratic Congress unilaterally lowered the U.S. tariff.

The outbreak of World War I in Europe in 1914, and the consequent disruption of ocean shipping, provided a new form of temporary protection to U.S. industries during wartime. But as the conflict came to an end, American business began to worry about cheap foreign competition—particularly from the German chemicals industry—and about how to negotiate access to closed European markets for U.S. exporters. The Wilson administration, preoccupied with its League of Nations and plans for global free trade, apparently hoped that international economic government would promote market access and reduce foreign trade barriers to American exports. They remained faithful to the traditional Democratic panacea of a tariff for revenue only, while endorsing the use of a non-partisan tariff commission to suggest tariff revisions.

Protection Restored

Skeptical of Wilson's motives, the Republicans skillfully campaigned in 1920 on public fears that "a flood of imports will cheapen our cost of living ... [and] destroy our capacity to buy." Soon after his inauguration in 1921, President Warren Harding asked Congress for emergency tariff legislation. "I believe in the protection of American industry, and it is our purpose to prosper America first," Harding said. In May 1921 Congress enacted an emergency tariff measure raising duties on agricultural products and amending the antidumping laws.[28]

Dumping occurs when a firm sells goods more cheaply in the export market than in the home market. Frequently it takes place at less than the cost of production. For the United States, dumping first became a disruptive factor before the American Revolution. After each war with France, British merchants unloaded inventories of unsold goods at bargain basement prices. Late in the nineteenth century, large American steel and German chemical companies engaged in differential pricing to penetrate foreign markets.

Canada enacted the first antidumping statute in 1904, authorizing the government to impose offsetting duties. In proposing the measure, the Canadian finance minister, W.S. Fielding, rebutted the argument of laissez-faire economists that cheap imports benefit consumers. He said:

> if we could be guaranteed for ever or for a long period that we would obtain cheap goods ... it would probably be wise for us to close up some of our industries and turn the energies of our people to other branches. But surely none of us imagine that when these high tariff trusts and combines send goods into Canada at sacrifice prices they do it for any benevolent purpose.... They send the goods here with the hope and the expectation that they will crush out the native Canadian industries.[29]

Fearful that German manufacturers might dump products such as chemicals, steel, and newsprint in the U.S. market after the war, Congress passed two laws. The first, the Revenue Act of 1916, provided criminal and civil penalties for predatory dumping. But this law proved difficult to enforce because it was necessary to show that importers had "intent" and "conspired" to destroy or injure an industry in the United States. As an alternative to criminal laws, Congress passed the 1921 Antidumping Act providing administrative remedies. This law gave the Treasury secretary broad discretionary power to conduct investigations and to impose duties offsetting the injurious effects of dumping. Avoiding the issue of intent, it focused on import pricing. In effect, it authorized the Secretary of the Treasury to conduct an inquiry to determine whether, as a matter of policy, merchandise was being sold in the United States at less than its "fair" value and whether such sales were injuring or threatening the injury of a U.S. industry. The 1921 law gave broad discretionary powers to the Secretary of the Treasury. It provided no standards for determining injury, imposed no deadlines, and authorized no outside review of injury findings. In effect, Congress made administration of the antidumping law an executive function and subordinated legal considerations to policy concerns. Nothing barred the Treasury from considering other relevant factors, such as how enforcement might impact bilateral political and military relations.

In 1922 the Republican Congress completed a comprehensive tariff revision—the Fordney–McCumber Act. It raised the average duty on all imports from 9.1 percent under Underwood to 14 percent. The final bill contained both a flexible tariff provision—permitting the independent Tariff Commission to recommend tariff changes to the president—and a retaliation provision. The latter authorized the president to retaliate unilaterally against foreign tariff discrimination.

In deciding how to administer the new tariff, the Harding administration made a fateful decision. In August 1923 Secretary of State Hughes announced that the United States would adopt the unconditional most-favored-nation policy. Eager to advance the principle of equality and to address the problem of growing discrimination against U.S. exports, the Republican officials effectively abandoned the long-established approach of extending concessions to third countries only after equivalent compensation. This process was tedious and time consuming, and the State Department hoped to encourage other nations to voluntarily provide equal treatment to all trading partners. They did not apparently foresee the situation where emerging competitors might become free riders—using the unconditional policy to gain access to the U.S. market while declining to provide reciprocal access to home markets. Eager to avoid commercial antagonisms, the Harding State Department also declined to invoke the retaliation provision. Reluctant to risk political relations for commercial advantage, the State Department was unsuccessful in the 1920s in opening the most important foreign markets to American exports—namely Canada, Great Britain, and France.

During the 1920s higher U.S. tariffs do not appear to have harmed the international economy. They had little impact on U.S. imports and economic growth. During the 1920 to 1923 recession, for instance, imports of dutiable goods fell less than duty-free imports (measured by value). Despite the price declines, the quantity of imports continued to rise. During the immediate post-war period, American private lending, direct investments in post-war Europe, and an outflow of tourists helped finance large merchandise trade surpluses: 2.6 million Americans traveled to Europe and the

Mediterranean during the 1920s; only 350,000 came to the United States. Paris was a popular tourist destination, and American tourists reportedly spent $180 million annually in France—more than offsetting the merchandise trade deficit. In 1929, for example, the United States experienced a travel expenditures deficit of $659 million, nearly offsetting a $734 million commodity trade surplus.[30]

Smoot–Hawley

One of the enduring myths concerns the Tariff Act of 1930, popularly known as the Smoot–Hawley Tariff. A widespread misconception—recycled in many newspaper columns and political speeches—holds that this tariff act represented the high-water mark of American protectionism, disrupting trade, exacerbating international relations, and contributing to the outbreak of World War II. Many of these claims rest on a misunderstanding of the 1930 tariff enacted after nearly eighteen months of hearings and debate in Congress from January 1929 to June 1930. Without a doubt, this last effort to effect a general tariff revision produced tense partisan debate, and a deadlock in Congress. In the Senate majority Republicans lost control of the bill to a coalition of midwestern Progressives and low-tariff Democrats. In effect, the bitter and protracted congressional debate, not the fear of higher tariffs, exacerbated the stock market collapse. Unable to forecast prices for inputs and end products, business might have postponed key investments and offered uncertain earnings forecasts to financial analysts.[31]

The 71st Congress did not enact the highest tariff in American history, as some texts and pundits assert. The highest was the Tariff of Abominations in 1828 at 61.7 percent. The average duty on dutiable goods enacted in 1930 was 44.9 percent, using 1930 trade data. It marked a return to Payne–Aldrich levels (40.8 percent), and did not exceed levels reached under the McKinley (48.4 percent) and Dingley tariffs (46.5 percent) in the 1890s. During the Great Depression, falling prices did ratchet up ad valorem equivalents for goods with specific duties (to a 59.1 percent average in 1932), but this would have occurred no matter what the tariff schedule. A 20 cent specific duty on an item priced at $1.00 effectively becomes a 40 percent duty if the good's price falls to 50 cents per unit. While Smoot–Hawley represents a return to the high Republican tariffs of post–Civil War America, there is one important difference. In the late nineteenth century roughly one-half of imports entered duty free; under Smoot–Hawley two-thirds did. Thus, the ratio of duties calculated to total free and dutiable imports is considerably lower under Smoot–Hawley (13.7 percent in 1930) than the Tariff of Abominations (57.3 percent), McKinley (23.0 percent), and Dingley (25.5 percent).[32]

Some writers have alleged the 1929–30 general tariff revision spooked the stock market and caused the Great Depression. Of course, the stock market collapsed in October 1929, about eight months before Smoot–Hawley cleared Congress and was signed into law. There is no evidence that the final act influenced the October equities sell-off and the resulting financial collapse. But there is testimony that the extended deadlock in Congress may have heightened business uncertainty, slowed investment, and complicated efforts to stabilize financial markets. It was not really fear of tariffs that spooked the market, but continued uncertainties. In 1929–30 business overwhelmingly favored a substantial protective tariff, but deplored political logrolling and capricious decision making.

How did Smoot–Hawley affect American commerce? Many economists and commentators continue to assert that the 1930 tariff disrupted world trade. But official data show that higher U.S. tariffs had little impact on American imports. From 1929 to 1932 imports of dutiable and duty-free goods fell almost the same percentage, suggesting that higher tariffs had little impact on most trading partners. Nor did foreign governments protest and retaliate against U.S. exports, as many pundits seem to think. While newspapers did warn of foreign protests and retaliation, as they do whenever Congress considers a trade bill, U.S. diplomatic records show that only two or three countries actually lodged formal diplomatic protests. Others may have sought to influence the policy process through leaks to newspapers, but exports to the countries most concerned about higher tariffs—Austria, Canada, France, Italy, Spain, Switzerland, and the United Kingdom—fell less than average. The sharpest drop in exports involved commodity-exporting countries, including some like Brazil, largely unaffected by higher U.S. tariffs.[33]

Finally, the political lesson of Smoot–Hawley. For years critics have alleged that the public was so dissatisfied with Smoot–Hawley protectionism that the authors of the act, Senator Reed Smoot of Utah and Congressman Willis Hawley of Oregon, lost their seats in the 1932 election. A review of local press suggests that the tariff had little effect. Hawley, the chairman of the Ways and Means Committee, lost a primary battle to a much younger opponent. He did not return to Oregon to campaign. According to Oregon newspapers a dispute over the location of a veterans' home as well as the battle over prohibition cost Hawley his elected position. Smoot, one of the leaders in the Mormon church, went down to defeat in the 1932 general election. He was a victim of the Roosevelt landslide, although popular enough to out-poll President Hoover and the Republican candidate for governor. His opponent also endorsed protectionism for Utah products like lead, copper, and sugar.

Secretary Hull's Trade Policy Revolution

The presidential election of 1932 produced a revolution in American trade policy. But that was not evident in the campaign. As might be expected, President Hoover defended Smoot–Hawley and warned that Democratic proposals for a revenue tariff would "place our farmers and workers in competition with peasant and sweated labor. . . ." The Democratic nominee, New York governor Franklin D. Roosevelt, followed his own pragmatic instincts attempting to satisfy both protectionists and free-traders. He endorsed barter trade and interpreted his party's platform as calling for a tariff that "equalizes the differences in the cost of production." During the campaign, it was apparent that Roosevelt wanted modified protectionism to safeguard his domestic policies intended to boost wages and prices.[34]

In selecting Tennessee senator Cordell Hull as Secretary of State, Roosevelt made a fateful decision. He turned trade policy over to the most determined tariff cutter and free trade idealist in the Democratic Party. During his service on Congressional oversight committees, Hull gained a reputation as a tariff expert. His views reflected the agricultural export orientation of his middle Tennessee district and Hull's experiences as chairman of the Democratic National Executive Committee (during the Harding administration). At a time when high-tariff industrial interests funded the Republican Party, he saw an opportunity to create a new export-oriented coalition with its base in southern agriculture and emerging mass-production industries, like automobiles.

In 1934 Hull persuaded Congress to enact his "reciprocal" trade program. The bill (H.R. 8687) contained no direct reference to tariff reduction as a goal. Instead it authorized "expanding foreign markets for the products of the United States . . . by regulating the admission of foreign goods into the United States in accordance with the characteristics and needs of various branches of American production." To achieve this goal, Congress granted the Executive Branch temporary authority, for three years, to *raise or lower* tariffs as much as 50 percent from 1930 levels. Hull explained the plan as "an emergency measure to deal with emergency panic conditions." He emphasized that the "entire policy of this bill would rest under trade relationships which would be *mutually and equally profitable* both to our own and other countries." In his transmittal message President Roosevelt emphasized the "no-injury concept." He said: "The successful building up of trade *without injury to American producers* depends upon a cautious and gradual evolution of plans . . . *no sound and important American interest will be injuriously disturbed*" (emphasis added).[35]

In effect, the 1934 act transferred tariff making from Congress, where the process was relatively transparent and the decisions made by elected officials, to the Executive Branch. Hull established two interdepartmental committees, composed of representatives of several Cabinet-level agencies and chaired by the State Department. In contrast to the congressional process, the powerful interagency committees operated anonymously. For twenty years Congress could not learn the identities of the middle-level officials who made life-or-death decisions about protection for American industries.

We now know that many members of the all-powerful Committee on Trade Agreements were recently hired academic economists without significant private sector experience. Given their academic backgrounds and Hull's disposition to lower tariffs as quickly as possible, it is not surprising that members of the Trade Agreements committee held that the "primary object" of the Reciprocal Trade Agreements Program (RTAP) "is to reduce trade barriers rather than to drive a sharp bargain." Their policy envisioned "permitting a greater increase in imports than in exports with a view to correcting the trade balance problem of the United States."[36]

In a series of so-called reciprocal trade agreements during the 1930s and during World War II, U.S. trade policymakers proceeded to roll back the American tariff system. From 1934 to 1947 the United States concluded thirty-two reciprocal trade agreements, all, except for Iran, being located in the Americas or Western Europe. A substantial number of the agreements, such as with Central American countries, Ecuador, Paraguay and Uruguay, as well as Turkey, Iran, and Finland, were shadow agreements without real substance. They contained duplicative or inconsequential concessions and lacked immediate commercial significance. For instance, the United States padded its list of concessions by binding coffee duty-free (par. 1654) in separate agreements with eleven countries. Such agreements constituted window-dressing for the reciprocal trade program. It allowed the State Department to claim momentum for the program.

In reciprocal trade negotiations U.S. officials offered and sought maximum 50 percent reductions; in negotiations with principal suppliers this was on an item-by-item basis. U.S. officials did not seek to drive hard bargains. Instead, they often accepted commitments to bind existing duties as consideration for real U.S. cuts! When reciprocal trade partners depreciated their currencies or imposed quantitative controls, as the Belgians and Swiss did, the State Department did not insist on reopening negotiations. It turned a blind eye.

After the February 1935 agreement with Belgium, the first with an industrial country, the State Department made a key interpretation about which countries could benefit from the lower rates. Although the United States had adopted an unconditional most-favored-nation policy in 1923, the United States might have denied concessions to many countries because they discriminated against U.S. trade. Industrialist George Peek, who sought to fashion New Deal trade policy, and President Franklin Roosevelt himself, favored the conditional approach, in which concessions were extended only to countries making equivalent concessions. He wanted the United States to get its money's worth for reductions. But, Hull's State Department insisted on continuing the unconditional approach and on withholding benefits only to countries flagrantly discriminating against the United States. This avoided the need for multiple follow-on negotiations with other trading partners and for weighing each individual concession carefully. Had Peek and Roosevelt prevailed, the United States might have limited concessions made in bilateral agreements to many third countries like Canada, Great Britain, Germany, and France—all of which discriminated substantially against U.S. trade. Instead, the State Department took a "conciliatory" approach and concluded that only Nazi Germany discriminated substantially against American trade and should be denied benefits. Even the Soviet Union, Italy, and Japan, among many nations, qualified for the lowest tariff rates.[37]

By 1937, when the program faced congressional re-authorization, the emergency trade program had become an instrument of foreign policy. During congressional oversight hearings, the State Department described reciprocal trade as both an "essential requirement of a full and balanced economic recovery" and as "a powerful instrument of *economic appeasement* and stability . . . to strengthen the foundations of world peace." The "successful" trade negotiations with Great Britain in 1938 reflected the influence of foreign policy considerations. In the months after Munich, when Germany presented a threat to European stability, diplomats from the British Foreign Office and the U.S. State Department insisted that the agreement could not fail. Although the United States achieved a major reduction in U.S. tariffs extending across hundreds of items (621 concessions on trade valued at $457.8 million in 1937, or 37 percent of U.S. dutiable imports), Washington was not prepared to press Britain for major modifications in the system of imperial agricultural preferences, nor for significant concessions on manufactured exports in the British market.[38]

Building the Bretton Woods World

Hull's vision of a peaceful, prosperous world without trade barriers guided America's post-war planners. From 1942 to 1945 they devised plans for three post-war international economic institutions—the International Monetary Fund, the International Bank for Reconstruction and Development

(World Bank), and the International Trade Organization (ITO). Each would operate under the auspices of the United Nations and have universal membership for its function. At Bretton Woods, New Hampshire, in July 1944, planners led by economists Harry Dexter White, representing the U.S. Treasury, and John Maynard Keynes, an adviser to the British Treasury, completed work on the post-war financial institutions. Preparations for the post-war trade organization, supervised by Hull's reciprocal trade policy team, lagged. But Hull's aides deemed it the centerpiece of the post-war economic order. It would establish the intergovernmental structure and rules for regulating world trade.

At a preparatory meeting in 1946, economist Clair Wilcox, leader of the U.S. delegation, asserted: "If political and economic order is to be rebuilt, we must provide, in our world trade charter, the solid foundation upon which the superstructure of international cooperation is to stand." A final proposal would not emerge until the winter of 1948 when trade policy officials met in Havana, Cuba, to complete this section of the post-war structure.[39]

American business favored trade expansion, and shared generally the Truman administration's enthusiasm for equal and non-discriminatory access to world markets. But big business disliked the charter for the International Trade Organization. Like the League of Nations charter a generation earlier, it was too grandiose and ambitious. In particular, business groups like the National Association of Manufacturers and the Chamber of Commerce of the United States worried that the ITO would prove too bureaucratic, too tolerant of exchange and trade restrictions, and too much a forum for developing and debtor countries. Big business worried that the investment provisions would complicate prompt and just compensation for expropriations. Said the NAM, the Havana charter promised to make the world "safe for socialistic planning" and a "very precarious place" for private enterprise.

Appreciating that the United States might need to increase imports to facilitate post-war reconstruction, big American business worried that an International Trade Organization in which the United States had one vote, like developing and war-damaged nations, would produce asymmetrical and unbalanced results. The charter established a structure and rules in which the United States would likely not receive "an adequate *quid pro quo* for any liberalization that it might adopt in its commercial policy." In essence, the ITO would accelerate America's market opening, but tolerate restrictions against American exports and investments.[40]

Like the League of Nations a generation earlier, the ITO seemed a grandiose abstraction. Business groups balked, disturbed over investment provisions and the proposed international bureaucracy. In the United States, Philip Cortney, a businessman, launched a successful campaign against the Havana Charter, claiming it condoned socialistic planning and had a bias toward full employment and inflation. He complained that the Charter authorized the use of quotas and exchange controls for balance of payments reasons. In ratifying the Charter, Cortney alleged, the United States would "surrender our main weapon against nationalistic economic wickedness, namely the power to retaliate."[41] The American Bar Association (ABA) also issued a critical assessment: "The ITO commits its members to action to conform their national policies and laws to the policies and decisions or findings or rules or regulations of the ITO, in the fields of trade, employment, and general economic development." Some ABA members commented that "the charter has more the appearance of a world-government constitution than that of an agency of the United Nations." Unable to persuade Congress, the Truman administration finally withdrew the ITO proposal in 1950.[42]

Five years later—during the Eisenhower administration—State Department planners revived the concept. After minor changes to the ITO proposal, they renamed it the Organization for Trade Cooperation.[43] Once again the sovereignty issue enraged Congress. In 1956 House Ways and Means Committee Republicans, including Howard Baker of Tennessee, complained, "authorization of United States membership in OTC will result in an almost complete transfer by the Congress to an international organization of its constitutional authority over United States foreign commerce policy."[44] Some Democrats had similar concerns.

To accelerate trade liberalization after World War II, the United States invited nineteen foreign countries, including the Soviet Union, to participate in the negotiation of a multilateral agreement at Geneva in 1947. Although the Soviets opted to pursue an autarkic course, twenty-three countries engaged in negotiations, conducted bilaterally on a product-by-product basis with principal suppliers. The various bilateral agreements became the multilateral General Agreement on Tariffs and Trade. Every country signing the agreement was eligible to enjoy the concessions of every other signatory and thus gained unconditional most-favored-nation status. Nine countries, accounting at that time for 80 percent of world trade, put the GATT agreement into effect on January 1, 1948. They were Australia, Belgium, Canada, Cuba, France, Luxembourg, the Netherlands, the United Kingdom, and the United States.

As a temporary forum for trade negotiations, pending creation of the ITO, the GATT endured for nearly a half-century until establishment of the World Trade Organization on January 1, 1995. Under GATT auspices a series of multilateral trade negotiating rounds took place beginning with the 1947 session in Geneva. The next four rounds, held in Annecy, France (1949), and Torquay, England (1950–51), Geneva (1956), and Geneva (1960–62), employed the same bilateral product-by-product negotiating approach. Beginning with the Kennedy Round (1962–67), negotiators adopted, with some exceptions, a linear formula for across-the-board percentage cuts, an approach that avoided some cumbersome bilateral negotiations with principal suppliers. In successive rounds more countries acceded, notably Italy (1949), West Germany (1951), and Japan (1955), and Israel, Switzerland, and Spain (1962). By the end of the Kennedy Round in 1967, GATT had 75 members. By December 31, 1994, GATT's final day, membership had expanded to 128 countries, and the most significant non-members—Russia, China, and Taiwan—wanted to join. In terms of duty reductions, the most important multilateral rounds were the ones ending in 1947 and 1967. The first Geneva Round and the Kennedy Round were the only ones in which the U.S. Congress authorized major duty reductions (up to 50 percent of existing rates), and in both the depth of tariff reductions averaged 35 percent. But these figures, which suggest reciprocal concessions, mask conspicuous asymmetries. In the first rounds after World War II the United States, of course, promptly implemented its concessions, but trading partners in Western Europe, who were recovering from the devastation of World War II, delayed the impact of their concessions, using exchange controls and quantitative restrictions. Obviously, given the enormity of war disruption and the problems of rebuilding economies, some controls were justified. But in some instances the perpetuation of controls into the late 1950s reflected the strength of local protectionist forces, or government enthusiasm for using national industrial policy to achieve competitive advantages. In Great Britain, for instance, agricultural interests used political pressure to discriminate against American apples, pears, grapefruit, and other products. Conceded trade official Reginald Maudling to Prime Minister Harold Macmillan in 1959: "The Americans have put more into G.A.T.T., and got less out of it, than any of the other big trading countries . . . by and large the Americans have kept their doors wide open to our trade (and at a time when they might have urged that we were shutting out their goods by quotas long after we were genuinely short of dollars to pay for them)." In the Kennedy Round, similar asymmetries occurred as Japan and most developing countries avoided meaningful reciprocal concessions.[45]

Marshall Plan Mentality

As noted, the ambitious plans for trade liberalization, conceived in Hull's State Department, soon took a back seat to recovery from World War II and to Cold War circumstances. During this period—unlike the period immediately after World War I—American political and business leaders chose to provide leadership and assistance to help devastated allies and defeated adversaries recover and become full participants in the global economy. But there was another key aspect—the emerging Cold War struggle with Soviet Russia. By late 1946 it was evident to leaders in Washington that the wartime alliance binding America, Britain, and Soviet Russia had disintegrated. In place of global peacekeeping solutions, the United States had to seek regional and bloc cooperation to offset and contain the threat of Communist expansionism.

The economic crisis of 1946–47 precipitated action. With wartime allies in Western Europe exhausted—their industries outmoded, their finances weakened—and with Axis nations enduring a bleak recovery from wartime devastation, the United States faced a tough challenge. It could disengage from events, as it did after World War I, or use its vast power and influence to help rebuild Western Europe and Japan and reconstruct the international economy. Adopting a "Marshall Plan mentality," American leaders chose the latter course. They pursued foreign economic policies designed to make U.S. allies self-sustaining participants in a thriving open international economy, even at the expense of domestic American economic interests.

American presidents in the post–World War II period from Harry Truman to Bill Clinton felt that America had a responsibility to lead the world economy, placing the interests of the system ahead of U.S. national interests. In the Cold War competition with the Soviet Union, foreign policy took priority. Reflecting pride in what publisher Henry Luce called the "American Century," Truman boasted, "Our industry dominates world markets ... American labor can now produce so much more than low-priced foreign labor in a given day's work that our workingmen need no longer fear, as they were justified in fearing in the past, the competition of foreign workers."[46]

It is not surprising that Truman's successor President Dwight Eisenhower, a former military leader, also gave priority to strategic considerations. Indeed, he criticized protectionist U.S. businesses for "shortsightedness bordering upon tragic stupidity." In the face of aggressive communism, he considered freer trade essential to help other nations "make a living." He emphasized: "We are not talking about trying to put American people out of work or undersell an American manufacturer and drive him to the wall or anything else. We are striving to make a better world for ourselves and for our children."[47]

Trade was important, Eisenhower thought, to sound political relationships. To secure allied support for strategic export controls against the

Soviet Union, the United States must provide alternative markets in the West.

This emphasis on opening the huge American market to aid foreign allies and promote international economic reconstruction surfaced during World War II and, publicly, during the 1947 Geneva trade negotiations. Eager to construct a liberal economic order without high tariffs and exchange controls, State Department planners contemplated drastic, and disproportionate, cuts in U.S. tariffs to stimulate imports and assist foreign reconstruction and participation in an open trading community. To them the statute requiring mutually balanced tariff concessions seemed overly restrictive and inappropriate to post-war circumstances.

Others in Congress and the private sectors were less sensitive to the dollar shortage and problems of international economic adjustment, less enthused about textbook solutions, and more cautious about the implications of opening the U.S. market for the sake of mankind. To the Republican Congress elected in 1946, further tariff reductions immediately after the war seemed imprudent and overly idealistic. The war had disrupted economies and created distortions. It was not clear whether previous cuts, especially the steep reductions effected in the 1938 reciprocal trade agreement with Britain, could be accommodated without injury to domestic industries and workers. Nonetheless, the congressional critics hesitated to vote down RTAP and to undercut Truman's effort to provide leadership. Instead, Senator Arthur Vandenberg, Chairman of the Senate Foreign Relations Committee, and Senator Eugene D. Millikin, Chairman of the Senate Finance Committee, negotiated with the administration. The Republicans would renew reciprocal trade tariff-cutting if President Truman reiterated the no-injury to domestic industry pledge of preceding Presidents. Truman promised that "domestic interests will be safeguarded in this process of expanding trade."[48]

GATT and Unreciprocal Trade

Notwithstanding President Truman's commitment, foreign policy considerations drove U.S. trade policy for the next forty years—and through the Uruguay Round. In a series of multilateral negotiations held under auspices of the GATT, U.S. negotiators yielded unbalanced concessions and tolerated free-riders. The Geneva negotiations of 1947 were a classic example. During these negotiations with fifteen countries, the primary U.S. goal was to bargain away what remained of the Smoot–Hawley protective system in exchange for the elimination of British preferences and discriminations against American exports. During the protracted talks, the Labor government of Clement Attlee battled to protect "at all costs the empire preference system," while U.S. officials took the view that this was an opportune time to break the preferential system. The United States claimed that the master lend-lease agreement obligated London to dismantle the preferential system, and they thought Britain's precarious financial situation and dependence on Washington for financial support and Marshall Plan assistance would tip the scales. When the Labor government refused, Washington chose in October 1947 to paper over differences with a thin agreement—one that provided major U.S. concessions on textiles and manufactures—the State Department acquiesced to a deal that failed to break down the preferential system. Four years later in the Torquay negotiations the British again attempted to win an agreement unbalanced in their favor, but this time the reciprocal trade program faced reauthorization scrutiny in Congress. The Truman administration pragmatically broke off negotiations, seeking to demonstrate toughness at the bargaining table.

For Presidents Truman and Eisenhower trade concessions represented an alternative to foreign aid, which never appealed to Congress or the voting public. Concerned about Soviet motives and the problems of recovery in Western Europe, the State Department worked to promote imports and acquiesced to discrimination against U.S. exports.

Perhaps the classic example of asymmetrical trade agreements involved the 1955 bilateral with Japan. Although Britain and some European countries attempted to block Japanese membership in GATT and to deny Japanese textiles access to international markets, the Eisenhower administration considered a trade agreement a high priority. As Eisenhower told congressional leaders, "all problems of local industry pale into insignificance in relation to the world crisis." He said that "Japan cannot live, and Japan cannot remain in the free world unless something is done to allow her to make a living."[49]

In light of later developments, minutes of the negotiating sessions make fascinating reading. C. Thayer White, the chief of the U.S. delegation, reminded the Japanese that "some of the most powerful support for the trade agreements program comes from American agriculture and the automobile industry." The minutes also cited international economic justifications for Japanese concessions. Arguing for a Japanese duty reduction on automobiles, White stated:

> [T]he United States industry is the largest and most efficient in the world; (2) the industry is strongly in favor of expanding the opportunities for world trade; (3) its access to foreign markets in recent years has been limited by import controls. . . . (4) although the United States Government appreciates that it is necessary for

> some countries to impose import restrictions for balance of payments reasons ... it would be in Japan's interest to import automobiles from the United States and export items in which Japan could excel.

On other occasions White referred to a statement that Japan only desired to establish industries that could compete in world markets and said "it would be inconsistent for Japan to attempt to establish an automobile industry because its prospects were not very promising for the future." He also urged a concession on machine-tool imports, doubting "that Japan could compete with the United States in world markets because of the difference in the relative efficiency of the industries in both countries." Establishment of "high cost industries behind a tariff wall does not contribute to the sound growth of national economy," White said.[50] He encouraged the Japanese not to use tariffs, but to increase productivity, favor foreign private direct investment, utilize technical assistance, facilitate domestic capital investment through tax incentives, and pursue a sound domestic fiscal policy.[51]

The Japanese had a different vision of their economy and their future in the international economy. Said K. Otabe, a Japanese delegate:

> (1) if the theory of international trade were pursued to its ultimate conclusion, the United States would specialize in the production of automobiles and Japan in the production of tuna; (2) such a division of labor does not take place ... because each government encourages and protects those industries which it believes important for reasons of *national policy.*

Urged to reduce import duties on synthetic textiles, Otabe declined, saying "the Japanese Government believes that a synthetic industry is necessary to diversify and promote the development of the Japanese economy." Asked to lower tariffs on handtools, Otabe refused: "the domestic industry was having difficulty competing and it was concerned over the competitive effects of increased imports." A lower duty on raisins would "interfere with the consumption of domestically produced sugar confectionery." Reductions on boots and shoes might "destroy" an industry composed of small firms.

Asked to reduce the Japanese duty on movie cameras, Otabe said his government "wished to advance the development of the Japanese optical industry." Asked about reductions on radios and television sets, Otabe demurred. The Japanese industry was at a "competitive disadvantage"; the government feared "political repercussions."

On electronic equipment the story was similar: "The Japanese Government believes that an electronics industry is essential to the development of the Japanese economy, the communications industry and national defense." Similar explanations applied to petrochemicals, tractors, and heavy machinery. Heavy machinery and machine tools were essential to the development and diversification of the Japanese economy and to a skilled labor force. Indeed, Otabe reminded the Americans "that a protective tariff had contributed to the development of new industries in the early history of the United States and that similarly a protective tariff could promote the development of the petrochemical, heavy machinery and other promising industries in Japan."[52]

What was the outcome? The Japanese press trumpeted their government's negotiating success. Privately, American officials conceded the Japanese had negotiated successfully and that they skillfully took advantage of American determination to make Japan a prosperous partner and ally supporting U.S. containment policy.

How did the 1955 bilateral agreement with Japan affect U.S. imports? Japan more than doubled its share of America's manufactured imports from 7.6 percent in 1955 to 15.4 percent in 1960. In essence, the 1955 trade negotiations with Japan, far more than the negotiations with Great Britain in 1938 and 1947, opened U.S. borders to imports of labor-intensive products and other manufactures. They also sparked a political reaction when reciprocal trade came up for renewal again in 1958. On this occasion, the Senate Finance Committee refused the Eisenhower administration's request for a five-year extension and authority to reduce tariffs an additional 25 percent. The White House agreed to shift trade-coordinating responsibilities from the State Department to the Commerce Department. In 1962, when President Kennedy requested a broad mandate permitting 50 percent reductions across the board, Congress insisted on establishing the office of Special Trade Representative with authority to negotiate and coordinate the interagency committees.

Kennedy Round Asymmetries

The most significant multilateral round of GATT tariff negotiations in the post-war period took place from 1964 to 1967. President Lyndon Johnson called the Kennedy Round the "most successful multilateral agreement on tariff reduction ever negotiated." The agreement, announced in May 1967, produced cuts of 36 to 39 percent in tariffs among participating industrial countries. But, on agriculture, a crucial long-term goal of U.S. trade negotiators, the United States failed to make any significant progress in persuading the European Community to liberalize restrictions. Nor did the Kennedy Round negotiators persuade Japan, the beneficiary of many concessions, to prove real reciprocity and open its protected home market to foreign competition. Forty-one developing countries, members of GATT, refused to participate. These included Singapore and Malaysia, future trade power-houses in the 1980s and 1990s. Another seventeen countries negotiated under special arrangements that did not require reciprocity. This second group included many big emerging markets such as Argentina, Brazil, India, Indonesia, Korea, and Pakistan.[53]

Despite evidence of unbalanced trade concessions, President Lyndon Johnson and the State Department wanted an agreement. The latter saw the negotiations as critical in promoting our foreign policy goal of a unified and prosperous Europe able to withstand Soviet pressure. The president, his leadership under assault at home, wanted a victory. In the Middle East, Israel and Egypt were on the brink of war. France's President Charles DeGaulle and some other governments wanted to impose discipline on the dollar's unique role in the world monetary system, and thus restrict a flood of American direct investments and influence.

Evidence of asymmetrical results can be found in the record of U.S. negotiations with Japan and nine important developing countries. Japan kept a low profile in the Kennedy Round, letting the Americans and Europeans slug out differences. Because of the unconditional most-favored-nation principle, the Japanese could anticipate benefiting from others' tariff cuts. Their negotiating tactic was to delay, knowing that the Americans faced a congressional deadline for concluding negotiations. Special Trade Representative (STR) Carl Gilbert told President Nixon later that "the Japanese took advantage of this situation along toward the close of the Kennedy Round." Congress weighed in with its own complaints. In the Trade Act of 1974, Congress inserted a provision requiring the president to determine after the conclusion of future negotiations whether any major industrial country (defined as Canada, the EEC, or Japan) had failed to make concessions "substantially equivalent" to U.S. concessions.[54]

Other evidence that the Kennedy Round left asymmetries in the U.S.–Japan relationship appears in bilateral trade data. In the three years before the Kennedy Round cuts took effect (1965–67), imports from Japan exceeded exports by 17 percent. A decade later (1975–77), imports from Japan exceeded U.S. exports by 50 percent. Much of this represented a surge in Japanese automobile exports as the energy crisis encouraged Americans to shift to fuel-efficient cars. But, a decline in the U.S. automobile tariff from 6.5 to 3 percent during the Kennedy Round, while Europe maintained 11 percent duties and quantitative restraints on Japanese cars, encouraged Japanese auto exports to the American market.[55]

With the developing countries the United States made concessions on $700 million in imports (most all of these being duty reductions of 50 percent or more). What did the nine developing countries provide in return?

They made concessions on $200 million in trade, but only $20 million of that amount involved actual tariff reductions. The rest consisted of commitments to bind existing tariffs. In the Kennedy Round, as in early tariff negotiations, the United States did not insist on parallel reductions. In 1967 American negotiators did not anticipate that one day Argentina, Brazil, and India might be big emerging markets for American exports. In effect, the Kennedy Round opened the American market to cheap imports from the world but did virtually nothing to open the markets of emerging countries. Instead, the United States reduced its tariffs, bound rates, and effectively gave away leverage that might over time have promoted free and balanced international trade.[56]

Under such circumstances it is not surprising that White House aides worked overtime to put the best face on results. According to journalist Steve Dryden, author of *Trade Warriors,* a history of the U.S. Trade Representative's office, Francis Bator, a National Security Council aide who briefed Johnson on the subject, instructed a young Oxford-trained economist on the staff to "use some creative thinking and make some new tables" showing a positive outcome. Imaginative staff work may have fashioned a paper victory, but the episode infuriated trade specialists in the Commerce, Labor, and Agriculture Departments who had negotiated for more reciprocal outcomes.[57]

More than any other single round of tariff negotiations, the Kennedy Round opened the American market to global competition and contributed to a growing merchandise trade imbalance. Said Secretary of Commerce Alexander Trowbridge, the "American domestic market—the greatest and most lucrative market in the world is no longer the private preserve of the American businessman." As the concessions were phased in over a five-year period, border barriers no longer shielded high-wage American manufacturing workers from global competition. The average ad valorem equivalent on dutiable U.S. imports fell from 12.2 percent in 1967 to 8.6 percent in 1972.[58]

Business leaders quickly understood that the Kennedy Round had changed the rules of the trading game. Previously, Fortune 500 firms generally produced domestically for the U.S. market. Those eager to participate in global markets established overseas production facilities, or exported. But the Kennedy Round created a global market for supplying U.S. consumers. Many big U.S. companies construed the results as evidence that the U.S. government wished to promote imports and would not employ import-remedy laws to shelter domestic industries from low-cost and unfair foreign competition. If U.S. manufacturers wanted to retain market share in the domestic market they needed to look abroad to take advantage of cheaper production costs.[59]

Production Sharing and Preferences

Two other U.S. government programs to stimulate exports from developing countries accentuated the trend toward global outsourcing and exacerbated trade imbalances in the 1970s. One was production sharing, the result of a congressional initiative that began somewhat innocuously to modify customs rules in order to permit automakers to process articles in contiguous areas of Canada during breakdowns or emergencies at their U.S. facilities. By the late 1960s production sharing had expanded to benefit low labor-cost countries like Mexico and Malaysia.

Malaysia illustrates the process nicely. Under Prime Minister Tun Razak's leadership, Malaysia offered foreign manufacturers generous incentives to encourage firms to export goods assembled in Malaysia. It also authorized a program of free trade zones to make use of Malaysia's low-cost labor. In an October 1971 speech to prospective investors in New York, Tun Razak said: "I hope to convince you all that Malaysia could be the answer to your problems of spiraling wages and increasing costs of production."[60] Labor-intensive industries responded, particularly makers of consumer electronics. By 1984, foreign trade zones provided employment to nearly 82,000 Malaysians. Fifty-two percent of Malaysia's exports to the United States ($1,421.7 of $2,721 million) qualified for production-sharing tariff treatment. Typically, semiconductors accounted for over 95 percent of these qualifying exports.

A related initiative was the Generalized System of Preferences (GSP), a program of one-way free trade designed to stimulate exports of manufactures from developing countries. In response to demands from the United Nations Conference on Trade and Development (UNCTAD), industrialized countries agreed to temporary incentives, rather than permanent concessions, to stimulate the trade and development of the world's most needy nations. It was consistent with the broad political theme of "trade, not aid." As it turned out, GSP proved a windfall for newly emerging industrial nations like Hong Kong, Singapore, Korea, Brazil, and Mexico, not the world's most backward nations, which had little to sell in world markets except commodities like rubber and palm oil. In 1995, the United States extended GSP duty-free entry to imports from 150 beneficiary countries. Of the $18.3 billion in benefits provided, 52 percent went to three rapidly industrializing countries—Malaysia, Thailand, and Brazil. Ten countries obtained 83 percent of GSP benefits, and all were big emerging markets. None were low-income nations from Africa or Central America. Some 28 percent of U.S. imports from Malaysia actually received GSP treatment, and this middle-income, rapidly industrializing country was the largest national beneficiary of the U.S. GSP program. It received 27 percent ($4,931 million) of total GSP benefits, ahead of Thailand's 13.1 percent ($2,394 million) and Brazil's 12.1 percent ($2,221 million). Meanwhile, many of these countries retained substantial restrictions on American commerce and investments, as detailed in the U.S. Trade Representative's annual reports on foreign trade barriers. Under pressure, developing countries liberalized somewhat their tariff regimes, but most maintain substantial restrictions on foreign investments and trade in services.[61]

Reacting to Free Riders

By the early 1970s the premises of U.S. trade policy seemed invalid. For years, as the Senate Finance Committee observed, the United States had "relied on a trade surplus to offset foreign aid, military expenditures abroad, as well as overseas private investment." But, in the early 1970s the trade surplus disappeared and the payments deficit widened. When European governments sought to convert accumulating dollar reserves to gold, the Nixon administration had little choice but to close the Treasury gold window in August 1971 and thus abandon the special gold-exchange obligations assumed at Bretton Woods. The resulting dollar devaluation had multiple roots—including Vietnam War–related domestic inflation and the emergence of new competitors such as Japan with state-of-the-art production facilities. But, in the opinion of the Senate Finance Committee, misguided trade policies shared responsibility.

> Throughout most of the postwar era, U.S. trade policy has been the orphan of U.S. foreign policy. Too often the Executive has granted trade concessions to accomplish political objectives. Rather than conducting U.S. international economic relations on sound economic and commercial principles, the Executive has set trade and monetary policy in a foreign aid context. An example has been the Executive's unwillingness to enforce U.S. trade statutes in response to foreign unfair trade practices. By pursuing a soft trade policy, by refusing to strike swiftly and surely at foreign unfair trade practices, the Executive has actually fostered the proliferation of barriers to international commerce. The result of this misguided policy has been to permit and even to encourage discriminatory trading arrangements among trading nations.

The Finance Committee attributed much significance to the free-rider problem. "The existence of many significant tariff and nontariff barriers in foreign countries and the very small reductions in tariffs of some industrialized countries in the Kennedy Round may be attributed to the realization by certain countries that they could automatically receive all the benefits of the trade agreement without paying any of the costs."[62]

On Capitol Hill the end of the Kennedy Round produced a tidal wave of condemnation. Evidence of the widespread dissatisfaction came from the flood of quota legislation introduced and the reluctance of Congress to extend the president's trade negotiating authority. Organized labor sponsored the Burke–Hartke bill, the Foreign Trade and Investment Act of 1972, which would have imposed mandatory quotas on all competitive imports and radically changed the tax-treatment of multinational corporations. Other evidence of congressional dissatisfaction with the Kennedy Round surfaced when the Legislative Branch refused to implement some of the key Kennedy Round agreements, particularly the antidumping code and repeal of the American selling price for certain chemicals. Not for six years did Congress offer the White House a new negotiating mandate and then on terms set by Chairman Wilbur Mills of the House Ways and Means Committee and Chairman Russell Long of the Senate Finance Committee. They insisted on a number of fundamental changes in the law to better safeguard domestic industries from import-related injury and to allow greater congressional and private-sector oversight of negotiations.[63]

From 1947 to the end of the Kennedy Round, Congress had insisted that trade liberalization not dislocate unnecessarily domestic industries and workers. The price for renewal of the trade liberalization program was the escape clause, permitting the withdrawal or modification of tariff concessions if imports surged causing injury, or threat of serious injury, to domestic producers. Distrustful of Executive Branch free traders, Congress insisted on an open and transparent process for assessing claims for escape clause relief, one that involved an independent agency, the Tariff Commission. It had responsibility for recommending any import-remedy relief to the President.

In practice, the process seldom functioned as Congress intended—and did so only in election years or when the trade agreements program faced congressional reauthorization. The State Department viewed the escape clause as an impediment to trade liberalization and as an irritant to diplomatic relationships during the Cold War years. From 1951 to 1962, the Tariff Commission conducted 112 investigations, but only 15 industries actually obtained some type of relief. During the Kennedy Round negotiations no domestic industry won relief, as a Tariff Commission loaded with free trade enthusiasts rejected thirteen successive petitions. But, as it turned out, modifications to the escape clause enacted in 1974 brought only temporary changes. During the decade from 1975 to 1984, 54 industries filed for escape clause relief and 18 (33 percent) gained some remedy from the process. Perhaps the most successful were the tariff on imported motorcycles that facilitated Harley Davidson's rejuvenation, and the Reagan administration's program of import restraints on steel products that provided a breathing space for industry restructuring. By 1985, however, the escape clause was a dead letter. During the second Reagan administration, individuals opposed philosophically to trade remedies administered the statute. The Bush and Clinton administrations also assigned top priority to preserving the multinational system and the open American market, not to helping domestic industries deal with import-related competition more successfully.

The 1974 act also renewed for five years the President's trade negotiating authority. It did so by establishing the fast-track process for considering trade legislation. In return for regular consultation with Congress and private-sector representatives, Congress promised the Executive to waive the usual congressional procedures and permit a vote within 90 days on implementing legislation. This agreed-upon procedure prohibited legislative amendments.

The act thus authorized U.S. participation in the seventh round of GATT negotiations, the so-called Tokyo Round. Unlike earlier rounds, these negotiations would emphasize non-tariff barriers, which many trade specialists thought had replaced tariffs as the primary obstacles to expanding world trade. Multinational corporations, which increasingly set the U.S. trade policy agenda, were especially interested in removing foreign barriers to their activities. Mirroring these concerns, Congress stated the U.S. negotiating objective as attainment of "more open and equitable market access and the harmonization, reduction, or elimination of devices which distort trade or commerce." Emphasizing the need for reciprocal outcomes, not simply reciprocal tariff reductions, the act stressed that a principal U.S. objective was obtaining competitive opportunities for U.S. exports to developed countries equivalent to the opportunities afforded in the U.S. market taking into account tariff and non-tariff barriers and "other distortions." But, for developing countries, Congress would continue past practice and not insist on full reciprocity. On the free-rider issue, Congress took a harder line. The Senate Finance Committee stated: "The United States should not grant concessions to countries which are not willing to offer substantial equivalent competitive opportunities for the products of the United States in their market as we offer their products in our market."[64]

Tokyo Round Promises

During the five years of negotiations, which opened in September 1973 at a ministerial meeting in Tokyo and ended formally on April 12, 1979, ninety-nine countries participated—up from forty in the Kennedy Round. Twenty-nine of these were either not members or only provisional members. This group included Mexico, the Philippines, and Thailand as well as a number of African and Latin American countries.[65]

Advanced countries agreed to cut tariffs about 33 percent on industrial goods, and for the United States this meant reducing tariffs on dutiable manufactures from about 8.1 percent to 5.6 percent. Some progress was made in agriculture—particularly in opening the Japanese market—but the European Community blocked any effort to roll back the variable levy system. Although the Ford administration, sensitive to the interests of mid-western Republican farmers, had pressed the Europeans for significant agri-cultural negotiations, the incoming Carter administration chose to subordinate this goal in order to break a negotiating impasse and restore momentum.

The Tokyo Round's principal outcome was an attempt to extend the GATT regime to cover non-tariff barriers. Delegates approved a series of specialized, non-tariff "codes" pertaining to subsidies and countervailing duties, antidumping duties, technical barriers and product standards, gov-ernment procurement, import licensing, customs valuation, and certain agri-cultural products. Reflecting a variety of philosophies and competing interests, these codes were intended to reduce the trade-distorting impact of domestic practices. The codes offered transparency, accountability, and dis-pute resolution. Because of differing national philosophies, some, such as the subsidies code, blurred differences with vague language. Each depended on the follow-through of participant governments for implementation. The dumping and countervailing duty codes, for instance, appeared to extend gov-ernment authority, while the code on government procurement represented an effort to deregulate certain types of trade, and to provide non-discriminatory national treatment to foreign suppliers. Unfortunately, relatively few coun-tries signed these codes, and even there implementation was limited. None-theless, the Carter administration assigned great significance to the codes and officials claimed the procurement code would "open up as much a[s] $25 billion a year in foreign government purchasing markets now closed to U.S. exports."

Interestingly, while GATT tariff negotiations proceeded on the basis of the unconditional most-favored-nation principle, the non-tariff code negoti-ations marked, in some respects, a return to the conditional approach. Hop-ing to limit the free-rider problem, which had distorted the results of previous multilateral negotiations, the Carter administration hoped to ad-minister the Code on Subsidies and Countervailing Measures in such a way to discriminate against countries not accepting the obligations of the code. Said USTR Bob Strauss to President Carter: "It is difficult to maintain a consensus for open trade if such countries continue to refuse to accept international discipline over their export subsidy practices." Also, he added: "We could not obtain congressional approval of the new subsidy code if a large number of countries were excluded from the discipline of the code (giving them a 'free ride')." In effect, he was saying that congressional dissatisfaction with the asymmetrical results of prior negotiations had compelled U.S. trade negotiators to insist on reciprocity among code signatories.[66]

In 1979, as at the end of previous negotiations, U.S. officials boasted about gains, and sold the agreement to Congress on the basis of the anticipated export opportunities. Once again U.S. leaders indulged in overselling a GATT agreement. President Carter called the MTN (Tokyo Round) results an "obvious advantage to American exporters" and stated that "obstacles to American goods going overseas will be removed or drastically reduced." Strauss's deputy Alonzo McDonald advised Congress that "the Tokyo Round result is potentially the most significant development in world trade since the GATT was established over 30 years ago." In particular, he identified the government procurement code as a major victory for the United States. "We have estimated that the code will increase U.S. exports by between $1.3 and $2.3 billion over the next three to five years and U.S. job opportunities by between 50,000 and 100,000."[67]

Spokesmen for multinational firms were ebullient. Lawrence McQuade, representing the Emergency Committee for American Trade (ECAT), a group of 64 multinational firms that employed 5 million people worldwide and had sales of $325 billion in 1977, was "very pleased" with the outcome. The subsidies code offered promise for counteracting government subsidies that distorted trade and gave some foreign competitors with government support a competitive advantage. Because U.S. firms were precluded from bidding for foreign government contracts, while foreign firms could solicit U.S. government business, the procurement code promised to removed asymmetries and to open about $20 billion in foreign government purchases to U.S. bidders. The standards code also appealed to ECAT, because it could help "stop the practice of using standards to inhibit or prevent imports." American labor had little enthusiasm for the Tokyo Round agreements. In particular it thought the procurement and standards codes could "jeopardize our national well-being." All agreed that the test of the agreements would be in the actual implementation, and accordingly Congress directed the U.S. Trade Representative to monitor compliance. In 1984 it would require USTR to prepare an annual report on significant foreign trade barriers.[68]

Using the fast-track procedure, Congress swiftly approved the accords with little discussion or dissent. The Trade Agreements Act of 1979 passed the House 395 to 7 and the Senate 90 to 4. The only substantial opposition came from Wisconsin cheese producers. But, recalling past White House efforts to pad trade agreements with optimistic forecasts, some in Congress remained skeptical of the stated advantages. Said Chairman Long's Senate Finance Committee: "The benefits to the United States from the various nontariff agreements negotiated in the MTN depend very heavily on the vigorous insistence by the United States that its rights be secured and that other countries carry out their obligations." In the absence of such insistence, the committee said, the agreements "will become largely one-way streets whereby the United States assumes obligations without reciprocity." Consequently, Congress amended Section 301 to give the President broad authority to enforce U.S. rights unilaterally under Tokyo Round agreements. The 1979 act directed the Chief Executive to take steps to "retaliate against unjustifiable, unreasonable, or discriminatory acts, policies, or practices that affect U.S. commerce."[69]

What was the long-term significance of the Tokyo Round? Some supporters of the multilateral process saw the results as "the most significant round of trade negotiations in history." They argued the substantive codes extended the GATT system to non-tariff barriers, and established the foundation for other substantive and organizational changes in the Uruguay Round of the 1980s. Trade law specialist John H. Jackson of the University of Michigan waxed enthusiastic about the far-reaching scope of the non-tariff codes. "The willingness of nations to yield 'sovereignty' . . . on such subject as government procurement, is impressive," he said.[70]

But, a decade after they went into effect, the six non-tariff codes had little formal acceptance outside the European Community, Japan, and the United States. As of December 31, 1990, merely 40 percent of GATT members (40 of 100) subscribed to the code on technical standards, a relatively innocuous agreement, that negotiators sought to broaden in the Uruguay Round. Only twelve countries adhered to the controversial code on government procurement, while twenty-five adhered to the codes on subsidies and dumping.[71] For the most part, developing nations declined to participate in any agreements that might tie their hands or handicap domestic producers. In light of promises made by Carter administration officials about export opportunities, the government procurement code proved the biggest disappointment. According to the AFL-CIO, "the U.S. opened up $18 billion in procurement opportunities to foreign suppliers, while only $4 billion was seen by U.S. suppliers." The General Accounting Office reported to Congress that these expectations were not realized because of the limited coverage included in the code, the small membership, and the reluctance of members to comply fully. The national procurement policies of France, Italy, and other countries remained significant barriers to American exports. As it turned out, the United States had opened up four times more of its government market than all other code signatories combined.[72]

Negotiation and implementation of the Tokyo Round accords occurred during awkward economic times. Oil-exporting nations succeeded in driving up petroleum prices after the 1973 Mideast War; and this imposed major adjustment burdens on all oil importers. Inflation surged; growth slowed; currencies fluctuated; and budget deficits swelled. Oil-importing developing countries were severely impacted, and the resulting debt-overload crisis disrupted world trade patterns. Viewed from twenty years later, it seems that supporters of the multilateral system pursued a successful holding action during the Tokyo Round. They continued to reward free-riding developing countries with tariff concessions. New Asian competitors and other developing countries were not obliged to offer substantially equivalent concessions. But, by *claiming* to seek reciprocity in the code negotiations, U.S. negotiators allayed some congressional concerns, and thus kept enough legislative support for the trade liberalization process. These efforts would bear fruit in the 1980s and in the Uruguay Round.

Meanwhile, exogenous events and new competition were transforming the environment for trade policy decision making in Washington and other capitals. When serious negotiations began in the Tokyo Round in 1975, the United States still bargained from some strength, despite dollar devaluation. It had an $8.9 billion merchandise trade surplus, and a current account surplus of $18.1 billion, both the largest in a thirty-year period extending from the 1960s to the mid-1990s. During these Tokyo Round negotiations the U.S. surpluses disappeared, replaced in 1978 with a $34 billion trade deficit and a $15 billion current account deficit. Higher energy costs initially exacerbated the deficits. The trade deficit with OPEC (the Organization of Petroleum Exporting Countries) more than doubled from $9 billion in 1975 to $20.8 in 1978, but so did imports of automobiles and consumer goods. The deficit with Japan soared from $1.7 billion in 1975 to $11.6 billion in 1978. The import surge in automotive and consumer imports continued in the 1980s, as foreign firms became more competitive in the U.S. market. U.S. trade and current account deficits peaked in 1987 for a while at $159.6 billion and $168 billion, respectively. The bilateral trade deficit with Japan was now $56.9 billion, but the deficit with OPEC, which crested in 1980 at $41.5 billion, had fallen dramatically by 1987 to $13.7 billion. In short, the composition and sources for the deficit had changed markedly. In 1987, the United States was running a $40 billion deficit on transportation equipment, a $19 billion deficit on clothing, and a $7 billion deficit on footwear—reflecting the rise of Asia as an export platform for consumer goods and cars. The deficit with Asia was $101 billion in 1987, compared with nearly a $1 billion surplus in 1975.[73]

What was the impact of U.S. tariff concessions in the MTN on these events? These reductions contributed to the surge in auto and consumer good imports, because the Tokyo Round lowered already low U.S. average duties on dutiable products from 8.2 percent to 5.7 percent. The MTN reduced U.S. textile tariffs from an average of 22.4 percent to 17.8 percent. Perhaps more significant, however, was the impact on U.S. exports. The Tokyo Round accords apparently did little to open Asian markets and to reduce non-tariff barriers, contrary to Carter administration assurances. Administration advocates had promised Congress that vast export markets would develop for American products as GATT members harmonized and eliminated non-tariff barriers. There is little in the record to suggest that the promised payoff was realized. In 1985 when the USTR began to publish the first of its annual volumes reporting on foreign tariff and non-tariff barriers, thirty-four major U.S. trading partners restricted or managed trade in one form or other. Problems with standards, procurement, subsidies, and investment policies, among other non-tariff barriers, severely handicapped U.S. exporters. A separate Congressional Research Service survey of 521 U.S. companies and trade associations identified 751 specific foreign trade barriers to the export of U.S. goods and services. This study, said a House Commerce subcommittee, found a "clear and incontrovertible pattern" in which "U.S. firms are systematically excluded from exercising their comparative advantages in the home markets of virtually all of our trading partners." But, foreign competitors "expand sales, generate investment capital and acquire new technology behind protectionist barriers, and bring these unfairly acquired advantages to the relatively open U.S. market to the severe disadvantage of domestic companies." Similarly, the Senate Finance Committee expressed concern that the Tokyo Round negotiations and efforts to implement them "have not had the effect of improving the American standard of living as intended." It added: "One way trade is not good for this country, and it is not good for the world either."[74]

As the trade deficit widened in the early to mid-1980s, many economists also pointed to a strong dollar brought about by higher interest rates resulting from inadequate domestic savings and a need to finance a burgeoning federal budget deficit. From a $40.7 billion deficit in FY 1979 the budget deficit grew rapidly to $207.8 billion in FY 1983. To finance the growing budget deficit the Treasury turned to Japanese buyers, enticed by high U.S. interest rates. In 1978 the Japanese replaced the British as the leading foreign holders of marketable Treasury bonds and notes. Heavy Japanese buying of U.S. securities helped prop up the dollar and finance the growing bilateral deficit. In 1985, for instance, Japanese investors bought $20.4 billion net in Treasury and other U.S. government bonds. That year the bilateral deficit was $43.5 billion. In effect, the U.S. budget deficit helped keep interest rates high, and the attraction of higher rates kept the dollar strong and the yen weak, benefiting Japanese exporters and American consumers, while harming U.S. producers and workers in import-competing industries. From an $8.6 billion trade imbalance in 1979, when the yen was relatively strong, the bilateral U.S.–Japan deficit rose to $21.6 billion in 1983 and $56.9 billion in 1987, when the overall merchandise deficit peaked at $160 billion. In 1997, the United States ran a $199 billion merchandise trade deficit, and a current account deficit of $166 billion.[75]

Capital flows were an important part of the story, but many experienced business leaders with firsthand experience competing for sales had a different explanation for the stubborn trade imbalances. Their interpretation focused on the impact of divergent government philosophies and policies. A Congressional Research Service study highlighted these differences. In the United States "free trade has been the overriding ideology guiding U.S. trade policy." Under this theory, market forces determined what each country would produce and trade, while government should, ideally, act as a neutral referee and "not actually use trade policy to promote the competitive position of U.S. industry." By contrast, the study concluded that "free trade ideology has not served as a strong guide for the overall trade policies adopted by the major U.S. trading partners." Japan's resurgence occurred "behind a protectionist wall," and other East Asian countries, such as South Korea and Taiwan, had "successfully copied" the Japanese model of "using controls over trade and investment flows to promote a strong export sector and to acquire technology." Discussion of whether the foreign protectionist policies were completely successful or not misses a critical point. "Closed foreign markets, restrictive investment practices, and subsidized exports can all produce serious economic hardship for individual U.S. producers and workers." The President's Export Council also emphasized the significance of industrial targeting, in which foreign governments and their domestic industries coordinated in attacking key foreign export markets. Japan, South Korea, Taiwan, Brazil, and West Germany were among the major competitors cited as employing such tactics.[76]

Nonetheless, during the 1980s the United States continued its efforts to lead the world trading system toward the laissez-faire ideal in difficult economic circumstances. The global recession of 1981–82 created dislocations and high unemployment in Western Europe and the United States. The developing country debt-overload crisis, exacerbated by a hike in oil prices and the fall in global demand for many commodities, contributed to a decline in world trade. Subsidized steel producers in Western Europe and some developing countries sought to adjust by boosting exports to the

United States. Japanese motorcycle makers and semiconductor makers did the same. The result was a tough test for the new antidumping and countervailing duty laws, written to implement Tokyo Round obligations. These laws, while cumbersome, costly, and legalistic, sometimes required the Reagan administration to impose a variety of import restraints. White House economic adviser William Niskanen later described Reagan trade policies as "strategic retreat." Although the president's goal was more free trade, he said that adverse circumstances compelled the administration to impose "more new restraints on trade than any administration since Hoover." Actually, this greatly overstated President Reagan's use of trade law remedies. The bottom line was that U.S. imports rose 99 percent during his administration, while exports grew only 43 percent.[77]

As it turned out, Reagan's occasional resort to safeguard relief produced some significant gains for domestic industries and workers. The administration's program of bilateral steel restraints bought time for domestic industry to downsize, modernize, cut costs, and become export competitive. The most successful example of escape-clause adjustment occurred on Ronald Reagan's watch. In September 1982 Harley-Davidson, the last American motorcycle maker, was in desperate straits as Japanese motorcycle imports cut into profits and market share. After an International Trade Commission investigation, Harley came roaring back. Within five years it was competitive and could even ask the government to lift the remaining import duties. President Reagan, the long-term exponent of free trade, went to the Harley production facility in Lancaster, Pennsylvania, and effused: "Like America, Harley is back and standing tall." He noted that "where U.S. firms have suffered from temporary surges in foreign competition, we haven't been shy about using our import laws to produce temporary relief . . . . You here at Harley-Davidson are living proof that our laws are working."[78]

FTA Blitz

Meanwhile, USTR Bill Brock, a former Republican senator from Tennessee, whose father voted against Smoot–Hawley in 1930 as a Democratic senator from that same state, pressed the free trade agenda that appealed to big business and the Washington trade-policy elite. Knowing from his years in Congress that the best way to contain protectionist pressures was to have ongoing multilateral negotiations, he urged GATT members to move forward with negotiations to improve the Tokyo Round codes and include other issues such as services, trade-related investments, and intellectual property under GATT supervision. But with Europe in a deep recession he found little interest at the 1982 Geneva ministerial in further negotiations.

Consequently, the United States began a two-track approach to freeing trade. On the one hand, it began to pursue bilateral free trade agreements and on the other it urged GATT members to authorize negotiations.

The bilateral path led first to a free trade agreement with Israel in 1985, then to one with Canada in 1987, and finally under President George Bush to the regional North American Free Trade Agreement (NAFTA) in 1992–93 with Mexico and Canada. President Clinton would push the regional approach with promises to extend free trade to the Western Hemisphere and to Southeast Asia in the twenty-first century. At a time in the mid-1980s when Congress was under enormous constituent pressure to restrict imports, free trade with Israel had political and strategic appeal. Economically, the case was less compelling. In 1985 this tiny middle-income country had a population of 4.2 million and a per capita gross national product only 40 percent of U.S. levels. In 1980, Israel sent 17.2 percent of its exports to the U.S. market some 6,000 miles away, while 52.2 percent went to Western Europe. Import statistics reflected a similar pattern. Europe supplied 52.2 percent of Israel's imports; the United States 19.3 percent. During the November 1983 visit of Israel's prime minister Yitzhak Shamir, President Reagan had promised to negotiate a free trade agreement (FTA), and the administration did so after obtaining negotiating authority from Congress in 1984. The agreement proposed to eliminate tariffs and non-tariff barriers on virtually all trade between the two countries over a ten-year period (1995). This first FTA also included items not covered in the GATT, such as trade in services, trade-related performance requirements, and intellectual property. But Israel retained substantial non-tariff barriers and levies on agricultural items, and the United States did so on textile and apparel imports.

What were the results of this first bilateral free trade agreement? At the signing ceremony in April 1985, Brock forecast that the current $3.5 billion in two-way trade between the United States and Israel would quadruple within three years as a consequence of the agreement. As it turned out, his forecast was far off the mark. Two-way trade increased only 51 percent in four years from 1984 to 1988, and in this period Israel's deficit with the United States turned into a strong merchandise trade surplus, reversing a trend that had existed since Israel declared independence in 1948. By 1997, the deficit had widened to nearly $1.3 billion. On a per capita basis the trade deficit with Israel was one of America's largest. The FTA appears to have increased the share of Israel's exports destined for the U.S. market from 17.2 percent in 1980 to 32.1 percent in 1997. The share of Israel's imports from America remained virtually unchanged—19.3 percent in 1980, 18.8 percent in 1997. The data seemed to indicate that U.S. trade officials had again oversold the gains from a trade agreement.[79]

President Reagan's second FTA initiative—the Canadian agreement—represented another attempt to fulfill nineteenth-century aspirations for a single North American market. The two countries shared a 3,000–mile border, spoke a common language, and had similar governmental institutions, laws, and business practices. Moreover, the two North American neighbors were mutually dependent, mature industrial economies with similar income levels. Each was the other's best customer. Canada sold 76 percent of its exports to the United States in 1985, while Canada took 26 percent of U.S. exports, more than the entire European Community.

Previous efforts to integrate the two economies had failed, mainly because of opposition from Canadian manufacturers concerned about competing with larger U.S.-based competitors. In the 1980s that mood changed. Dependent on access to its neighbor's market, ten times the size of the home market, Canadian business grew alarmed over increasing U.S. use of countervailing and antidumping remedies and fearful that the European Union might turn inward. To remain competitive and to benefit from economies of scale, Canadian firms needed more secure access to the American market. For the United States the attraction of an FTA with Canada included an opportunity to strike a blow at non-tariff barriers and investment restrictions, and to establish rules regarding services, intellectual property, and subsidies that might impact multilateral negotiations.[80]

The final agreement, formally signed on January 2, 1988, provided for elimination of tariffs and non-tariff barriers by January 1998. In the controversial agricultural area all tariffs would be eliminated during the ten-year period and non-tariff barriers would be reduced. The FTA retained the 1965 U.S.–Canada Automotive Products Trade Agreement (APTA), which provided for a limited form of free trade beneficial to existing producers. Other provisions concerning government procurement were intended to serve as an impetus for the "multilateral liberalization of international government procurement policies to provide balanced and equitable trade." The FTA also established dispute settlement procedures intended to provide effective and expeditious dispute settlement procedures, which included use of binational dispute resolution panels. While each country would continue to apply its own antidumping and countervailing duty laws to imported goods, a new procedure provided for a special binational panel to review appeals.

Certain sensitive issues were not resolved in the negotiations. These included Canada's desire to preserve and maintain its unique cultural heritage. As a result, publishing and communications were generally excluded from non-tariff provisions of the FTA. Nor was there agreement on financial services or on subsidies.[81]

Viewed from a decade after the negotiations, the U.S.-Canadian FTA appears to have had some adverse impact on the U.S. merchandise trade deficit and current account. The bilateral deficit in goods widened after implementation of the agreement and reached $24.0 billion in 1996. U.S. surpluses on services and investment income only partially offset that amount, and the current account deficit for 1996 amounted to $10.7 billion. Because the two countries have a long and open border, trade account statistics contain discrepancies and must be used cautiously. Because the FTA negotiations did not produce fixed exchange rates, Canada has used exchange rate depreciation to accumulate merchandise trade and current-account surpluses with the United States.[82]

NAFTA Oversell

The most controversial bilateral free trade initiative involved Mexico. Like President Taft who pressed Canadian reciprocity, President George Bush apparently hoped that trade deals with neighboring countries would leave a lasting imprint on his place in history. Unlike Israel and Canada, which had much smaller populations than the United States, Mexico was a relatively large country (85 million estimated population in 1990) with a per capita gross national product of $2,360, about one-tenth of the U.S. level. Unlike Canada and the United States, which had similar political and legal systems with checks and balances, Mexico had a strong presidency, one dominant political party, and a political tradition without much local democracy. After joining GATT in 1986, Mexico had moved to reduce its tariffs and to attract foreign capital needed to stimulate domestic growth and employment for a rapidly growing population. Its leaders hoped to attract European capital and technology to offset the influence of American investors. But the collapse of the Soviet Union and the liberalization of Eastern Europe forced President José Salinas de Gotari to look northward. In President Bush, an adopted Texan and former business associate of his father's, Salinas found an American president receptive to an FTA.

In February 1991, leaders of the United States, Canada, and Mexico jointly announced their intention to pursue a trilateral FTA intended to liberalize trade in goods and services, foreign investment, protection of intellectual property, and dispute settlement. Eighteen months later, in August 1992, the three governments announced the successful conclusion to negotiations. The two presidents and the prime minister of Canada initialed the NAFTA text at a ceremony in October 1992, a month before the U.S. presidential election.

Tariff eliminations were a small part of the overall deal, since by 1992 average U.S. duties on imports from Mexico were 3 percent and Mexican duties about 10 percent on U.S. products. Far more important were the investment provisions. Until NAFTA, Mexico had strictly regulated foreign investment and prohibited or limited investment in many sectors. Generally, foreign ownership had been limited to 49 percent in a company. Activities in some 141 areas—including transportation equipment, transportation services, petrochemicals, mining, and autoparts—remained classified and subject to government regulations. NAFTA, while making exceptions for activities in a few key sectors reserved to the Mexican state, encouraged the liberalization process. It ensured that foreign investors would receive national treatment, prohibited expropriation except for "public purpose," and provided in those cases for prompt compensation at market prices.

Another important goal was mandatory dispute settlement. NAFTA provided for a five-member arbitration process, and for binational panels to review antidumping and countervailing duty determinations. While the FTA considered a range of issues outside the GATT framework, some of the more innovative provisions related to the movement of professional workers and to rules of origin that operated against investors from outside North America.[83]

After the presidential election, President Bill Clinton revisited the NAFTA agreement, negotiated modest side agreements involving labor and environmental issues in an effort to placate some opponents, and submitted the agreement to Congress under fast-track procedures on November 4, 1993. Many Democrats opposed NAFTA, including House Majority Leader Richard Gephardt together with the AFL-CIO and Ralph Nader. Ross Perot was the most strident opponent; he predicted a "giant sucking sound" of jobs moving south of the border. The U.S. House of Representatives approved implementing legislation on November 17 by a 234 to 200 vote, although a majority of House Democrats opposed. Three days later, the Senate approved 61 to 38.[84]

During the NAFTA debate, proponents engaged in overselling the benefits of a trade agreement. With NAFTA low in the polls, the Clinton administration attempted to showcase endorsements from every living ex-President, 41 governors, 7 environmental organizations, and 284 economists, including 12 Nobel laureates. On the employment issue, Treasury Secretary Lloyd Bentsen and Trade Representative Mickey Kantor told the Senate that "there will be 200,000 more export jobs, which pay 12–17 percent higher than other jobs in our economy, in the next two years if the NAFTA comes into being." Secretary of State Warren Christopher called NAFTA a "turning point" in relations with Mexico that is in the "overriding national interests of the United States." Rejection of NAFTA, he said, "will seriously damage our relations with Mexico and erode our credibility with the other nations of the hemisphere, and, indeed, of the world."[85]

NAFTA's proponents did not hesitate to offer enthusiastic praise for President Salinas and the Mexican government. Said former Secretary of State Henry Kissinger, "I know of no government anywhere that is more competent [than Salinas's]. . . . NAFTA's defeat . . . would humiliate President Salinas in his bet on trust and cooperation with the United States." The pro-NAFTA press warned about the horrible consequences of congressional rejection. *Business Week* hypothesized anti-Yanqui protests, a plunging peso, capital flight, and a dramatic jump in interest rates. The *Washington Post* warned that "investors may begin to hold back their money—resulting in great distress among Mexicans."[86]

As it turned out, NAFTA passed, but some of the dark prophecies came true. The merchandise trade surplus with Mexico soon reversed after peso devaluation. A $4.9 billion surplus in 1992 became an $18.4 billion deficit by 1996, arguably involving a loss of some 450,000 job opportunities. In 1997 the deficit fell to $14.5 billion. A study done in the U.S. Department of Labor subsequently suggested that U.S. exports to Mexico would have grown more rapidly had NAFTA never passed and produced its bubble of speculative foreign investment and subsequent devaluations in Mexico.[87]

Interestingly, the FTAs with Israel, Canada, and Mexico (NAFTA) represented significant departures from U.S. commitment to the multilateral GATT process. FTA provisions digressed somewhat from the principle of nondiscrimination, but arguably they complemented the overall objective of liberalizing trade in that bilateral FTAs sought to address specific issues not handled successfully in the GATT forum—agriculture, services, investments, intellectual property, and other non-tariff issues. In providing for appeals to special bi-national panels (Chapter 19), the Canadian FTA represented a novel experiment. It replaced domestic judicial review with review by ad hoc panels of five individuals, composed of both Canadians and Americans. Sponsors of this approach sold it to Congress and Parliament with representations that such panels would continue to apply the domestic law and standards of judicial review of the country whose determination was being reviewed. But it did not work that way. In a controversial softwood lumber case, three Canadian panelists voted to reverse the U.S. Commerce Department's subsidy determination. They did so after making their own evaluation of evidence and insisting on their own methodologies, rather than deferring to the factual findings of administering authorities. A dissenting U.S. panelist said that the majority opinion "may violate more principles of appellate review of agency action than any opinion by a reviewing body which I have ever read." Later, it was learned that two of the Canadian panelists failed to disclose matters that might affect their impartiality. One of the Canadian panelists had been an employee of the

Canadian government at the same time he was serving as a panelist to decide claims put forth by that government. Another was a partner in a law firm that advised Canadian provincial governments and Canadian lumber companies on trade work.[88]

Uruguay Round "Victory"

The FTA negotiations served Brock's free trade strategy. Not only did they deflect congressional initiatives to address the growing trade deficit, they spurred the GATT process. Concerned that the United States had embarked on a bilateral course, which might include other preferential arrangements with the Association of Southeast Asian Nations (ASEAN) and Latin American nations, Europe relaxed its objections to new multilateral negotiations. Also very important was the debt-overload crisis of less developed countries (LDCs). It threatened the big international banks, the overseas investments of multinational corporations, and trade relationships generally. In the early 1980s there was a widespread fear in multinational circles that LDC debt servicing problems could lead to a 1930s-style collapse of world trade and finance. International bankers and multinational CEOs feared that resurgent "protectionist pressures" in Europe, the United States, Latin America, and elsewhere would precipitate another Great Depression. Unfortunately, they paid much less attention to America's growing structural trade deficit. The tradition of American economic "leadership" was so well established that officials in Washington believed the United States had a "responsibility" to put the perceived interests of the economic system ahead of the short-term concerns of U.S. producers and workers.[89]

In September 1986, a GATT ministerial at Punta del Este, Uruguay, approved the eighth round of negotiations. This one, the Uruguay Round, would focus on efforts to improve GATT rules, particularly those pertaining to agriculture, subsidies, safeguards, dispute settlement, and non-tariff measures. The last item included several topics not raised in the Tokyo Round—services, intellectual property, and investment measures.

For U.S. trade officials, negotiations to improve the GATT system had several specific objectives. The first was "more effective and expeditious dispute settlement mechanisms and procedures" within the GATT. Interestingly, Congress did not specifically mention mandatory dispute settlement in the 1988 act authorizing U.S. participation. Reflecting its traditional concern about free-riders and asymmetries, Congress insisted that developing countries provide reciprocal benefits and assume equivalent obligations. It urged establishing procedures for "reducing nonreciprocal trade benefits for the more advanced developing countries." Among the other negotiating objectives that Congress identified were "more open and fair conditions of trade in agricultural commodities" and improvement of GATT provisions to define, deter, and discourage unfair trading practices.

As it turned out, the Uruguay Round negotiations moved slowly and did not end as anticipated in 1990. Clayton Yeutter, a Nebraskan who succeeded Brock as trade representative, pressed Europe for major concessions in agriculture. Europe strongly resisted, as it had since the beginning of multilateral negotiations. An effort to reach final agreement in Brussels in December 1990 failed when Europe refused to substantially liberalize agriculture. The complex negotiations, which began in the Reagan years, dragged on under George Bush and his USTR, Carla Hills, and finally came to a "successful" close on April 15, 1994, after intensive bargaining and extensive concessions by the United States. One hundred eleven countries signed the Final Act in Marrakech, Morocco.

The outcome established the World Trade Organization, a permanent organization to serve as a forum and a vehicle for implementing trade agreements, to replace GATT. The package also contained thirteen different agreements covering trade in goods and agreements on agriculture; sanitary and phytosanitary measures; textiles and clothing; technical barriers to trade (standards); trade-related investment measures (TRIMs); antidumping, customs valuation, preshipment inspection, rules of origin, import licensing procedures, subsidies, and countervailing measures; and safeguards. In addition, there was a General Agreement on Trade in Services (GATS); an Agreement on Trade-Related Aspects of Intellectual Property Rights (TRIPs); a Dispute Settlement Understanding; Trade Policy Review Mechanism; and four plurilateral trade agreements covering government procurement, civil aircraft, dairy, and bovine meat. The plurilaterals, however, did not involve all members. The final act also set a further negotiating agenda to include financial services, basic telecommunications services, and civil aircraft, but these matters were left largely unresolved.[90]

Transmitting the package to Congress in September 1994, President Clinton called the Uruguay Round Agreements "the broadest, most comprehensive trade agreements in history." When fully implemented, he claimed, the agreements would "add $100–200 billion to the U.S. economy each year and create hundreds of thousands of new, well-paying American jobs." The president noted that U.S. exports to the Asian Pacific economies and Latin America were growing rapidly. "Uruguay Round Agreements will ensure that these fast-growing markets will be open to international competition and that all of our trading partners will play by international trading rules." Stressing that the end of the Cold War and the rise of the global economy had created new opportunities, he called on Americans to implement the Uruguay Round Agreements and so ensure that "we rise to the challenges of this new era and lead the world on a path of prosperity."[91]

Like the Kennedy and Tokyo Rounds, as well as NAFTA, the Uruguay Round produced rosy administration estimates about American export gains. Trade Representative Mickey Kantor forecast that the pact would contribute a minimum of $1 trillion in additional income to the U.S. gross national product over ten years. This estimate was 525 percent greater than the next largest estimate by the OECD, and appeared to reflect wildly optimistic gains from the sale of financial and business services, telecommunications, and public procurement in developing markets.[92]

The history of previous negotiations, and their implementation, suggests that such optimistic estimates are unrealistic. But big business was delighted. In a draft statement, the National Association of Manufacturers applauded the outcome but expressed a "number of serious concerns." While approving establishment of the World Trade Organization, the NAM expressed concern that the bureaucracy might become "unduly independent and champion of its own agenda." The intellectual property rights (TRIPs) agreement could "dramatically enhance" protections for U.S. patents, trademarks, and trade secrets, but the NAM was "distressed" that developing countries would have ten years to implement provisions. "This will mean that certain U.S. companies and U.S. products may effectively have no intellectual property rights protection for a decade or more in several important markets in Asia, Africa, and Latin America." The agreement on trade-related investments seemed "limited." "We are concerned by the number of trade distorting performance requirements and other market skewing government policies that would still be permitted under the Agreement on Trade Related Investment Measures."[93]

Among the most controversial aspects of the package were the new World Trade Organization and mandatory dispute settlement. In the WTO, the United States obtained only one vote, despite its role as the leading trading nation. The European Union, which negotiates in GATT as a single bloc, received fifteen separate votes (one for each member nation). More important, developing nations control 83 percent of votes in the proposed WTO, and thus hold more than the three-quarters majority needed to interpret WTO legal provisions. In what must be considered a fantasy of diplomacy, eighteen WTO member nations with less than one million people would cast votes equal to the United States, Japan, Canada, Germany, France, and Great Britain, the largest trading nations. In such circumstances, it is not unreasonable to suppose that the WTO would become another vehicle for Third World causes, like UNCTAD. Unlike the United Nations Security Council, the United States would have no veto. Unlike the International

Monetary Fund and the World Bank, the economically powerful would not benefit from a weighted voting formula.

For the United States and other industrial countries the WTO regime brought other changes. Powerful nations like the United States could no longer take unilateral action to enforce rights under trade agreements as they pertained to members of the WTO. As a result, developing nations could block efforts to enforce international property rights or to open Third World markets to trade in merchandise, financial services, or telecommunications where the United States had some competitive advantages.

Also troubling was Article XVI of the proposed trade pact. It stipulated: "Each Member shall ensure the conformity of its laws, regulations and administrative procedures with its obligations as provided in the annexed Agreements." This provision appeared to allow the WTO to override the U.S. Constitution and domestic laws. Members of the WTO could use the agreement to challenge national laws, including those of local governments, that appear inconsistent with the trade-liberalization purposes of the WTO. Critics say that local health and safety concerns will take a back seat to trade liberalization and the harmonization of rules.[94]

Finally, the WTO also continued the use of panel dispute settlement procedures, similar to those of the FTAs. Panels of trade experts, not necessarily independent and experienced jurists, would make prompt decisions in secret, avoiding public accountability. The governments affected have no effective choice but to implement such decisions, or open themselves to trade sanctions by other nations.

What did the American people obtain from the Uruguay Round agreements? U.S. trade negotiators, pursuing a trade-policy agenda supporting the interests of large multinational corporations eager to expand further abroad, yielded effective sovereignty to an international commercial organization (the WTO). Phasing out existing tariffs on textiles and apparel meant that hereafter the jobs of nearly one million apparel workers in the United States would be vulnerable to competition from low labor-cost countries. Remaining U.S. apparel makers viewed the outcome as a green light for moving their plants to cheap labor countries like Pakistan and Bangladesh. The mandatory dispute settlement mechanism seemed designed primarily to serve the interests of multinational corporations concerned about receiving fair treatment in developing countries. Although the Uruguay Round placed some agricultural issues under further WTO negotiation, once again the United States and other major agricultural exporters gained little in terms of market access to major protected markets such as the European Community and Japan. In essence, the Uruguay Round Agreements, like the previous U.S. "reciprocal" and multilateral negotiations, seemed the inspiration of a confident trade-policy elite committed to implementing and managing economic internationalism. A global free trade regime managed by MNC-oriented lawyers and economists would strongly protect MNC interests. Their vision stressed so-called economic integration, internationalism, and "global competition." The Uruguay Round agreements, however, did nothing to eliminate large U.S. trade and current account deficits, to eliminate asymmetries, or to achieve a level playing field for manufacturing workers. Understandably, opinion polls showed substantial opposition to free trade agreements, like NAFTA and the Uruguay Round GATT Agreement, among the unskilled and less educated, the class that experienced reduced incomes and extensive job dislocations. A Louis Harris poll for *Business Week* in September 1997 found that "despite a robust economy, a majority of Americans oppose trade expansion." A "significant majority—54 percent—don't want the pact [NAFTA] extended to other Latin American nations." Trade expansion won "majority support only from younger (ages 18–29), more highly educated (those with post-graduate degrees), and higher-paid Americans (those earning over $75,000 a year)."[95]

As the twentieth century moved to a close, the American market was asymmetrically open to global competition and to multinational corporations. From 1947 to 1967 six successive multilateral rounds of GATT negotiations had removed American tariff barriers, and programs targeted at developing nations—particularly production-sharing and GSP—added substantial incentives for the private sector to shift labor-intensive assembly abroad. The watershed, perhaps, was the end of the Kennedy Round. In the twenty years from the Korean War to 1970, despite increasing imports, the U.S. economy had experienced reasonably strong economic growth, averaging 3.5 percent annually. In constant dollars, median family income rose about 80 percent, and weekly earnings for production workers in manufacturing climbed 55 percent. For young men—many of them high-school drop-outs—who bravely went to war in World War II and returned home, after defeating Hitler and Tojo, to take assembly-line jobs in manufacturing, this was still the American dream of higher wages and steadily improving living conditions. But in the quarter-century after 1970 the good times ended as surging import competition forced plants to close and companies to restructure. During this period the industrial economy stagnated, and U.S. economic growth slowed to a 2.8 percent average. Over the period real median family income increased only slightly, even though more members of each household worked. Real weekly earnings for individual workers fell significantly. Income distribution became more uneven. The gap widened between the incomes of skilled and unskilled workers. As the federal government continued to spend more than it generated in tax revenue, this country became hooked on budget deficits, imports from abroad, and foreign capital to finance budget and trading deficits. Persistent, large trade and current-account deficits significantly depressed domestic growth—as much as 3 percent in 1986, a year when real gross domestic product rose 3.1 percent. Rather than providing a net stimulus to the American economy, recent Commerce Department data suggest that surging U.S. imports substantially shifted domestic resources out of productive, high-wage manufacturing into lower-wage service jobs insulated from global competition. No wonder many American middle- and lower-class families lost ground.[96]

Unbalanced trade concessions clearly exacerbated the merchandise trade deficit and depressed job opportunities for manufacturing workers. U.S. merchandise trade turned from a strong surplus to a persistent deficit as the Kennedy Round concessions were implemented. From 1976 to 1997 the United States has experienced twenty-one successive merchandise trade deficits—when imports exceeded exports. The cumulative trade deficit amounted to more than $2,000 billion and averaged about $125 billion annually since 1983. Assuming, as the Department of Commerce does, that each one billion dollars in trade affects 17,000 to 20,000 job opportunities, the U.S. trade deficits probably cost American workers at least millions of good-paying job opportunities in manufacturing. Because a trade deficit depresses gross national product [GNP = C + I + G + (X - M)], it is apparent that the chronic deficit has suppressed real domestic growth substantially in recent years.

Although some celebrate the ideal of free trade and freedom for the individual to trade, a large portion of global commerce does not correspond to conditions of the classical free trade model. In most developing countries the governments continue to regulate and manage commerce in substantial ways. In Japan and Europe trade is still not as free as in the United States. Does this free trade legacy still make sense in the post–Cold War era? To answer this question intelligently, we must review carefully the best accumulated insights of economists on trade policy. When and in what circumstances can free trade really improve the mutual welfare of nations and their peoples?

3

RICHARD L. BRINKMAN

Freer Trade: Static Comparative Advantage

Overview

Adam Smith urged the liberalization of commerce from guild restrictions, monopolies, and feudal privileges. Increased output and greater specialization derived from laissez-faire policies would improve the wealth of nations, especially for domestic industries and trading. But Smith accepted four major limitations on free international trade: (i) retaliation tariffs as a matter of statesman-like deliberation; (ii) protection for industries vital to national defense; (iii) navigation laws to promote the merchant marine and maritime commerce; and (iv) extensive public works (roads, canals, harbors, and waterworks) (Smith 1937, 429–436, 410–414, and 651–716). Thus, while Smith broke with earlier, naïve mercantilist thinking, his support for internal improvements allowed scope for nation-building policies like those used in Britain (1650–1840s) or the United States (1791–1920s). Alexander Hamilton and Friedrich List later argued for substantial tariff protection to nurture manufacturing development, although accepting widespread laissez faire *within nations* in accord with Smith's liberal thinking.

But Britain, in the 1840s after their Industrial Revolution, decided that policies of freer trade, not protection, would better serve national interests. Britain's need was no longer to protect the economy from foreign manufacturing, because Britain enjoyed broad industrial ascendancy, but rather to open more global markets for expanding British industrial production. Adam Smith is widely credited with pioneering economic theory in support of freer trade. Yet Smith's support for laissez faire allowed considerable leeway for nation-building policies. In addition to support of policies promoting national defense as "more important than opulence," and with views that the "act of navigation is perhaps the wisest of all commercial regulations," as Jacob Viner noted, Adam Smith also made "concessions to the mercantilistic policy of regulation of the foreign trade" (Smith 1937, 431; Irwin 1991, 111). Of course, Smith had written the *Wealth of Nations* in a context of widespread mercantilism in the 1770s.

It is often maintained that the free trade advocacy that took place in Britain during the 1830s and 1840s was supported by the comparative cost theory.[1] Ricardo's cloth/wine arguments served as the foundation for what later came to be called the "Pure Theory of Trade." Historically, this theory, in turn, has come to be used to justify and rationalize a policy derivative of free trade. Given their respective hegemonic positions, Britain (1840s–1880s) and the United States (1940s–1970s), both nations embarked upon policies allowing the extreme of one-way or unilateral free trade. Unfortunately, one-way free trade policies did not maintain their respective industrial-maritime predominance. Accordingly, support for such unilateral free trade policies, in disregard of global asymmetries and non-reciprocity, waned as each country lost ground against more protected rivals. Both countries delayed, considerably, in recognizing their vulnerability that was manifest in growing economic asymmetries.

By the 1970s, however, the American economic malaise was recognized even among the orthodox (Haberler 1979). While causality and cures might be debated, the empirical facts indicative of economic malaise and maladjustment could not. After an apparent turning point, circa 1973, U.S. rates of economic growth became anemic in comparison to the historic long-term trends (Madrick 1995). This provided evidence of American long-term economic decline. In addition and as an explanation, many conclude that our problems are structural in nature (Bernstein and Adler 1994). Troubling economic indicators appear in productivity decline, balance of payments deficits, international indebtedness, a decline in real wages, and so on.[2] Consequently, industrial renewal and a restoration of global competitiveness have as yet to fully materialize for the U.S. economy (Mishel, Bernstein, and Schmitt 1997).

Such a period of maladjustment is indicative of a cultural lag. The basic cultural lag that we now face pertains not only to trade policy, but also relates to the trade theory upon which such policy is based.[3] There is a need to develop "new" theories of trade to serve as a basis for the formulation of a rational trade policy relevant to the current economic problems that America faces. There is a need for a new game plan to address the new ball game now being played in the competitive, global arena. In the vernacular of Woody Hayes, when "three yards and a cloud of dust" no longer produce victory, it is time to change the game plan and throw a few passes (Thurow 1996, 1–19; 1992, 259–299).

Origins of Free Trade: Theory and Policy

Trade theory experienced an historical transformation. Starting with Adam Smith and through the works of David Ricardo, John S. Mill, Alfred Marshall, and on to the contributions of Eli Heckscher, Bertil Ohlin, and Paul Samuelson, orthodox trade theory in support of free trade has experienced significant changes, refinement, and narrowing.[4]

The story that unfolds in the literature is that Adam Smith argued the case for free trade based on absolute advantage. David Ricardo explained "what" was traded in terms of the "Doctrine of Comparative Costs," which in turn came to serve as the basis for relative comparative advantage. John S. Mill offered an explanation of the "international price" at which goods were exchanged in terms of reciprocal demand. Marshall, in *The Pure Theory of Trade,* provided a base for analytic synthesis, as a framework to put it all together in the direction of general equilibrium theory, and a more rigorous foundation for theory. Gottfried Haberler introduced "opportunity costs" to replace the classical and Marxian labor theory of value and its associated measure of labor costs. The orthodox pure theory was added to by the works of Heckscher, Ohlin, and Samuelson, explaining "why" a given nation had a comparative cost advantage as well as directing more attention for the results and "gains" to be derived from a policy of free trade.[5]

To understand Adam Smith one must appreciate the gradual Industrial Revolution from which these ideas sprang. The process of trade itself served a dynamic function and catalytic role in cultural evolution in the later Middle Ages. It can be argued that the expansion of trade constituted a significant factor in the breakdown of the feudal system. After a long era of feudal stagnation from the fall of the Roman Empire up to the bubonic plague (1349–50), a period designated as a gradual Commercial Revolution (circa 1350–1750) followed. And it was the overly restrictive "mercantile system" of the Early Modern period (1550–1750) that Adam Smith attacked in the *Wealth of Nations.*[6]

The Commercial Revolution can be conceptualized as "early capitalism," or using Rostow's classification, a stage of "preconditions" allowing for the subsequent "take-off" into modern industrial growth (Rostow 1968). A seed bed was nurtured for the ultimate flowering of what later came to be called the Industrial Revolution (circa 1750–1850). The Commercial Revolution was interrelated to many inventions of the period, both social and material, such as the compass, larger sailing ships, banking, double entry bookkeeping, improved iron-making, greater use of coal, and so on. Among the most important technological advances was the printing press. All this advance in turn was instrumental in the innovation of one of the greatest social inventions of all time. We speak here of the invention of the method of invention, better known as the institution of science. This process of invention became institutionalized during the period which Kuznets has designated as a "scientific epoch."

The science being nurtured during the period was not confined simply to material culture, but spilled into social culture as well. Enter Adam Smith, the *Wealth of Nations,* and the modern science of economics. By comparison, earlier mercantilist writers are viewed as pamphleteers seeking personal gain and mercantile profits. The theory behind mercantilist policies is allegedly sparse and not really representative of a unified matrix (Marshall 1927, 719–720). By contrast, Adam Smith offered a path for policy to be predicated on "scientific" inquiry. As Max Lerner states: "Like all great books, *The Wealth of Nations* is the outpouring not only of a great mind, but of a whole epoch. The man who wrote it had learning, wisdom, a talent for words; but equally important was the fact that he stood with these gifts at the dawn of a new science and the opening of a new era in Europe" (Smith 1937, v).

But crucial to the mercantilism that evolved during the Commercial Revolution was the nation-state. "The emergence of national states governed by rulers who exercised sway over large areas, was perhaps the most important political development of the early modern period" (Heaton 1948, 221–222). And from this new structure of social organization, the nation-state, came forth the policies later referred to as mercantilism. The actual policies included state corporations, franchises or guild privileges, substantial excise taxes, tariffs on imports, overseas colonies (if possible), and favors to domestic as opposed to foreign artisans, merchants, and shipping activities.

Though crude and somewhat oppressive, mercantilist policies did work in terms of state building.[7] And this meant *nation*-state building. This integrative process served as a sine qua non for the *First Industrial Revolution.* Mercantilist policies had an impact even beyond that of state building in that they also served as policies of transition into modern economic growth and industrialization.[8] It was not the domestic policy of laissez faire, nor its international extension as British "free trade," that served to foster the Industrial Revolution. Rather, it was the policies of mercantilism and the emergence of science during the later Commercial Revolution which fostered a "scientific epoch" and, ultimately, led to the dynamics of modern and industrial economic growth. It was after the British Industrial Revolution when the nation-state, Britain, achieved a measure of global hegemony, that Britain tried freer trade with the repeal of the Corn Laws in 1846. Similarly, for the United States, it was the Hamiltonian internal improvement and external tariff policies embedded in the "American System" that promoted national unification and power, and gradual U.S. industrialization, not external free trade. Again, it was only after the fact of achieving global industrial and economic hegemony that the United States embarked on policies directed toward free trade, mainly after World War II.[9]

What then is Adam Smith's framework? Wealth for a nation resides in production, not gold. Production rests on labor productivity, which is based on the division of labor. Specialization, inherent in the division of labor, is promoted by larger market size. Large market size is partly related to the accumulation of capital, but large market size is also a function of trade. The policy orientation that was to hold the whole system together was a general laissez faire.[10]

There are three basic legs to Adam Smith's theory of international trade: (i) absolute advantage; (ii) outlet or vent-for-surplus; and (iii) productivity doctrine (Myint 1958). Why nations trade particular items and what allows for lower costs is a function of "absolute advantage." Given static and fixed conditions of climate and resources, it does not make sense to produce strawberries and bananas in a hot house. A static conception of absolute advantage is the one usually offered in the literature. But given an absolute advantage in both industrial and agrarian pursuits, why then should a nation engage in trade and import goods produced less efficiently abroad? This question, outside the boundaries of Smith's matrix, led to the introduction of Ricardo's Doctrine of Comparative Costs. By comparison, the framework of comparative costs explains that it is possible in some circumstances to benefit from importing a good that is more costly in its production abroad—a possibility overlooked by Adam Smith, but recognized by Ricardo.

The outlet or vent-for-surplus theory is stressed more recently by Hlya Myint as perhaps more relevant in relating the classical theory of trade to the problem of economic development (Myint 1958). In allowing a vent, or outlet, for surplus production, free exports permit a nation to improve position on its efficiency locus, better known as the production-possibility or transformation curve. The outlet-for-surplus reasoning accounts for a movement from unemployed to fully employed resources at zero opportunity costs. The outlet-for-surplus theory, however, also supports the dumping of surplus goods abroad, with frequent disruptive impacts upon other nations.

But the reasoning in support of freer trade offered by Adam Smith was not merely confined to a static analysis embedded in absolute advantage and the outlet-for-surplus theories. Adam Smith, importantly, also provided a dynamic theory of international trade with the "productivity doctrine." Laissez faire and broader trade are a dynamic force which, by widening the market and scope for the division of labor, raises the skill and dexterity of the workman, encourages technical innovation, overcomes technical indivisibilities, and generally enables a trading country to enjoy increasing returns and economic development (Myint 1958, 318–319).

The free trade position of Adam Smith has historically been submitted to a whole variety of criticism and limitations. These views have also evolved over time but include attacks originating from Alexander Hamilton, Friedrich List, Raul Prebisch, and Gunnar Myrdal, among others. Trade theory, more relevant to the dynamics of development, will be dealt with more specifically in the next chapter. But another critique concerned the oppressive results of a free trade policy. Mercantilism was critiqued for its colonization and because benefits mainly accrued to the mother country. With classical free trade all nations were supposed to benefit. In actuality, however, the end result was sometimes more colonialism, on a larger scale. Colonialism as imperialism was often associated with the policies of free trade.[11] The earlier colonialism of mercantilism paled by comparison to imperialism of the late nineteenth century. The pattern that emerged was that the "relatively most efficient in industrial production (by good fortune Britain) would continue to industrialize while the most relatively efficient hewers of wood and drawers of water would go on doing just that" (Dowd 1993, 17).

Pure Theory of Trade

It was the Ricardian framework, the static "Doctrine of Comparative Costs," which gave rise to *The Pure Theory of Foreign Trade* (Marshall 1949). The epithet "pure" theory, according to Bhagwati, is derived from the work of Marshall, which postulates a separation of "trade" theory from "monetary" theory.[12] In the Marshallian offer-curve framework, "trade balances for each country. . . . There is no possibility of international borrowing. . . . Ricardo postulated balanced trade and maintained that international capital movements did not take place" (Robinson 1980, 138).

Over time, as a theory of comparative advantage evolved, neoclassical economists developed a variety of ancillary analytical tools in their attempts to argue the correctness of free trade policy. "The pure theory of international trade has been most thoroughly refined in terms of static general equilibrium analysis" (Meier 1968, 10). Haberler's introduction of opportunity costs during the 1930s served to substitute for the classical tradition, which focused on a measure based on labor productivity and a labor theory of value. Over time, the maturation of the pure theory of trade, in its evolution, produced the current standard textbook treatment, which includes a composite mix of several additional tools. Among them are the production-possibilities curve; Marshallian offer curves; as well as an indifference map to serve as a basis for value theory.

From these abstract, esoteric tools of neoclassical economics, a basic analytical and methodological sequence follows. Its overall composition constitutes the "Pure Theory of Trade." "What" is traded is a function of the domestic terms of trade. The domestic rates of exchange are derived from a given nation's production-possibilities (P-P) or transformation curve. These domestic rates of exchange are then used to determine a nation's relative comparative cost advantage. When the dust settles among the production functions in the Edgeworth–Bowley box diagram, the efficiency locus, so achieved, provides for the derivation of a nation's P-P curve. But the P-P curve is not only important in determining the domestic terms of trade. In the framework of the neoclassical pure theory of trade, the P-P curve serves a very important function in relation to the conception and meaning of economic growth and development.

Crucial to the pure theory of trade is the demonstration of the "gains" to be derived from international trade and further that the "gains" be shown to serve as an improvement in human welfare. How then to demonstrate the "gains" from trade in relation to the processes of economic growth and development? Certainly, an assumed gain would be that trade, more correctly free trade, would promote development for both nations engaged in trade. This is especially of importance and relevant to an agricultural or LDC nation. Therefore, what conception of development does the pure theory of trade offer? "We can now extend the analysis to development problems by first interpreting a country's development in terms of outward shifts in its production frontier."[13] These shifts, in conjunction with an indifference map, were used to indicate the welfare aspects of economic development, the "gains" supposedly wrought in the crucible of free trade.

Meier's neoclassical conception of economic development is essentially synonymous with the comparative statics of economic growth. And this "growth" is then made to be the conceptual equivalent of economic development. But how, then, in the matrix of neoclassical theory is the outward shift of the P-P curve explained and thereby, the realization of economic development (in a more complete, institution-building sense)?

The domestic terms of trade are derived from the P-P curve (efficiency locus) and are used to determine the ratios of exchange between cloth and wine, and to determine the "what" is traded. Comparative costs do not determine the international price or the international terms of trade. John S. Mill answered this question with the conception of reciprocal demand. Enter Alfred Marshall and the offer-curve analysis. The equilibrium position obtained from the offer-curve analysis provides for the derivation of the international terms of trade (ITT). This new rate of exchange is of great importance in the context of the pure theory of trade and is demarcated in

Figure 3.1. **Marshallian Offer Curves and the "Engine of Growth"**

A. <u>Marshallian Offer Curves</u>

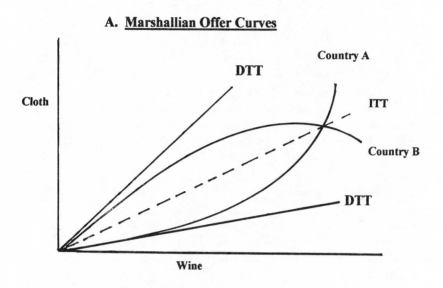

B. <u>Gains from Trade: "Economic Development"</u>

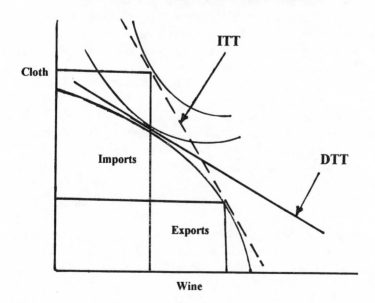

Figure 3.1A as the line ITT. The ITT is not based upon labor productivity, but represents new rates of exchange offering an improvement over the domestic terms of trade (DTT) for both nations. This has a "real income effect, the same *as if* there had been an outward shift in its production frontier" (Meier 1968, 20, italics added).

Especially to be noted, therefore, is that the newly formulated ITT serves the same function, *as if* there had been a real shift in the production frontier when in actuality all that had occurred was a change in price manifest in the newly originated international terms of trade. Reciprocal demand (not the dynamics of technological change) was assumed to be causal in promoting economic development through the newly formulated ITT, which served the same function *as if* the production-possibilities curve had shifted outward when in actuality it had not. Increased specialization in the production of more wine simply results in a movement along the given P-P curve, but not in an actual outward shifting of the curve (see Figure 3.1B).

Changes in resources, factor inputs, or technology (the basis for an actual or real outward movement of the production frontier) are assumed not to have taken place and are taken to be given. Ceteris paribus, it becomes necessary to show how the introduction of international trade, as the isolated and independent variable, promoted growth (development) that is the outward shift of the P-P frontier. The *as if* shift was accomplished via a newly formulated international terms of trade. Consequently, what the analysis boils down to is that a favorable change in the international terms of trade is the conceptual equivalent of *an assumption of economic development,* given the offer-curve methodology as an explanation of the "gains" from free trade.

Price changes and static economic efficiency of given and existing resources, in the context of a given structure, have always constituted the major concern of neoclassical economic analysis. The upshot of the pure theory of trade manifests and continues this focus in the context of international prices and the improved terms of trade, not the dynamics of development. The paradigmatic boundaries and predilections demarcated by the analytical tools of the neoclassical pure theory of trade, consequently, preclude an analysis of the dynamics of economic development. The pure theory of trade, by focusing on the gains that accrue from the production of more and more wine or cloth, offers a restricted, static function of trade as an "Engine of Growth." The relevant question, however, is to demonstrate how trade serves a dynamic function as an "Engine of Development."[14]

And finally to round out the framework, "why" did a nation have a relative cost advantage to begin with? The Ricardian "Doctrine of Comparative Cost," as theory, explained "what" was traded but did not really explain at all "why" a particular nation had such a relative cost advantage. The Heckscher–Ohlin model tried to offer an explanation in terms of the quantitative supply of labor and capital, as the basic factors of production. These factors in turn, serve to demarcate the basic analytical boundaries of the E-B box diagram. The efficiency locus of the E-B box in turn determines the P-P curve, which, in turn, is used to determine the domestic terms of trade.

"Heckscher's innovation was to attribute disparities in comparative costs and hence in the pattern of trade, to dissimilarities in factor endowments. . . . Ohlin recognized the revolutionary nature of Heckscher's brilliant idea, married it explicitly with general equilibrium, neoclassic theory" as the pure theory of trade.[15] The Heckscher–Ohlin theory evolved into what has come to be called the Heckscher–Ohlin–Samuelson–Jones theory of international trade (Heckscher and Ohlin 1991, 1–30). The neoclassical analytical circle from causality to results, and starting with the E-B box diagram in the orthodox pure theory of trade, was thereby given its logical completion with the introduction of the H-O model.

Of the two basic theorems of the H-O model to be explicitly stated, one was associated with an explanation as to why a nation had a relative cost advantage in the production of a given commodity. The second explicit theorem of the H-O model was related to an explanation as to why a free-market system, of laissez faire and its international concomitant of free trade, tended to provide for factor-price equalization. Factor-price equalization is not to be equated with a tendency toward an international leveling or equalization of GNP/capita. But rather that factor payments, per se, in a specific area of production or country would move toward equality. The conclusion reached was that all nations would improve their positions in terms of economic growth and welfare, and be better off, *but not necessarily equally.* The question then becomes, Is the pure theory of trade sound in terms of its internal conceptual orientation and logic, and especially, in terms of its basic and underlying assumptions?

Static Comparative Advantage Under Siege: Errors and Omissions

The siege has actually had a long history; even in 1937 Viner noted that historically, the theory had been under attack—"Never widely accepted on the Continent, the doctrine is clearly on the defensive everywhere" (Viner 1965, 438). The cannonade continues today with increased intensity, only now there are more cannons and with increased firing power. A fundamental critique is that a pure free trade policy ignores and discounts the obvious global asymmetries that exist today. And whereas global realities indicate the need for policies of reciprocity, actual policy recommended by pure free-traders moves in the direction of unilateral free trade.

Unilateral, unrestricted free trade takes a head-in-the-sand view of reality. This outlook assumes that one policy prescription for the United States is immutable and will work for all nations for all times and all places, yet "there is no one template that fits all industries" (Robert Kuttner in Blecker 1996, 31). To assume that a policy of unrestricted laissez faire will resolve all of the current global maladies is analogous to believing in that old snake-oil medicine sold in the Wild West of the past. Laissez faire does not work even in the far less complex arena of the domestic economy let alone the heterogeneous complexity of international cultures, at different stages of development, characterizing the asymmetrical global economy. Samuelson is correct: "undiluted laissez faire died before Queen Victoria died" (Samuelson 1979, 820).

The crucial flaw usually cited is that the pure theory of trade rests upon a foundation of "Magnificent Assumptions," which can also be classified simply as "whoppers" (Salvatore 1998, 110).

1. Only two nations, two commodities, and two factors of production (labor and capital) exist.
2. Production functions are homogeneous; all nations use the same technology.
3. One commodity is labor intensive (X) and the other capital intensive (Y) in both nations.
4. Commodities in both countries are produced under constant costs.
5. There is incomplete specialization in production in both countries.
6. Tastes are the same in both countries.
7. Perfect factor mobility exists within nations; no mobility is international.
8. There is perfect competition in commodity and factor markets.
9. There are no transportation costs, tariffs, or other obstructions to free trade.
10. All resources are fully employed in both nations.
11. International trade is balanced.

It is an understatement to say that these assumptions constitute a rationalization of neoclassical theory. In that the Heckscher–Ohlin model is predicated on the quantitative base of factors in explaining the basis of comparative costs for a given nation, the assumption of immobility of factors must be made in order for the theory to hold. But even in the latter part of the nineteenth century, when the static framework of Marshall's pure theory was being formulated, reality and the empirical record revealed large migratory flows of capital, labor, and technological diffusion. The same prevailed for the assumption of full employment. During this period, the periodic ups and downs of the business cycle frequently indicated high levels of unemployment, quite apart from the massive unemployment of the Great Depression.

It appears that every assumption on the list of the eleven basic assumptions stretches the bounds of relevancy and credibility. But one that deserves special attention, and related to the dynamics of the economic process, is the assumption of homogeneous production functions. In plain English, this means that technology everywhere is assumed to be the same. This assumption is founded on the further assumption that since knowledge is free and accessible to all, that every nation is capable of acquiring its fair and equal share. And since knowledge constitutes the fountainhead of technology, all nations have homogeneous production functions. All of which then further assumes that all nations are at the same level of economic development, and ignores the great technological and developmental asymmetries that exist among the United States, Japan, Somalia, and Ethiopia, not to mention the obvious asymmetries in the comparative levels of technology and development that exist between the United States and its Mexican neighbor.

How, then, to explain such flawed assumptions, which are offered in support of the pure theory of trade? Marshall perhaps provides the answer. "A politician is compelled to seek his allies among those who desire the same ends as his; and therefore political influences on economic studies are not always wholesome" (Marshall 1927, v). Perhaps the economists who originated the theory placed the cart of politics and the policy of free trade before the horse of relevant, systematic, and scientific inquiry. It is duly noted in the literature that the Ricardian theory of static comparative advantage served as the underlying rationale for the politics of the free trade battle that ultimately resulted in the repeal of the Corn Laws in 1846 (Condliffe 1950, 203–236; Cunningham 1904).

It is far more publicly palatable and practical for power elites to have their policies directed and rationalized by systematic "scientific" inquiry, rather than that of political maneuver organized by blatant political interests and power. It is no wonder, then, that Viner states: "many of the best expositions of the classical theory of international trade were made in the course of discussion of proposals for legislation, and that, *Hansard,* the record of the British parliamentary debates, is not a bad source from which to learn what classical theory of international trade was and that it . . . was formulated primarily with a view to its providing guidance on questions of national policy" (Viner 1952, 15; 1965, 437). In their desire for implementation of the free trade policy agenda, and to provide the validity of their theory, maybe orthodox economists lost sight of empirical economic realities, especially in relation to their underlying assumptions.

And while the list of the eleven assumptions is fairly long and unbelievably out of sync in terms of relevancy to the real world, more could be added, such as the assumption of rational *homo economicus,* and that the real world is static and fixed rather than dynamic and evolving.

Another extremely important assumption, and one not usually given its warranted attention, is that economic growth as an outward shifting P-P curve is assumed to be the conceptual equivalent of economic development (recall Meier 1968, 22). But as Schumpeter among others has observed, economic growth is not synonymous with economic development.

Static Versus Dynamic Issue

A central issue deserving of further explication relates to static nature of the pure theory of trade. This problem is universally recognized in the literature, and not simply by those of heterodox predilections, but orthodox economists themselves.[16] To begin with, the concepts static and dynamic are not without normative connotations. People tend to admire the dynamic, for example, a dynamic speaker. The dynamic is symbolic of action and motion—something exciting and good is happening. By comparison, the static and the stagnant are assessed in negative terms. This underlying evaluation carries over into the assessment of theories of economic theories wherein the dynamic appears meritorious and the static as somehow being faulty. But both the static (replication and reproduction) and the dynamic (transformation and metamorphosis) are necessary for scientific inquiry relevant to analysis of an evolutionary process. The problem with "pure" trade theory is that it tells only a limited fragment of the story, the static, and avoids the dynamic evolution (the whole story unfolding).

In the neoclassical literature, a passage of time is usually exemplified by the movement from one equilibrium position to another and is conceptualized as "comparative statics" (Salvatore 1998, 733). But to consider "comparative statics" to be the conceptual equivalent of a dynamic process would be tantamount to assuming that shuffling a deck of cards, or moving marbles around in a fish bowl from one equilibrium position to another, given a prerequisite change and intervening motion over time, represents a dynamic process. Change in a sense has taken place, a new equilibrium is achieved, but nothing has really changed. The structure under analysis is still the same. In such cases, motion in terms of change within a given structure has taken place, but the structure has not. This important and relevant distinction has been noted by Frank Knight: "one of the major errors of the classical tradition [is] that it failed, and still largely fails, to make a sharp and correct theoretical distinction between the working of a system under given conditions and, including the movement towards equilibrium, changes in the given conditions or content of the system itself."[17]

This perspective is expressed by LDC nations. "[D]eveloping nations attack traditional theory as static and irrelevant to the development process. They view traditional trade theory as involving *adjustment* to existing conditions, while development requires *changing* existing conditions" (Salvatore 1998, 331). Consequently, a dynamic process entails a process of metamorphosis and transformation of structure. A dynamic process leads to something structurally new and qualitatively different (Schumpeter 1983, 63).

To Schumpeter, the dynamics of the economic process are contained in the conception of economic development as a qualitative process of structural transformation. And development entails the social and cultural and the dynamics of institutional adjustment (Kuznets 1930, 432). How, then, to fit the complexity of the dynamic process of development into a matrix of Marshallian offer curves? The neoclassical analysis and pure theory of trade comprising an "as if" conception of growth, which in turn is viewed as the conceptual equivalent of economic development, is simply not relevant to the dynamics of development.

In the literature, economic development is usually relegated to technological advance. "Economic development is fundamentally a product of technological change. . . . Yet traditional economic models provide little help in understanding this process" (Dosi, Tyson, and Zysman, 1989, 19). The pure theory of trade handles this complexity again with the "Magnificent Assumption" of homogeneous production functions and that technology is basically assumed to be given. In addition, the social, institutional, and the culture are also taken as givens.

A common critique pressuring the need for the pure theory of trade was that Adam Smith's theories of free trade lacked "analytical rigor" (Bloomfield 1994, 109). But in their quest for a more "rigorous" economic analysis, neoclassical economists drowned the dynamic baby in the static, unrealistic bathwaters they introduced. In making the theory more "rigorous," the pure theory of trade obfuscated and avoided any realistic understanding of the dynamics of economic development.

It appears that Ricardo's static theory of comparative advantage shunted classical trade theory off the potentially dynamic track laid by Adam Smith and on to a static way station (or cul-de-sac) in the structure of the pure theory of trade. That wise old Scot, Adam Smith, was maybe the wisest after all. Adam Smith did indeed have broader vision and a nascent dynamic theory of international trade. It is obvious that the "productivity doctrine," referred to previously, provided a matrix relevant for the introduction of technological advance into trade theory. Not so obvious is the relevancy of absolute advantage to the dynamics of the economic process.

Usually discussions of absolute advantage relate to growing strawberries or bananas in a hot house. This relegates absolute advantage to the statics of a given climate, resource endowment, or particular geographical conditions. These conditions do explain part of a nation's absolute advantage. But Adam Smith also drew attention to the fact that a nation's absolute advantage rested on the vanguard position of a nation's overall position in the stage of modern economic growth. "Most opulent nations . . . generally excel all their neighbours in agriculture as well as in manufactures; but they are commonly more distinguished by their superiority in the latter than in the former" (Bloomfield 1994, 111).

The United States in the past, and Japan recently, achieved positive trade balances and international creditor positions based upon the absolute advantages achieved through broadly superior technological advantage and scale economies. It is absolute cost advantage which cuts the competitive edge, not comparative costs. Arguments are currently being presented for "A Rehabilitation of Absolute Advantage" (MacDonald and Markussen 1985). "Our hypothesis is thus that absolute advantages *dominate* over comparative advantages as determinants of trade flows" (Dosi, Pavitt, and Soete 1990, 148–151). That Britain once exported textiles and dominated the global economy in production and trade, the hegemonic Pax Britannica of the nineteenth century, was not a function of relative or comparative costs, but rather, and obviously, that Britain had innovated the *First Industrial Revolution*. The patterns and expansion of industrial trade relate to the dynamics of technological evolution, which in turn reflect absolute advantage.

But this is not to assume that unilateral, unrestricted, or unbalanced free trade serves as the best agency in the promotion of absolute advantage. In fact, the basic message of this book is that a policy of one-way, nonreciprocal, or unbalanced free trade generally serves to retard and inhibit a nation's drive toward higher levels of absolute advantage. Certainly this realization did not escape Hamilton, List, Prebisch, or Myrdal. Neither has it escaped the trade policies of America's Asian competitors and new industrial countries (NICs) generally.

The pure theory of trade, and any other naïve version of one-way or unilateral laissez faire, no longer serves as a basis to promote a rational or sound trade policy. A sound trade policy requires a dynamic theory of international trade. If the United States is to play in the dynamic game of global competitiveness, we need more realistic theories of dynamic comparative advantage to provide for a rational and sound trade policy.

4

RICHARD L. BRINKMAN

Dynamic Comparative Advantage

In evaluating "gains" from trade, a major concern relates to the impact of trade on economic development. As Gerald Meier wrote: "Dominating all issues. . . . Can foreign trade have a propulsive role in the development of a country?" (Meier 1968, 215). And the problem of development is not only for the LDC world, but also includes the ongoing development of mature countries like the United States. But the pure theory of trade, which historically provided the rationale for freer trade, is based upon static and doubtful assumptions. Consequently, trade theory needs a better understanding for economic development. The current global reality constitutes an evolutionary dynamic of development and transformation.

Structural Transformation: The Secretary–Lawyer Analogy

This analytical conundrum, in applying a static framework to a dynamic process, is illustrated in the secretary–lawyer analogy. Granting that a lawyer has absolute advantage in both legal and secretarial work, Friedman draws the conclusion, widely supported in the literature, that "both he and the secretary are better off if he practices law and the secretary types letters" (Friedman and Friedman 1980, 45). The rationale, somewhat intuitively obvious, is that a lawyer would be better off by specializing in legal work and having the secretary specialize in typing and secretarial work (Bloomfield 1994, 111). This problem was also addressed by David Ricardo with the "Doctrine of Comparative Costs."[1] But do the conclusion and logic, based upon static assumptions, necessarily follow?

Case 1, from Table 4.1, "Statics and Dynamics of the Secretary–Lawyer Analogy," illustrates a situation in which the lawyer has absolute advantage in both legal and secretarial work. It is assumed that the secretary and lawyer work one-half time at both legal and secretarial work for a total and combined income of $80,000. After reading about comparative cost

Table 4.1 **Statics and Dynamics of the Secretary–Lawyer Analogy**
(dollars/year)

Static Comparative Advantage

Case # 1 Nonspecialization

	Woman (Nation A)	Man (Nation B)	Total
Secretary (wine/agriculture)	$10,000.00	$16,000.00	
Lawyer (cloth/industry)	$ 4,000.00 $14,000.00	$50,000.00 $66,000.00	$80.000.00

Case # 2 Specialization

	Woman (Nation A)	Man (Nation B)	Total
Secretary (wine/agriculture)	$20,000.00	*********	
Lawyer (cloth/industry)	********* $20,000.00	$100,000.00 $100,000.00	$120,000.00

Dynamic Comparative Advantage

Case # 3 Rational-Structural Transformation

	Woman (Nation A)	Man (Nation B)	Total
Secretary (wine/agricultural)	*********	*********	
Lawyer (cloth/industry)	$100.000.00 $100,000.00	$100,000.00 $100,000.00	$200,000.00

Source of data: The empirical accuracy of the data is not necessary in order to validate the internal logic or conclusions derived therefrom; compare Ricardo 1912, 81–83, as a basic exemplar of the intuitive and deductive logic and methodology.

advantages, they both now work full time, one specializing in legal work and the other in secretarial. The comparative cost logic seems vindicated, in that total income increases from $80,000 up to $120,000. Both receive increases in income, though not necessarily equally. Case closed? Not quite.

The secretary might have become a comparable lawyer, if only the circumstances and dynamics of life had been different. Case 3 presents such an outcome. Given a dynamic solution, and structural change, the secretary in becoming a lawyer could make $100,000. Total income for both, consequently, goes up to $200,000. (This assumes that both can be lawyers, and that other secretarial support can be mobilized somehow.)

Although American experience seems to be moving this way, admittedly we cannot all become lawyers. But this is not to say, however, that all nations cannot achieve the dynamics of modern economic growth. If further, we equate the lawyer with an industrial nation (Britain) and the secretary with an agrarian nation (Ricardo's Portugal or current LDCs), total world income as well as the income of individual nations would be advanced via the dynamics of structural transformation. LDCs are cultures specializing and locked into an agrarian (secretarial) stage of economic development. Such cultures are limited in economic capacity and characterized by lower standards of living.

Under comparative cost ratios the lawyer employs the secretary and buys (imports) those services, though less efficient. In this "fallacy of composition," what seems correct for individual behavior is transferred to the well-being of a whole nation. This logic supposedly explains why it would be rational for a nation to import goods, even though they are produced less efficiently abroad. Assuming that inefficiency usually means production at higher costs and higher prices, given the "Doctrine of Comparative Costs," this suggests it would be logical to import goods that are more expensive and cost more (granting ceteris paribus assumptions). This is an irrational, not rational, conclusion. Does this mark the final folly of the rational species *Homo economicus?* To assume that wheat costing $2.00 per bushel, produced less efficiently abroad, would be imported, even granting a more efficient domestic producer (having an absolute advantage) offering wheat at $1.50 per bushel, defies the basic logic contained in downward-sloping demand curves.

Absolute advantage and costs are more important to determine the absolute level of prices and the flow of goods between countries than are relative cost ratios. What Britain produced and exported, in the form of textiles, was not based upon relative cost considerations. Rather, Britain got absolute advantages from having transformed itself in the Industrial Revolution. As the lawyer, Britain was assumed to have an absolute advantage in both agricultural and industrial production.[2] Therefore "what" is produced and sold in international markets resides in the dynamics of development. By comparison, specialization based upon static comparative costs offers a danger of backwardness and economic fossilization. "Regions or nations which remain tied to a single export commodity almost inevitably fail to achieve sustained expansion" (North 1961, 3).[3] Consequently, we need economic development. And dynamic comparative advantage must be interrelated to the processes of economic development and progress.

Dynamics of Development

Understanding America's economic decline and its current economic malaise, requires a recognition that the economic problems facing the United States are long-term and structural in nature (Bernstein and Adler 1994). The Nobel laureate economist Gunnar Myrdal offered a conception of economic development that included the dynamic processes of structural transformation. The social and cultural were not taken as given or fixed parameters by Myrdal, but treated as qualitative, "non-economic" variables. Myrdal's conception—*"the movement of the whole social system upward is what all of us in fact mean by development"*—is clearly outside the neoclassical paradigm limited to an outward shift of the P-P curve and Marshallian offer curves (Myrdal 1974). Myrdal's conceptualization, as to the substantive nature of the process of economic development, coincides with the seminal anthropological conception of culture "as that complex whole," offered by Edward Tylor in 1871 (Kroeber and Kluckholm 1952). Consequently, it is culture that constitutes the substantive grist for the mill of the process of economic evolution. Humankind's culture comprises what grows and develops in the process of economic evolution (Brinkman 1992). Material aspects of culture—bridges, boats, buildings, and technology—as capital and consumer goods, along with their social concomitants, advance as an integrated whole in the overall dynamics of cultural evolution.

But if a culture grows, does it also experience development? Schumpeter clearly drew a distinction: "Nor will the mere growth of the economy . . . be designated here as a process of development. For it calls forth no qualitatively new phenomenon . . . " (Schumpeter 1983, 63). Orthodox economists, by comparison, and not only related to trade theory, but growth theory in general, often assume that "they are in essence synonymous" (Meier and Baldwin 1959, 2; Meier 1968, 22). But why not assume that economic growth is the conceptual equivalent of development? For if an economy, nation, or culture achieves the level of approximately $20,000 GNP/capita, is not such growth also indicative of some development? Culture does not mark time and stand still in a static mold or given structure but, rather, evolves over time. And though evolution is comprised of the processes of both growth (reproduction) and development (transformation), it is the latter process that dominates the dynamics of structural transformation (and big improvements in productivity).

But as culture evolves, how then to identify or describe its gradual transformation? Sociologists identify the evolutionary and structural transformation of culture in the form of a sequential pattern of "logistic surges" in which one "S" curve is superimposed on another.[4] The result is manifest in an accelerated evolution of culture. Empirically, this pattern of "logistic surges" relates to the overall whole of culture as well as to parts (Hart 1946).

Humankind achieved growth in the speed of travel to the current level of 20,000 miles/hour not by growing more feet and running faster. That speed was achieved through a structural transformation of transportation technology from that of foot travel to that of space rocketry. Similarly, the pattern prevails for culture as a whole. Humankind did not achieve $20,000 GNP/capita levels of income by "growing" more hoes and plows or more bows and arrows. Humankind achieved the $20,000 level through a structural transformation of culture from "hunting and gathering" to that of, ultimately, an "Industrial Revolution" characterized by modern economic growth (Epoch III) (Easterlin 1996, 16).

Ongoing growth within the confines of a given structure cannot continue indefinitely. A dugout canoe cannot grow to the size of a *Queen Mary*. "Growth of a university from 5,000 to 50,000 students is clearly not just a linear increase in size but a massive upheaval in structure as well" (Bell 1973, 174). Given the "Principle of Similitude," ongoing, *sustained* growth implies a need for structural transformation.[5] Growth, as the quantitative, constitutes a process of reproduction and replication, whereas development, as the qualitative, relates to processes of structural transformation and metamorphosis. Consequently, there can be only limited "growth" without development; the two concepts are not synonymous as neoclassical trade theory and as most mainstream economists might lead us to believe (Clower, Dalton, Hawitz, and Walters 1996; Brinkman 1995).

Economic development entails a process of structural transformation fed by the dynamics of technological advance. According to Schumpeter, "Add as many mail coaches as you please, you will never get a railway thereby" (Schumpeter 1983, 64). Similarly, in the antebellum, agrarian South, the production of more and more cotton, a staple trap, led to a sclerotic reinforcement of slavery and the plantation system. Such a culture was not suitable for modern economic growth. Comparable systems of serfdom or slavery, and their embedded illiteracy, resist the science-based technology characterizing modern economic growth (Kuznets 1973, 247). This is the plight of LDC (secretarial) nations that specialize in a static structure of agrarian production. Such static specialization explains the structural rigidity of Rostow's traditional society and places a ceiling on its capacity to continue to grow and develop.

More cocoa beans, or more wine produced by Portugal (the Ricardian case), in the promotion of a staple trap of specialization, may actually retard the structural dynamics characteristic of economic development. The "Magnificent Dynamics," associated with the process of economic development, constitute the basic heterodox position associated with the contributions of Hamilton, List, Myrdal, Prebisch, and on (Baumol 1951, 6, 11–51). But their contributions are neglected in the textbook literature, and especially in the field of international economics. By comparison, John S. Mill, in stating that "foreign trade . . . sometimes works sort of an industrial revolution in a country whose resources were previously undeveloped," falls flat (Mill 1911, 351).[6] Consequently, we see that merely increasing production in a static structure is not synonymous with economic development (Brinkman 1995).

It is almost universally conceded that the dynamic behind the process of economic development resides in the advance of technology. To Kuznets, modern economic growth was spawned in the crucible of a "scientific epoch." Science-based technology constitutes the key to the understanding of the dynamics propelling modern economic development and growth. The additions to human knowledge are of major significance and importance in the shaping of the course of modern economic growth. And modern economic growth, in turn, is characterized by increases in production, social transformation, and a global spread.[7]

Kuznets's emphasis on the advance of science appears on firm ground in that technology is universally conceptualized as applied knowledge. And technology constitutes the dominant variable invoked by economists to explain the dynamics of development and evolution. A conception of technology, consequently, is crucial. Both Kuznets and Myrdal, among others, understand technology to include both the material and the social.[8] The steam engine as material technology also required the factory system in order to function. Thus, technology should be seen in holistic terms, comprised of both material and non-material culture. Such a culture-conception of technology helps explain why some cultures (civilizations) rise and fall and/or stagnate, potentially the United States included.[9]

This explanation of the process of economic development and the dynamics of cultural evolution, and the emphasis provided for by Simon Kuznets in terms of the advance of useful knowledge and technology, provides a framework upon which to build the dynamic theory of comparative advantage. Our problem is how, then, to relate international trade to a theory of the production and accumulation of useful knowledge and technology? Such dynamic theory is outside the paradigm of the H-O model and the static pure theory of international trade. Currently, it is no wonder that the static theory of comparative advantage is under siege (Thurow 1996, 65–74). This is manifest in myriad attempts to formulate "new" theories of trade. "The Need for a New Paradigm" appears warranted (Porter 1990, 1–30).

"New" Theories of Trade: Toward Dynamic Comparative Advantage

Economic development does not relate simply to a more efficient allocation of resources within a given structure (Arndt 1981, 463). To understand the dynamic processes of development there is a need to explain the structural transformation of social institutions. It is essentially this process that relates to the achievement of higher levels of absolute advantage and that constitutes a prerequisite for the formulation of a dynamic theory of comparative advantage. Consequently, the neoclassical paradigm that equates an outward shift of the P-P curve with the process of economic growth (assumed to be synonymous with economic development) appears as an overly simplistic abstraction, and far too primitive as a conception. This is recognized by "new" theories of trade appearing in the literature which attempt to incorporate "new" theories of economic growth. Of special interest is that this literature originates not simply from heterodox economists, but comes from neoclassical and mainstream economists themselves.

For example, Robert Solow employed technology as an exogenous variable (Solow 1957). Solow's theory, itself, came under siege by other mainstream economists who directed attention to the origination and innovation of theories incorporating technology as an endogenous variable. These new theories are associated with the contributions of Maurice Scott and Paul Romer, among others (Grossman and Helpman 1991, 22–42). However, while making an attempt to step into the "black box" of technological change, they "forgot to bring a flashlight."

Thus, in attempting to make technology endogenous, Scott offered a conception of technology which is equated to that of gross investment. "Indeed, with my definition of investment, separation is strictly meaningless," he wrote, and "inventions are best regarded as a form of investment . . ." (Scott 1989, 95, xxxii). Alternatively, however, in that technological advance is fundamentally predicated on the evolution of science and useful knowledge, this process might be "quite unrelated to the terms of factor supply"

(Abramovitz 1993, 237). Rather than manifesting new forms of technological innovation, capital accumulation may simply represent a quantitative growth process in the replication of a technology already in existence.[10] Further, these so-called new theories of growth still carry forward the underlying neoclassical assumption that mere growth is synonymous with development (Lucas 1988).

Consequently, through a conceptual slight of hand, given the assumption that economic growth is synonymous with development, theories and policies of economic growth are assumed, ipso facto, to be theories and policies of economic development. The emphasis by Grossman and Helpman upon technology and the role of knowledge, the diffusion of knowledge, and making trade theory permeable to a "dynamic evolution of comparative advantage," is highly commendable (Grossman and Heldman 1991, vol. XI, 177–205). However, the conclusions reached by Grossman and Helpman are somewhat predictable: "Strikingly, we found that long-run patterns of specialization and trade are determined solely by countries' relative factor endowments" (Grossman and Helpman 1991, 206). Yet others emphasize that "comparative advantage based upon the factors of production is not sufficient" and, "insufficiency of factor advantage in explaining trade is widely accepted . . ." (Porter 1990, 12, 16). Unfortunately, some attempts at "new" trade theory still end up with the same old paradigmatic blinders contained in the "flawed" Heckscher–Ohlin matrix and theory.[11] "[S]uch new trade theory pushes the limits of traditional thought . . . but it still reflects many of the assumptions and foundations of such thought . . . the theory is centrally concerned with the problem of the optimal allocation of resources" (Dosi, Tyson, and Zysman 1989, 11).

But the fact that a nation has an abundance of capital, as a factor input, and consequently absolute advantages in the production of knowledge and technology, is not given by nature, but rather is a function of the level and dynamics of economic evolution. Therefore it is more the stage of economic development that determines absolute advantages, manifest in what is traded and trade patterns, not comparative costs. This dynamic position is consequently more in line with the contributions of Hamilton and List rather than that of Ricardo, as well as some attempts to formulate "new" trade theories by Grossman and Helpman.

Trade between Somalia and Ethiopia, the agrarian (secretarial) LDCs, is naturally limited in product diversity and volume. In terms of "what" is traded, how can an LDC country export a product that it is technologically incapable of producing and for which a comparative cost ratio is nonexistent? The "what" is traded by advanced countries has much wider diversity as to product content and volume. In explaining trade patterns, we should note that the largest volume of trade takes place between the mature industrial countries, rather than between mature nations and the LDCs, or among LDCs themselves. Those trade patterns are explained by absolute cost advantages much more than comparative costs.

By comparison, Friedrich List related trade theory and trade patterns to a stage of economic and cultural development. The stage methodology is still widely ignored in the current literature of mainstream trade theory. But the level or stage of economic development is of central importance to an explanation of a nation's relative absolute advantage. In contrast, Ricardo's static comparative cost doctrine is based on an abstract methodology that is ahistorical, non-evolutionary, and consequently not related to economic development or changing structures of technological capability.

Ricardo's static view was reinforced by free trade orthodoxy; heterodox views were largely ignored. But this was a mistake. In this context, Marshall noted: "But killing the messengers did not kill the hostile troops of which the messengers brought record . . . and therefore never properly refuted . . ." (Marshall 1927, 759–762). Heterodox messengers of dynamic concerns—for example, such as those embodied in the infant industry argument—were essentially ignored. The infant industry argument of Hamilton and others was initially ignored but finally accepted, much later, by Mill and Marshall. Similarly, while the infant industry argument was ultimately recognized as a limitation on freer trade policy, the message and messengers in support of an evolutionary framework and more active development policy are still being ignored in the current orthodox literature, textbook or otherwise, in dealing with trade theory.

In explaining the relation of trade to development, Jacob Viner failed to fully understand the stage of economic development and absolute advantages generated in the processes of modern economic growth. "That agriculture is not necessarily associated with poverty becomes obvious when one considers Australia, New Zealand, Denmark, or Iowa and Nebraska" (Viner 1952, 62–73, 144). Economists "should insist that scarce resources shall be allocated to their socially most productive use, and wasting resources on romantic dreams is not such a use" (1952, 73). But Iowa, California, New Zealand, Denmark, and on are not mainly agricultural cultures, but are parts of regions that have utilized modern technology extensively, and which have industrialization as a general characteristic. Thus, Viner stressed, there is not "any marked backwardness in the technology of the agriculture of Denmark, New Zealand, of England or of Iowa" (Viner 1952, 144).

The key to a rational trade policy is that it be based upon dynamic, not static, comparative advantage. It appears that the best theoretical foundation, in explaining what is traded, trade patterns, and relevant to the modern issue of international competitiveness, would be more associated with the contributions of Adam Smith rather than those of David Ricardo. Recall that two legs of Adam Smith's theory of international trade related to absolute advantage and the productivity doctrine. In relation to the productivity doctrine, an increase in trade through the expansion of market size encourages technological advance as well. Such an increase in trade need not be "free" entirely and in fact the historical record demonstrates that tariffs often nurtured new industries. Mill and Marshall accepted this logic. In fact, the main industrial revolutions for Britain, the United States, Japan, South Korea, Taiwan, and on, were preceded by tariffs, protection, and governmental promotion, rather than that of a completely laissez faire–oriented free trade policy. It is the rapid process of industrial development which spills over into the international arena in the promotion of trade (Easterlin 1996, 41). But an access to expanding trade in turn promoted further technological advance and higher levels of production. Given the larger market size so nurtured, enter Joseph Schumpeter and the dynamics of entrepreneurial innovation.[12]

Consequently, it was the Industrial Revolution which imparted absolute advantages to Britain, and in the process accounted for hegemony and trade dominance during the nineteenth century. The epicenter of modern economic growth in shifting to the United States, in turn, accounted for U.S. hegemony and Pax Americana in most of the twentieth century and the ensuing high volume of U.S. trade. To some extent, further shifts in technological dynamism have been occurring to Japan and elsewhere in recent years. Therefore it is mainly the internal development process, the achievement of absolute advantages, and higher levels of productivity that account for what is traded as well as the volume and enhanced global competitiveness.

Basically, given the conception and theory of modern economic growth offered by Kuznets, for trade to serve a dynamic function in the domestic economy, it must reinforce Adam Smith's "productivity doctrine" in the advance of useful knowledge and technology. Thus, capital flows, technology licensing, and other diffusions of knowledge may be very helpful to countries trying to upgrade or maintain their industries, productivity, and economic growth. Trade flows *may be* involved significantly with such technology transfers. But industrial decline in advanced countries may represent stagnation, if not retreat, from the development process, and may manifest a neglect of a long-term productivity potential.

Hence, trade can, especially in the context of one-way free trade or unbalanced trading policy, operate negatively and retard economic development and prosperity, as Britain and the U.S. have come to realize. In rationalizing the benefits from unrestricted free trade, orthodox economists have become too limited and unrealistic.[13] "The economist's case for free trade is essentially a unilateral case: a country serves its own interests by pursuing free trade regardless of what other countries may do" (Krugman 1997, 113). The "unilateral" version, however, ignores wage stagnation and weak productivity performance in the U.S. since the early 1970s, and chronic U.S. trade and current account deficits in the 1980s and 1990s.

Now more economists are challenging this naiveté. *"The pattern of foreign trade that resulted from the failure of the United States to have a trade policy that protected its national interests . . . was the central and decisive cause in the economic decline of the United States"* [emphasis added] (Culbertson 1989, 23, 3–40).

Toward Improved Trade Policy

From a political standpoint, unrestricted free trade policies, especially on a unilateral basis, are becoming more difficult to sell. Even after being inundated by an MNC media blitz, presidential hype, and a public relations overkill, we still find that "Free Trade Gets an Unfriendly Reception" in the United States (Hammonds 1997, 34). Polls abound which indicate negative attitudes toward complete free trade vis-à-vis the negative impact on jobs, wages, and the environment.[14] Consequently, other than free trade-oriented textbook writers, who really endorses an unrestricted free trade policy orientation?[15] Another way of raising the same question is: Who benefits from a unilateral free trade policy? The answer seems to be multinational corporations (MNCs) and their lobbyists—an increasingly influential network of interest groups.

Another problem for unilateral free traders is that MNCs are conceded to hold market or price power in situations of imperfect or monopolistic competition. Textbooks are now admitting this is a problem for trade policy. Also, there are an increased number of books drawing attention to the political clout of MNCs.[16] Currently, the larger MNCs are as big and as powerful as nations. This power is translated not only into economic power, administered prices and market control, but political and legislative power as well. But why, then, do the MNCs use their political muscle to favor an unrestricted free trade policy orientation? Should not U.S. MNCs look toward more reciprocal trade policies as a means to secure a maximization of U.S. corporate profits?

The problem perhaps is best addressed in what might be called *CEO-Corporate Profits: A Vicious Circle.* Granting American technological superiority during the immediate post–World War II period, the earlier Bretton Woods era, it was widely assumed that even the unilateral opening of American markets, regardless of non-reciprocity, would still produce favorable results for the American economy (Atlantic Institute 1970). However, it became increasingly evident since the 1970s that as the world economy became more and more internationalized, the U.S. was not meeting the increased global competition. The U.S. share in global markets was declining, and since the late 1970s the U.S. has suffered serious merchandise trade imbalance problems—an economic malaise for the American economy from which the U.S., apparently, has as yet to recover.

The predominant solution taken by corporate America has apparently been to cut costs, move plants abroad, and downsize. This jump-start policy was sold to the American public as a necessary need for pain in order to regain global competitiveness. Rather than pursuing the "high road," as noted by Dan Luria, policies embracing a "low road" of cost reduction ensued (Madrick 1995, 78–83). Costs were cut by lowering wages through downsizing, more part-time work, cut-backs in pensions, a reduction in health and other benefits, union bashing, and on. The linchpin of this policy was provided for by the MNC orientation toward unilateral free trade and the use of cheap foreign labor. This "Race to the Bottom" is predicated on an untapped global supply of cheap labor potentially of enormous proportions (Korten 1996, 229–238).

The next phase of this policy evolution is manifest in the results derived from "low road" policies. The empirical record here of "pain" is clear in that real wages since 1973 have stagnated or declined (Mishel et al. 1997, 131–233). This contradicts the goals and policy recommendations set forth by the President's Commission on Competitiveness. A restoration of American global competitiveness should not be predicated on a reduction in American standards of living (President's Commission 1985, 6). An alternative "high road" solution would be to invest in skilled American labor as an asset to be developed through improvements in productivity, not as a burden to be reduced. But the basic result and upshot of "low road" policies has been, of course, to increase corporate profits, at least temporarily.

Corporate profits are in turn reflected in stock market prices. The scenario here is all too well known. The impact of corporate profits in recent years was reflected in a bullish stock market that has been running for a decade. Unfortunately, there are growing signs of speculative excess. This vicious circle is now clear and within our grasp. From all this are we to assume, in contradiction to Berle and Means, that corporate leaders and their policies really reflect and are controlled and managed by the wishes of their stock owners? Perhaps. But the bottom line in all of this includes "golden parachutes" and CEO bonuses and benefits that are tied to stock prices. A bonus situation allowing for stock to be purchased in the future at today's prices often results in bonanzas for corporate CEOs. An increase in stock prices, predicated on increases in profits, and in turn predicated on cost reduction, has an appealing logic for corporate CEOs.

All of this constitutes a virtuous circle for the corporate CEOs and the elite top 3 percent benefiting from the profits and wealth redistribution now taking place in the United States. For everyone else, the middle class and the poor, the circle is vicious. Current CEO greed and selfishness borders on the obscene. Even J.P. Morgan, hardly the stereotype for a friend of labor or altruist, felt that a ratio between salaries and wages in the neighborhood of 20:1 was fair and adequate. Currently, Germany has a ratio of approximately 20:1 and Japan 16:1. The U.S., led by corporate America, now has a ratio of 180:1. *The Search for Excess* dominates the current American economic landscape (Crystal 1991).

With all this widespread "pain" for the American middle class and working America, there has been insufficient "gain," and American competitiveness and economic renewal have yet to show any fundamental recovery.[17] U.S. balance of payments deficits are among the highest. Trends in relation to long-term rates of economic growth, rather than short-run cyclical upturns, are still sluggish (Madrick 1995; Bernstein and Adler 1994). A policy orientation toward unilateral, non-reciprocal free trade will only produce a continuity and exacerbation of the current economic malaise. As so-called free trade is promulgated as policy, not that anyone abroad really wants it or intends to practice it, it can be translated into an avoidance of warranted regulation of MNC power and policy. The government, as a humane referee in the economic process, is thrown out in the free trade bath water. Unrestricted, one-way laissez faire in trade policy becomes very costly negligence, and enforces national decline.

A neoclassical synthesis, emphasizing exchange rate depreciation, coupled with restrictive monetary and fiscal policy, is not sufficient.[18] Exchange rate depreciation constitutes only palliatives or band-aid solutions. Given that substantial depreciation of the American dollar since 1971 has proved ineffectual in eliminating U.S. competitiveness problems and deficits, the need is for structural change and trade policy reforms. Ongoing and unresolved trade deficits and current account deficits will ultimately be translated into a reduced American economic growth, more structural unemployment, and risks of renewed stagflation—with increased social discord.

The problem facing America is a basic cultural lag. There is a need for fundamental institutional adjustment manifest in a new trade policy. We need to re-emphasize dynamic comparative advantage to serve as a basis for a rational trade policy.

"In the institutional view, international trade is a dichotomous process in which technology tends to outpace the ability of institutions to adapt to the new exigencies" (McClintock 1996, 240, 242). Dynamic comparative advantage requires the rebuilding of industrial strength in connecting trade to the dynamics of economic and cultural evolution.

The opening of the American economy, on a non-reciprocal basis, served to promote the current American economic malaise. Consequently, current U.S. policies oriented toward perpetuating unilateral free trade and indifferent to reciprocity have tended to hold back and retard American economic recovery and development. And it is technological advance, embedded in the social developmental process, that in turn serves as the fountainhead for increases in productivity—the key for improving global competitiveness.

But the overall goal is not simply economic efficiency, increased rates of productivity, improved competitiveness and the advance of economic development. Economic advance and sustainable development provide a necessary, though not sufficient, condition for ongoing human development and well-being. How should we make the evolutionary economic process sustainable so as to also promote basic human needs and rights? In all of this there is the need for a broader "human development strategy." Significant work is suggested by the United Nations Development Programme (Griffin and McKinley 1994).

There is a need to address more realistically the issues of U.S. living standards, jobs, education, health, and environmental sustainability. The process requires a participatory democracy, by and for all the people and not simply for a privileged few. The process also requires skillful government rather than a mystical laissez-faire ideology, be it domestic or international (Schafer and Faux 1996, 321–333). What unilateral free trade advocacy really serves to accomplish is to grant greater license to MNC power. And multibillionaire George Soros has much to say about what this concentration of power and laissez faire policies portend for the democratic process (Soros 1997).

Currently "flawed" trade policies based upon "flawed" trade theory produce "flawed" results. Old-fashioned trade theories emanating from the Ricardian era are not up to the challenge of providing for a rational trade policy that will nurture American economic renewal and restore American competitiveness. How then to implement a rational trade policy? And, especially, how then to address the current dominant problems in the areas of trade asymmetries, manifest in trade deficits and imbalances, and the lack of reciprocity embedded in our current trade policies?

"The debate on trade policy has been constricted by a narrow, often ideological focus on rules of trade *rather than results for the United States.*

An ideal set of 'free trade' rules guarantees neither trade balances for the United States nor prosperity for the world. . . . Our ultimate goals remain the same, more trade, more competition, more access to U.S. producers, the only difference is how to get there . . ." (Cuomo Commission 1992, 200, 202). The overall objective of a rational U.S. trade policy is not to hold back or retard trade but rather to enhance the positive potential to be derived from increasing trade and spreading technology as means to global peace and economic well-being. Clearly, U.S. trade must be better balanced with more effective reciprocity and supervision.

5

WILLIAM A. LOVETT

Rebalancing U.S. Trade

Stubborn trade imbalances challenge America's role in the global economy. These imbalance and asymmetry problems grew more serious in the 1980s and 1990s. Between 1981 and 1997 the United States suffered a total of $2,000 billion in accumulated trade deficits, and $1,500 billion in current account (balance of payments) deficits. As a result, the U.S. transformed itself from the world's largest creditor nation (+$325 billion) to become the biggest debtor country (–$1,250 billion) in these years. Because of weak U.S. trade policy, the U.S. suffered a net loss of at least 10–12 million manufacturing jobs, substantially reduced economic growth, and painful demoralization in some areas. With a stronger, reciprocity-based trade policy, U.S. GNP would have been 10–20 percent higher.[1] Instead, weak U.S. trade policies increased the nation's structural unemployment, long-term poverty, and aggravated crime. Enhanced inequalities and social conflict followed for many communities. In addition, the U.S. industrial, technology, and mobilization base has been weakened by this failure to enforce reasonable reciprocity and by all these excessive, and really unnecessary, trade and current account deficits.

Also, many U.S. environmental and consumer interests insist that important U.S. trade concessions, especially in the GATT 1994 and WTO agreements, undermine a generation of hard-won progress in setting higher standards for U.S. environmental protection and regulatory supervision.[2] Thus, weak U.S. trade bargaining eroded responsible safeguards for the environment and consumer protection in the United States and abroad. The problem is that multinational corporations (MNCs) can now move their plants to low-wage, poorly regulated, and minimally protected areas with complete freedom under GATT 1994. Environmental, labor, and consumer interests complain that wage freezes, reduced standards, and weaker protection are the inevitable results. From their perspective, only if imports can be limited from areas with weak environmental protection or minimal safeguards can we restore confidence in U.S. environmental standards, consumer laws, and more reasonable protection for wages and salaries in U.S. manufacturing. A new, reciprocity-based U.S. trade policy is needed for these purposes, and to restore overall balance in U.S. trading relationships.

U.S. industrial decline and job losses in the manufacture of watches, photographic equipment, clothing, shoes, appliances, and other consumer industries were already occurring between the late 1940s and the early 1970s. This could be traced to previous trade concessions, and a failure to enforce reciprocity in the GATT rounds between 1947 and 1967. But in those years, the U.S. at least maintained an overall trade balance (or modest trade surpluses), most of the time. Thus, while Americans accepted somewhat less overall industrial and economic growth as part of their Cold War strategy, and conceded industrial expansion to key allies and trade partners (especially Germany, Switzerland, Scandinavia, France, Italy, Japan, Taiwan, and Korea), the overall balance of U.S. trade between 1947 and 1974 suggests that the U.S. was living "within its means" from a merchandise trade point of view.[3]

Although the U.S. invested a bit more abroad between 1958 and 1974 than it "earned," this extra outlay to promote industrial expansion and growth among U.S. allies, *and to support naval, ground, and air forces in defense of free world interests,* was largely welcomed by most of America's friends abroad.[4]

But the subsequent years (1975–97) brought aggravated, and more recently chronic, U.S. trade and current account deficits (see Tables 1.1 and 1.2 in Chapter 1). Certainly it seems fair to say that the U.S. began to "live beyond its means," in an external account sense, in the mid-1970s, and particularly so in the early 1980s through 1997. Unfortunately, as a result of accumulated U.S. structural trade concessions from the Kennedy, Tokyo, and Uruguay Rounds (along with the NAFTA and WTO agreements), Americans have created for themselves a very bad problem of entrenched asymmetries and trading imbalances.

To be sure, increased U.S. budget deficits, especially between 1983 and 1996, did aggravate U.S. external account and trade imbalance problems (see Table 1.3, Chapter 1). But the direct and more substantial cause of these large, chronic external deficits was U.S. trading policy. For the sake of Cold War alliance politics and defense of free world interests, the U.S. simply accepted these trade imbalances without much protest. Why? Clearly Cold War politics was at work, but also, U.S. trading policy was influenced, to an increasing degree since the 1960s, by major multinational corporations and banks. So far as U.S. trade policy-making was concerned, big business (the MNCs) have become the main constituency on the details of American foreign economic relations.[5]

This situation, chronic and excessive U.S. trade and current account deficits, cannot continue much longer. Sooner or later, large and sustained balances of payments must be eliminated by countries suffering with them. Eventually, all nations are forced to live within their means from an external accounts perspective. Somehow U.S. imports must be cut back and/or U.S. exports increased (or some blend of the two must occur). By what adjustment process should this reconciliation be accomplished?

Alternative Solutions

Three strategies *(or some combination)* are available to the United States for its external imbalance predicament:[6] (1) Substantial dollar devaluation and a likely weakening of the dollar's role as the major reserve currency. (2) A new reciprocity-based U.S. trade policy that emphasizes bilateral and regional relationships and enforces reasonable balance in U.S. trading. (3) Comprehensive renewal of U.S. technology, manufacturing, and export expansion.

Dollar Devaluation

Currency realignment is a normal adjustment process (in the era of floating exchange rates since 1971). Most countries must accept devaluation of their currencies when they suffer large and/or chronic external deficits. And, in fact, the U.S. already has suffered long-term dollar devaluation as against the strongest currencies (Swiss franc, German Deutschmark, and Japanese yen) (see Table 1.4 in Chapter 1). But why has dollar devaluation not completely eliminated U.S. external deficits in the 1990s? One reason is that key export surplus countries (especially Japan, China, and other Asian nations) would not allow their currencies to appreciate sufficiently. In other words, they were afraid to weaken their exports into the United States. A substantial part of the continued U.S. trade deficit in the late 1990s might be explained this way. Thus, while the Japanese yen appreciated by 300 percent between 1983 and 1995, more recently the yen has fallen, from 1 dollar/80 yen in April 1995, to roughly 1 dollar/130 yen by the spring of 1997. Second, the dollar remained the most reliable reserve currency in the world (especially as against currencies of developing countries). Large capital inflows keep coming into dollar accounts, U.S. government securities, and the U.S. stock and bond markets.[7] No other currency and capital market has had comparable size, reliability, or prosperity in which to allow foreign investors "to park" their medium-term assets. Only the EU's "euro" could become a serious rival for the dollar as a reserve currency and challenge U.S. capital markets as a convenient parking place for secure investments of liquidity. All this explains why the normal process of exchange rate realignment has not proceeded to completion in the 1990s. Key export surplus countries are afraid to let their currencies appreciate sufficiently, and heavy foreign capital inflows prop up the dollar because of its unique reserve currency "attractiveness."

To what extent, then, can the U.S. expect to utilize dollar devaluation (or currency realignment) as the cure for its structural trade imbalance problems? So far, at least, although the dollar declined greatly from 1971 (in the era of floating exchange rates), U.S. trade imbalance problems gradually got worse (see Tables 1.1, 1.2, and 1.4). Even the Plaza Agreement, an orchestrated, two-year effort to bring the U.S. dollar down from an excessive, unsustainable level in 1985 to 1987, failed to eliminate the U.S. structural trade deficits. Some improvement occurred in U.S. trade balances during the late 1980s, but not enough. In fact, asymmetrical openness (with the U.S. more open than most foreign markets) continued from the mid-1980s onward, *and got worse* as a result of GATT 1994 and the WTO Agreement (see Tables 1.1, 1.2) While NAFTA was sold as a *mutually balanced* trade expansion deal, after the Mexican peso devaluations of 1994–95, the U.S. trade deficit with Mexico increased dramatically.[8] And, most recently, when Southeast Asian nations (Thailand, Philippines, Malaysia, and Indonesia) developed large export surpluses into the U.S. like Mexico in 1990–93, these "New Tigers" became hot emerging markets for foreign investment. But speculative excess again led to overinvestment, significant losses, and a corrective reaction. Devaluations and stock market declines have followed for Thailand, Malaysia, Indonesia, and to a lesser extent, the Philippines.[9] Thus, these new industrial countries must retrench imports, and hopes for bigger exports from the U.S. have been set back substantially; continued trade surpluses with the U.S. from Southeast Asia will be hard to eliminate quickly.

Accordingly, significant relief for the U.S. balance of payments does not seem likely soon. Many U.S. interests—banking, securities, insurance, importers generally and MNCs relying on foreign parts or components— would also be upset by any big U.S. dollar devaluation. And politically, large-scale dollar devaluation will greatly weaken any incumbent presidential administration, whether Democratic or Republican. Devaluation does not seem realistic now as the main vehicle for U.S. external account adjustment. The U.S. must use other channels to correct and eliminate its large trade and current account deficits.

Reciprocal Trade Policy

The United States should recognize that the major and continuing source of its external deficits is a lack of effective trading reciprocity.[10] Although the

U.S. began to open its markets under "Reciprocal Trade Agreements" (see Chapter 2), in fact, American trade negotiators generally accepted less than full reciprocity. As a result, asymmetries and trade imbalances developed between the United States and many of its trading partners. Some asymmetries still operate between the U.S. and EU, especially in more heavily subsidized EU agricultural markets, quicker access to EU antidumping settlement relief, and more extensive industrial and regional subsidies in the EU. But, apart from agriculture, the U.S., EU, Canada, Australia, and New Zealand are fairly open to each other, and trade has been substantially balanced most of the time (see Table 1.2).

With Japan, unfortunately, trade remains heavily unbalanced. This pattern has persisted since the early 1980s. Although Japan dropped its tariffs to low levels after the Tokyo Round (1975–79), foreign manufactured imports are disfavored under restrictive Japanese marketing customs and through a mix of language, cultural loyalties, and administrative guidance. U.S. manufactured exports to Japan are much smaller than U.S. manufactured imports from Japan. And, as a result of asymmetrical policies with respect to foreign companies, Japanese enterprises are allowed a much bigger role in the U.S. than American companies in Japan (see Table 1.2). U.S.–Japan trade has been out of balance for nearly twenty years, with U.S. trade deficits averaging $50 billion or more annually since 1985.

With respect to new industrial countries (NICs) like Taiwan, South Korea, China, Thailand, Malaysia, Brazil, and Mexico, U.S. markets are open. But NICs generally employ substantial tariffs (averaging 15–25–35 percent), extensive subsidies,[11] non-tariff barriers, restrictive regulations; some use exchange controls and/or capital market regulation; and most limit access to their service markets. Intellectual property is often a problem for U.S. companies, with extensive misuse without adequate compensation. For many NICs, therefore, it was only natural that export surpluses would develop against the U.S. (see Table 1.2). In 1996, U.S. trade deficits were $42 billion with China, $17 billion with Mexico, and $12 billion with Taiwan. Total U.S. trade deficits for Malaysia, Singapore, Thailand, Indonesia, Philippines, India, and Sri Lanka were $28 billion in 1996. In that year U.S. imports from all of Asia were $317 billion while U.S. exports to Asia were $187 billion (with an all-Asia deficit of $130 billion). In less developed countries (LDCs) similar asymmetries operate. But most LDCs have not yet expanded their manufacturing and exports enough to have big trade surpluses against the U.S. Many would like to do so, and hope to emulate NIC success stories. Yet most LDCs are simply NIC "wannabes."

Obviously, asymmetries distort investment and trade flows; they are the main cause of U.S. "structural" trade deficits. Multinational corporations naturally locate manufacturing plants in lower-wage, more convenient, protected, and often subsidized national settings. If major U.S. markets are completely open to the output of "favored" foreign operations, we have established a major, systemic bias toward deindustrialization in the U.S., and toward relocation of U.S. manufacturing, industrial technology, and engineering capabilities. Unfortunately, this has been the growing impact (though not intended) of U.S. industrial–trade policies over the last 15–20 years. If the U.S. persists in this unequal, perverse policy, the inevitable consequence will be further erosion in the U.S. industrial, technology, and prosperity base. Not only are such U.S. policies self-destructive economically, they ultimately undermine the mobilization base of the U.S. for national security purposes (and America's ability to stay at the forefront of military, naval, and communications technology).[12]

U.S. trade policy accepted some erosion of its U.S. industrial-technology lead (after World War II) in helping U.S. allies in the Cold War, when U.S. per capita incomes remained well ahead of most nations. But circumstances have changed. Now the U.S. has lost its lead in many areas of industry and technology, and U.S. per capita incomes no longer exceed average OECD levels by significant margins. Furthermore, growing U.S. poverty pockets and distress for the American low-middle class are very serious, deeply troubling problems.[13] No longer can the U.S. afford to "subsidize" its competitors in the global marketplace with non-reciprocal trading policies.

So what changes in U.S. trade policy make sense? An urgent goal must be to restore effective, overall reciprocity. Fortunately, for *most* OECD countries (apart from the EU's Common Agricultural Policy), something close to reasonable trade balance and mutually open markets prevails (see Table 1.2).[14] Thus, for countries with reasonably balanced and/or open trade with the U.S. no significant change in treatment is needed.[15] The big imbalance problems in 1996 were with Japan, China, Mexico, Taiwan, Malaysia, Thailand, Philippines, India, and Sri Lanka (see Table 1.2). (In 1997 the pattern was similar, except that trade deficits with China and Japan got worse.)

Worst of all, certainly, are the China and Japan imbalance problems. But these other countries—Mexico, Taiwan, Malaysia, Thailand, Indonesia, Philippines, India, and Sri Lanka—also had large, *disproportionate* trade surpluses with the United States (although their trade volume does not bulk so large as that of Japan or China).[16]

Clearly, if U.S. trade policy-makers had enforced strong reciprocity with important U.S. trading partners, these large, excessive, and now chronic U.S. trade deficits could have been prevented. But, even though belated, strong U.S. reciprocity measures should now be imposed within a reasonable transition period, say three to five years.

	1997 balances		
Country	Exports to U.S.	Imports from U.S.	U.S. Trade Deficit (Surplus)
Japan	$124b.	$66b.	$58b
China	66b.	13b.	53b
Hong Kong	11b.	15b.	−4b
Mexico	87b.	71b.	16b
Taiwan	33b.	20b.	13b
Malaysia	19b.	11b.	8b
Thailand	13b.	7b.	6b
Indonesia	10b.	5b.	5b
Philippines	10b.	7b.	3b
India	8b.	4b.	4b
Sri Lanka	1.7b.	0.2b.	0.2b
Total	$393b.	$219b.	162b

More specifically, what is the best, most efficient way for effective U.S. reciprocity to be enforced at this stage? A new U.S. trade policy must set overall balance in its external accounts as a top national priority, and a major goal for macroeconomic policy. Fortunately, all other countries in the world are forced to live under comparable external account discipline. So, most countries will readily understand the U.S. predicament, and accept the need for the U.S. "to put its own house in order." They will, in many cases, enjoy a wry satisfaction that the "mighty U.S., too," must submit to the disciplines of world currency markets and the IMF. A few countries, led by Japan, China, Taiwan, Malaysia, and others, may plead special circumstances, and try to justify their disproportionate trade surpluses. But U.S. trade policy must focus on the larger, most disproportionate, and longer-lasting trade surpluses as needing correction. A reasonable time, say three to five years, should be allowed for the corrective process. And countries (and companies) that collaborate should be given easier, more flexible treatment. But nations (and corporations) that resist or stonewall should be dealt with more harshly, with shorter deadlines. Thus, "playing ball" with the U.S. in solving its external account problem must be rewarded; but antagonism, non-cooperation, and recalcitrance should be discouraged and pay higher prices for access to U.S. markets.[17]

So, here is how the new, reciprocity-based U.S. trade policy should work: "From this point forward continued access to U.S. markets will be governed by overall reciprocity, and the need to eliminate, within several years, U.S. trade and current account deficits. Countries already equally open to U.S. companies and exporters, and those maintaining something close to overall balance, will enjoy continued access to U.S. markets. But corrective action will be taken under U.S. trade laws to enforce reciprocity and achieve reasonable trade balance within a few years against any and all countries that enjoy large or disproportionate trade surpluses with the U.S. Their collaboration will be solicited, and greatly appreciated, but the U.S. will protect its vital national interests and achieve an overall balance in U.S. trade within a few years."

Against large, disproportionate trade surplus countries, consolidated action should be brought by the U.S. government under Section 301—U.S. Trade Act of 1974 (as amended), and GATT Article XII—Balance of Payments Relief. If appropriate, GATT Article VI—Countervailing Duties for Subsidies or Dumping with Injury to U.S. producers, should be added against some countries. Normal U.S. relief against large, disproportionate trade surplus countries should be a 10–15 percent import surcharge, continued until the disproportionate trade surpluses are eliminated. *Note:* The United States should no longer allow unconditional MFN treatment to large, disproportionate trade surplus countries.

A *crucial* implementing measure for the new reciprocity-based U.S. trade policy will be to *discontinue* MFN treatment for all countries that have large, disproportionate trade surpluses (e.g., Japan, China, Taiwan, Malaysia, etc.) with the U.S., *until these disproportionate trade surpluses are eliminated.* Justification for this enforcement measure shall be based upon GATT Article XII—Balance of Payments Relief; Article VI—Countervailing Duties Against Dumping and Subsidies; and Article XXI—National Security. Under U.S. trade law the relevant statutory authority will be the Trade Act of 1974, Section 125 (presidential authority to terminate international agreements), Section 122 (balance of payments relief), Section 232 (national security), Section 301 (unjustifiable trade practices and discrimination), and a new U.S. Trade Reciprocity Act (outlining a congressional mandate for reciprocity-based trade policy).

Certainly the U.S. has strong economic justification for discontinuing MFN treatment for nations that accumulated and maintain large, disproportionate trade surpluses against the U.S. Unconditional free-rider privileges make no sense for non-reciprocal trading partners. But sound legal justification also can be employed under GATT Articles XII and XXI, because the U.S. needs to eliminate large, excessive trade and current account deficits for its long-term economic prosperity and national security interests. Asking U.S. trade partners to open markets without limiting their exports to the U.S. simply has not worked at all. This is why U.S. trade policy must now "enforce" reciprocity, and this reciprocity discipline should be focused on whatever countries happen to be running large and/or disproportionate trade surpluses with the U.S.[18]

But the U.S. must insist upon its legitimate freedom to charge import fees under GATT Article XII and U.S. trade laws (Sections 122, 125, 232, and 301 of the Trade Act of 1974, and if appropriate, U.S. antidumping and countervailing duty laws) against large, disproportionate trade surplus countries. Under no circumstances should GATT Article II (the unconditional MFN provision) be a constraint upon the new reciprocity-based trade policy. If necessary, the U.S. must withdraw promptly from the WTO on these grounds, that is, due to the need for the U.S. to enforce overall reciprocity discipline in its trading policy. (Withdrawal from the WTO only requires six months' notice to the UN Secretary General and the Director General of the WTO.) The U.S. also could seek explicit amendment or interpretation of GATT Article II (the MFN provision) to allow these reciprocity enforcement measures against countries with large, disproportionate trade surpluses. If the WTO does not accept this amendment or interpretation, the United States must promptly withdraw. (See the upcoming section, "Cleaning Up Legal Underbrush.")

Industrial Rejuvenation Efforts

America's industrial and technology base has suffered erosion in some sectors, although others have been adequately cared for. Industries losing ground in the U.S. include parts of metallurgy, machinery, electronics, transportation equipment, textiles, fisheries, shipbuilding, and shipping. On the other hand, most of U.S. agriculture is still sound, aerospace was well financed through the Cold War; computers, software, and applications flourished, although global competition has been increasing lately. Health care was well financed in the United States, and its pharmaceutical sector has been strong. Petroleum and chemical technology is highly developed in the U.S., too.

Bear in mind that, in most really healthy industries, wherever located in the world, the strong companies are progressive, export oriented, and ample R&D investment continues (by the companies themselves and/or with government support). Weak or declining industries normally are not investing enough, lack government nurturing, and often become defeatist through neglect.[19]

An important feature of declining industries, quite frequently, is stronger support abroad, with government subsidies or scale economies, protected home markets (with higher prices and profits), and marginal cost discounting into the more open countries. Thus, maintaining healthy competitiveness in the open market countries is a serious challenge. While it is unwise to be overly protective and shut out foreign imports completely, a sensible mid-range solution is likely to be the most productive. This welcomes foreign joint ventures, especially for improved technology, and accepts rising imports on an average cost basis. But to avoid a total wipeout of the domestic industry, a blend of voluntary restraint agreements (VRAs), and substantial offsets to foreign dumping or subsidies may be needed. This requires subtlety, pragmatism, quick business–government decisions, and "fast track" import relief and settlements. But heavy, sustained high-tariff protection is often unwise and counterproductive.

Unfortunately, U.S. government–industry–trade practice has tended to be simplistic. More frequently, in recent years, U.S. trade policy reflected a naïve, completely open "unilateral free trade" mentality. By contrast, Japanese, European, and NIC practices (in the more successful nations), tend to strike a more skillful balance. Most U.S. trade policy-makers frame their choices in a black-and-white "free trade" versus "protection" dichotomy. Furthermore, U.S. trade administrators (especially from the USTR) saw the government's role as a neutral, hands-off, minimal function—solely to maintain "the integrity" of free trade. This outlook, while fashionable among "post-industrial age" writers in late-twentieth-century U.S. politics, does not understand the collaboration, at times even government–industry partnerships, that are common in Europe, Japan, and many new industrial countries.

All too often, U.S. trade negotiators failed to grasp the degree of teamwork, support, or nurturing by foreign governments for their significant industries, companies, or entrepreneurs abroad. Thus, government procurement practices abroad still favor domestic companies; any other result is difficult to achieve. "Opening the market" assurances were given by foreign trade officials with the knowledge that not too much disruption from unwanted foreign imports could occur. In fact, these divergent outlooks between U.S. trade officials and foreign trade networks are a large part of the ongoing asymmetry problem, that is, structural trade imbalances. The U.S. State Department, its various embassies abroad, and the Foreign Service officer establishment, tend to favor the local ally–client state's interests, their export programs, and their overall economic growth agendas. Few in the U.S. foreign policy, State Department, or USTR network see the object of U.S. trade practice as a tough, day-by-day struggle for export expansion, requiring loyalty to U.S. industries, in which success is measured by eliminating U.S. trade deficits, and if possible, by achieving solid U.S. trade surpluses. Obviously, for reciprocity-based U.S. trade policy to be implemented successfully, our network of administrators in the United States and abroad must really change their thinking, operational goals, and performance standards.

Also, successful industrial competitiveness and rejuvenation for the United States requires a more "industry-friendly" enthusiasm generally. Traditionally, Americans enjoyed an industrious, hard-working culture that took pride in technical skills and ingenuity from the Revolution through World War II and on into the 1960s. More recently, however, significant elements of the U.S. industrial base are viewed with disdain, or simply taken for granted. In a rather odd, selective way, some technical skills are glamorized—computers, "high tech," health care, finance, many professional services, lawyering, and even small-scale handicrafts. But basic industries, machinery, factories, chemicals, and manufacturing are viewed negatively by much of the public and the media.

To be sure, most modern people realize that far greater care, increased investment, and safeguarding are needed for the natural environment, especially in areas of the world where population growth and crowding are evident. But intelligent environmental policy realizes that broad prosperity, full employment, and social harmony still require ample industrial production. Yes, that output must be cleaner, environmentally respectful, and better engineered. There should be a realistic view of total, long-term effects on our habitat. But general deindustrialization as a mindset undermines general prosperity and employment.

So the U.S. must overhaul its industrial nurturing systematically, and provide comprehensive support to productive, efficient, and environmentally respectful activities. The full range of engineering and technology should be exploited, with good teamwork between universities, R&D organizations, government, and industries. The externalities of a broad, complete technostructure are very substantial, and greatly enhance the potential for sustained success across the front of science and engineering. The most successful nations (the U.S. from the 1860s–1970s), modern Japan, those in the EU, and the more dynamic NICs (China, India, Brazil, Korea, Taiwan) illustrate this approach.

The most important ingredients of a good, industry-friendly environment include (i) a healthy tax structure that encourages productive investment, and sustains vigorous enterprise teamwork; (ii) a strong educational system that provides a solid foundation of literacy, math abilities, and technical potential, with upgrading for the more talented, higher skilled professions in reasonable proportions; (iii) healthy labor relations that encourage productive teamwork, job mobility, full employment, and industrial progress (not sluggishness or resistance to productivity improvements); (iv) a good social insurance, pension, and health care system that makes the best of improving technology, builds upon healthy family life, and helps people to take better care of themselves (without undue waste, overpricing, or inefficiency); and (v) sound macroeconomic coordination, involving responsible fiscal, monetary, wage–price, and external account disciplines (and the avoidance of substantial inflation, unemployment, disruptive slumps, heavy budget deficits, and large or chronic external account deficits).[20]

Unfortunately, modern politics (*in many countries*) makes implementation of these goals controversial, at least in some respects. But for countries *at the top of their games,* in their more successful eras, there is a general sense of progress. Rational compromises spread through the system (e.g., the U.S., Scandinavia, W. Germany, Switzerland in the later 1940s–1960s, or Japan in the 1950s–1980s.) Unfortunately, as countries falter they suffer more internal conflict, unemployment, stagnation, poverty, and demoralization. The quality of these compromises often erodes, leading to decline and reduced national teamwork.[21]

One way or another, industrial and technological progress is a prime feature of every successful nation. Governments should play an active, sustaining role in broadening this progress, and overcoming sectors of backwardness with realistic aid and reforms. Responsible politics should include industrial prosperity, full employment, and strong environmental protection as a harmonious, mutually reinforcing agenda. Industries are not enemies of humane progress, they are essential ingredients of sound social policy—in every country of the world.

This is why most "backward," less developed countries set a priority on general industrialization, and improved rates of economic growth. They learned from Britain's Industrial Revolution from 1750 to the 1880s, and the somewhat later industrial successes of the U.S., Germany, Japan, and others, that encouraging a broad front of industrial progress generated more rapid, mutually reinforcing prosperity. In most of these success stories a substantial degree of tariff protection played a crucial, positive role. Government subsidies, bureaucratic awards, and central planning are a lot less productive most of the time. A key advantage of moderate to substantial import tariffs, set in place long enough so that investments in manufacturing plans and marketing operations can flourish (from infant industries into healthy, self-sustaining maturity), was that myriad independent business enterprises take faster, more productive decisions than a few top level government officials. Industrial success requires a great deal of decentralized initiative. The beauty of general tariffs (whether at 15, 20, or 25 percent) is that domestic industrial expansion efforts can rely upon a reasonable, steady cushion or safeguarding from the bigger, stronger industries of the leading nations. For these reasons, most LDCs and NICs have been reluctant to give up the freedom for infant industry tariffs, and this outlook was recognized in GATT 1947, GATT amendments in 1965 (Articles XXXVI–XXXVIII), and GATT 1994–WTO Agreement. Thus, trade asymmetries favoring developing nations have become strongly entrenched in the present multilateral trading regime. It was not realistic to believe these tariffs and other restrictions to promote industrial progress will be abandoned any time soon by most LDCs and the majority of NICs.

But this leaves an awkward, interesting question for mature, somewhat stagnant industrial nations (like most OECD bloc countries today). If the mature nations lose too much ground, and excessive deindustrialization occurs, shouldn't they be allowed to use tariffs again, at least selectively, to rejuvenate their industrial base? Thereby over the longer run, the redevelopment cycle could be started again and rejuvenation tariffs be justified. Countries that have slipped back too far, with imprudent reliance on industries from LDCs and NICs, and excessive imports, trade deficits, and chronic balance of payments problems, need a significant renewal of tariffs (like the LDCs and NICs used to catch up). The U.S., in fact, may suffer this predicament to some extent already. Fifteen years of increased, large, and stubborn external deficits suggest that, to some extent at least, rejuvenation tariffs are needed by the U.S. for its industrial renewal. Should not GATT 1947, the 1965 GATT amendments, and GATT 1994 be interpreted, reasonably, to authorize rejuvenation tariffs where too much industrial decline has occurred? Or, doesn't this logic suggest that unconditional MFN must have natural limits for countries like the United States, which gave up too much industrial ground by not insisting on more effective reciprocity? Certainly, as against trading partners with large, disproportionate, and extended trade surpluses, this logic justifies moderate rejuvenation tariffs (in addition to remedies outlined previously—see the section "Reciprocal Trade Policy").

Clinton–Perot: A Mandate Not Implemented

In 1991–92 unease was developing among a majority of the American public about slowed economic growth, reduced job prospects, and a decline in real wages (discounted for inflation). In spite of euphoria over Allied victory in the Gulf War (defeating Iraq's army and liberating Kuwait), and a surge of free world confidence after the collapse of Russian communism (1989–91), the American public mood turned pessimistic on the economic front. President George Bush had become overconfident, and during the spring of 1992 three strong challengers hammered away at U.S. deficits, job losses, and reduced confidence among the middle class. They exploited a slump in the U.S. economy, and raised serious objections to the conduct of U.S. foreign economic policy and the cumulative effects of U.S. industrial decline. For the majority of Americans, it was evident that U.S. kindness and Cold War politics allowed foreign exporters more access to the U.S. marketplace than we enjoyed in many markets abroad. The Conservative populist, Pat Buchanan, attacked "King George" [Bush] in New Hampshire and later primaries on these issues, which hurt Republican momentum that year. The moderate populist and billionaire, Ross Perot, attacked excessive U.S. deficits, weak trade policy, and urged health care reform for a broken system. Perot threatened an independent, third party ticket, and bitterly attacked NAFTA, saying that it would bring a "giant sucking sound" of U.S. jobs moving south. And within the Democratic party, Bill Clinton proved to be the most resilient, toughest campaigner. Clinton focused on "jobs, jobs, jobs," and "it's the economy, stupid" as his mantras; and he also promoted health care overhaul. Meanwhile, Paul Tsongas and Warren Rudman (former U.S. Senators) of the Concord coalition, strongly attacked excessive and chronic budget deficits. All this led to widespread dissatisfaction with the sluggish U.S. economy, weak jobs performance, and concerns about U.S. trade policy.[22]

When Bill Clinton (43 percent) and Ross Perot (19 percent) defeated George Bush (38 percent) in the November 1992 election, a mandate seemed reasonably clear, at least up to a point. Americans wanted a stronger economy, more jobs, reduced deficits, health care reforms (cost reductions and broader coverage), and a tougher trade policy. Most Americans were alarmed about rising crime, and wanted stronger action on that front, too. In the spring of 1993 Clinton enjoyed the normal, brief "honeymoon" for newly elected presidents, but this ebbed by mid-summer. Meanwhile, fierce fights erupted over Clinton's economic and trade policies within the administration. An advantage for Clinton, at least initially, were Democratic majorities in both House and Senate.

But Clinton's economic policy gradually crystallized as a moderate, somewhat Wall Street–oriented view on budget deficits, specifically, the need to gradually reduce them, which would allow lower interest rates. Most of his economic advisers (Bentsen, Rubin, Rivlin, Altman, and Greenspan) urged that outlook, and they also supported freer trade. Although Clinton's U.S. Trade Representative, Mickey Kantor (his initial campaign manager and leading fundraiser), was not a trade policy expert, Kantor soon took a largely free trade line. Clinton quickly approved mild Side Agreements with Mexico on NAFTA, which supposedly dealt with Import Surges, Labor Rights, and Environmental Protection; but they did not seriously limit or alter the NAFTA agreements as negotiated by the Bush administration. Clinton's Side Agreements just set up more formalized mutual consultations for "problems" in these areas. And, more importantly, Kantor pretty much accepted the draft Uruguay GATT Round deal as negotiated by his USTR predecessor, Carla Hills. The only important change, at the last moment, was to rename the Multilateral Trade Organization (MTO) as the World Trade Organization (WTO). These U.S. trade negotiating decisions were essentially complete in the summer of 1993. In

fact, Kantor promised in spring 1993 that the Uruguay Round GATT negotiations would be completed by that fall. Unfortunately, this eliminated any
effective bargaining leverage to substantially improve upon the Dunkel
draft deal. In this way, sadly, the Clinton administration gave away its best
opportunity to substantially improve U.S. reciprocity.

The bigger questions for the Clinton White House were political. And this
caused some real agonizing, especially over NAFTA. During the spring and
summer of 1993 Clinton handled trade matters in a low-key way, allowing
many Democratic Congressional leaders to believe that Clinton's political
commitment to NAFTA was weak and limited. In this context, House Majority
Leader Richard Gephardt and Whip David Bonior took strong public stands
against NAFTA; the AFL-CIO launched an expensive campaign against
NAFTA; and Jesse Jackson and Ralph Nader opposed it, as did the majority of
environmental organizations. By August 1993, Clinton faced a tough political
dilemma. Should he let NAFTA "fail," which would weaken his prestige as
"an international leader," or should Clinton divide his own party with a bitter
fight over trade policy? Newt Gingrich and the House Republicans offered to
help Clinton pass NAFTA, knowing this would help drive a sword of division
into the belly of House Democrats. By September Clinton decided that he had
to go ahead with NAFTA, and make a strong effort for Congressional approval
under fast-track procedures. Interestingly, the final Uruguay Round GATT deal
was scheduled to be finalized shortly after the NAFTA vote. (Much more
complicated, and hard for Congress and the public to understand, the Uruguay
GATT Round deal was hardly mentioned by the administration, nor even much
discussed by the NAFTA opposition. This lack of serious attention or debate
proved to be a major U.S. trade policy blunder.)

As Clinton focused on the crucial House NAFTA vote (in mid-October
1993), Vice-President Al Gore was selected by the White House to debate
Ross Perot on prime time TV, *mano a mano.* The gamble paid off. Polls
reported Gore "won" the debate. (Interestingly, the somewhat cranky Perot
was picked to personify the opposition to NAFTA, rather than Ralph Nader,
Jesse Jackson, Pat Buchanan, Richard Gephardt, or Dave Bonior.) Once
Gore *won* the debate, NAFTA was approved by the House (although nearly
two-thirds of the House Democrats still opposed it.) Shortly thereafter Kantor announced that the Uruguay GATT Round agreement was signed. But
little discussion, detailed analysis, or debate followed on the GATT deal.
And, most interestingly, a special Congressional vote on the Uruguay
Round GATT deal under fast track was scheduled eventually for late November 1994, *after the fall 1994 congressional elections.*

Meanwhile, during 1994, political attention shifted to the health care
package, which had been carefully developed under the leadership of Hillary

Clinton, with a great deal of fanfare and publicity. Unfortunately, the plans proved too complicated, required large new budget outlays, featured threatening new regulations for health care providers, and yet did not achieve substantial savings in the short run. Congress was never consulted adequately about the package, and as the summer of 1994 wore on it became apparent that the Clinton health care overhaul effort had failed, with great embarrassment for the administration.[23]

But that summer and fall, Republicans under Newt Gingrich were mounting a strong national campaign to carry the House of Representatives. They proposed a Contract with America—a ten-point agenda of balanced budget, fiscal, tax, family, crime control, and other measures that would be pushed by a Republican Congress. To the surprise of most observers, Republicans carried in November not only the U.S. House of Representatives, but also the U.S. Senate.

In the immediate wake of that Republican mid-term electoral victory, Congress reconvened (as previously agreed) to vote on the Uruguay Round GATT deal—now referred to as "GATT 1994 and the World Trade Organization Agreement." Hardly any national debate, minimal Congressional hearings, and only brief, conclusory "reviews" of the deal were offered by the USTR in support. So little discussion occurred in the media, it was evident that few press people were up to speed on the many technical issues dealt with by the GATT round (between 1985 and 1991).[24] There was almost no historical literature on U.S. trade policy in recent years, especially for the post–World War II era.[25] Intriguingly, Newt Gingrich had complained openly, in a June 10, 1994, House Ways and Means Committee Hearing, about the lack of serious debate and literature on the Uruguay Round deal. He, quite properly, compared the U.S. decision on GATT 1994 and the WTO to Britain's entry into the European Common Market in 1973. Certainly, he said, the U.S. should be thinking through, systematically and carefully, the ramifications of the new GATT 1994 and WTO Agreement. But few other members of the House expressed serious concern. In this context, it was not really surprising that Congress would give fast-track approval to GATT 1994 and the WTO agreement. The surprise, frankly, was that a third of the Congress, from both Republican and Democratic ranks, voted *against* GATT 1994 and the WTO Agreement. Without much debate or leadership involvement, this Congressional vote really reflected broad unease over U.S. trade policy and accumulated asymmetries.[26]

Department of Industry, Technology, and Trade (DITT)

Many experts on industrial development, engineering, and technological progress believe that governments have an active, continuing, and essential role to play in fostering these activities.[27] Certainly tax policies should encourage productive investments, ample incentives for engineers, designers, production workers, and marketing organizations. Intellectual property, patents, trademarks, and copyright protection are valuable incentives, too. But government support for engineering schools, research and development projects, and scientific expertise have played a significant role as well. In periods of national emergency, like World Wars I and II, the Cold War, or severe economic dislocation (e.g., the OPEC I and II energy shortages), government R&D programs, mobilization efforts, and coordination have been crucial. And, of course, long-standing U.S. tariff policies, from Alexander Hamilton through World War II, strongly nurtured U.S. manufacturing, mining, and agricultural industries. Other industrial (OECD) nations, new industrial countries (NICs), and less developed countries (LDCs) have employed comparable industrial and technology encouragement policies, to the extent that their resources and stage of development allowed.

The organizational structure used by the U.S. government was comparable to that of other nations in fostering this industrial expansion and technological progress. Congress established and regulated the tax and tariff structure, with guidance at times from Presidents. War and Navy Departments were created initially, along with a Treasury Department, Departments of Commerce (for business and industry), Agriculture (for farming), and Interior (for mining and resources) were set up later on to promote economic development. The Department of Labor was established to protect worker interests. During World Wars I and II emergency industrial mobilization and coordination agencies were created, more elaborate for the longer World War II effort (1940–45), including a War Production Board, Labor Board, and Office of Price Administration. Smaller and ad hoc institutions were needed, among the most striking being the Manhattan Project (atomic energy research to develop the first nuclear bombs). After World War II, major demobilization of the armed forces occurred, although reorganization split off the Air Force as a separate service (formerly the Army Air Corps). But the new Department of Defense and collateral agencies, including the National Security Agency and the Central Intelligence Agency, and long-term procurement relations with many defense equipment suppliers (aerospace, naval, shipbuilding, electronics, computers, tanks and armored vehicles, lighter arms, and munitions of all kinds) took on important roles in sponsoring industrial progress, engineering improvement, and the maintenance (as far as possible) of a U.S. technical edge in most aspects of weaponry.

In defense-related sectors, the U.S. maintained a systematic industrial policy, at least through the Cold War era (1946–91). The Department of

Agriculture, farm lobbies, and their influence in many states supported efforts for progress, efficiency, and prosperity in that sector. And in the minerals sector, tax and other policies promoted production, emergency stockpiles, international investment, and adequate supplies for industry.

But for the rest of U.S. industry and manufacturing, little need was seen for government nurturing. World War II left America with a lead in many industries. This allowed U.S. trade policy to open its manufacturing markets (far more than other nations) as part of U.S. Cold War politics, helping Allies and developing nations to prosperity by leading the way toward a more integrated free world economy.

The chief instrumentality for this "trade not aid" policy was a small section of U.S. trade negotiators in the State Department.[28] Later, as part of the Kennedy Round enabling legislation, these people staffed up the new Office of the U.S. Trade Representative (USTR). Subsequently, the USTR became dominant in U.S. trade policy. Unfortunately, the USTR personnel did not see themselves as guardians of trade reciprocity or overall balance in U.S. export/import flows. Quite the contrary, the USTR saw use by the U.S. of its own trade laws to limit imports, enforce fair trade, or require effective reciprocity *as an interference with free trade.* Typically, the USTR accepted foreign pledges to gradually open markets and reduce trade barriers abroad *as the equivalent* of U.S. openness. In effect, the Office of the USTR became the primary architect of asymmetries in U.S. trading relationships, further entrenched by the GATT 1994 and WTO agreement negotiated by the USTR. The USTR became the steadfast foe of any effective U.S. "industrial policy," and the USTR insisted that it be the only significant voice in shaping detailed U.S. trade policy or negotiations (within the U.S. government).

Because of the USTR's institutional bias and well-established track record on their view of "free trade," it is evident that this agency could never accept or implement a new, reciprocity-based U.S. trade policy that emphasizes the goals of overall balance in U.S. trade flows. Therefore, the USTR must be abolished. The USTR and its "culture" are simply not consistent with a stronger, reciprocity-based policy.

Accordingly, all U.S. trade negotiation and oversight functions and responsibilities should be transferred to a new, larger, and stronger agency, the Department of Industry, Technology, and Trade (DITT).[29] Portions of the Department of Commerce, for the most part, should be the core of the new DITT, but energized with a new and stronger trade policy mandate. The DITT should take over most of the business, industrial, and trade statistics gathering responsibilities in the U.S. government (except for financial markets, which should be left to the Federal Reserve, SEC, and other financial market supervisors). Agricultural data should be left to the Department of Agriculture. A new mission statement must be developed for the DITT that emphasizes as national policy goals: (i) the promotion of U.S. industry, technology, and trade; (ii) effective trading reciprocity and overall balance in U.S. export/import flows; (iii) achieving fair shares for U.S. business, commerce, and industry in world markets; (iv) careful monitoring and reporting on industrial developments in the world marketplace, observing technology trends, trade barriers of all kinds, and relative access to foreign markets by U.S. companies, investors, and workers; (v) skillful enforcement of U.S. trade laws, and representation of the U.S. in foreign trade dealings (including working with the WTO, NAFTA, and any other trade organizations); and (vi) collaboration with other government agencies and departments that impact industry, technology, and trade, including the Departments of Defense, Agriculture, Interior and Labor, the Environmental Protection Agency, the Federal Reserve, Treasury, and a new Maritime Department (which should take over the Maritime Administration and Maritime Commission—presently in the Commerce Department).[30]

Thus, DITT becomes the new, predominant lead agency for U.S. trade policy (replacing the USTR). It will rival, and be a counterpart of, the Japanese Ministry of International Trade and Industry (MITI). DITT should (like Japan's MITI) have a coordinative role in representing the interests of U.S. industries, companies, communities, and workers. A clear commitment to U.S. trade reciprocity, and overall balance in U.S. imports/exports will make it clear to all other nations that a new U.S. trade policy has been installed. The U.S. will be friendly, fair, and evenhanded. But the U.S. will no longer "accept the short end of the stick." America will no longer be the World "Chump" of trade.

In this regard, we must emphasize that a strong, coordinative role for DITT does not replace vigorous, dynamic U.S. companies and manufacturers as the primary vehicles of industrial success and prosperity. No—the function of DITT is *not to control or dictate,* but to aid, encourage, and promote U.S. manufacturers, plants, companies, and workers. Very importantly, DITT's mandate is also to offset the strong, widespread industrial support systems of many OECD nations, and the majority of NICs and LDCs. This offset responsibility is now generally neglected by the U.S. government. Under the ideologically biased world view of the USTR, this lack of U.S. response was rationalized as a "commitment to free trade." The real, important, and continuing contribution of foreign industrial support systems was heavily discounted and minimized by naïve free trade enthusiasts. Sadly, this mentality only helps to sustain asymmetries widely appreciated abroad, but not adequately understood by many in the U.S. government (especially within the USTR).

However, we must realize that the growing spread of multinational corporations (MNCs), their subsidiaries, investments, and allies, does make it more complicated to trace relative market shares and influence. And MNCs, especially the larger ones, are taking a bigger share of world trade in recent years. Much of the growing volume of world trade, in fact, represents intra-corporate (and inter-affiliate) trading, investment, and financial flows. Routings through tax havens to divert profits into minimal or no-tax environments add fog to the data problems, especially for capital flows, financial services, and "royalty" payments, particularly for intellectual property.[31] Nonetheless, some countries are far more effective "(e.g., Japan) than others in making sure that *their multinationals* get a good, fair share of the transactional pie. Those nations get a "higher yield" in real benefits, market shares, and trade flows, of course, and enjoy faster overall real GNP growth (with less risk of stagnation). Thus, the role for DITT must be actively pursued, with savvy and long-term determination. In the modern global economy, DITT must be a permanent feature of sound, effective U.S. trade policy.

It is interesting that the first major proposals for a new U.S. Department of International Trade and Industry (DITI) came during the 1983–85 period.[32] Secretary of Commerce Malcolm Baldrige proposed to transform the Commerce Department into a DITI as a necessary counter-measure to deal more effectively with Japan's MITI and comparable industrial-trade policy efforts in other countries. (An earlier, more limited version of this effort was made under Secretary of Commerce Maurice Stans in early 1969, but President Nixon chose not to press the matter after some congressional misgivings.) Not surprisingly, of course, the USTR lobbied strongly (though not too publicly) to head off this idea and prevent its implementation; it would have been a major threat to continued USTR dominance over the details of U.S. trade policy.

Cleaning Up Legal Underbrush

An essential chore for new, reciprocity-based U.S. trade policy is to clear away the legal underbrush that gets in the way. U.S. trade laws, so far as they go, are reasonably adequate.[33] The Trade Act of 1974, including Section 122 (balance of payments relief), Section 125 (presidential authority to terminate agreements), Section 232 (national security), and Section 301 (unjustifiable trade practices and discrimination), together with Section 337 (actions against unfair trade practices—mainly involving intellectual property), along with the antidumping and countervailing duty for subsidy laws, make sense. The main problem with U.S. trade laws has been great timidity in their enforcement. Thus, for example, as part of their Uruguay Round "standstill" pledge in 1985–93, U.S. trade negotiators promised that they would minimize the development of any significant import restrictions *(or trade barriers)* under U.S. trade laws.

Fortunately, the recent Uruguay Round Agreements Act of 1994, the U.S. implementing act for GATT 1994 and the WTO, made it very clear that *U.S. trade laws prevail* over the WTO Agreement.[34] Even though explicit language in the WTO Agreement expresses a contrary idea—that is, that the WTO Agreement prevails over all national laws—the U.S. implementing act explicitly rejects this impact. Thus, an evident conflict has been created between U.S. implementing law and the text of the WTO agreement. The U.S. must insist that U.S. trade laws prevail, and if any WTO panel decision or interpretation fails to sustain this priority for U.S. law, the U.S. should promptly withdraw from the WTO (and give the Secretary General of the UN and the Director General of the WTO the six months' notice as required.[35]

It is important also that the new reciprocity-based U.S. trade policy be enunciated in strong, fresh, and clear legislation. The goals of enforcing effective trade reciprocity and of achieving overall balance in U.S. imports and exports must be set forth in no uncertain terms. For these reasons, a new "Reciprocity Trade Balance Act" must be enacted as the charter and explicit mandate for the new U.S. trade policy. And the fundamental rationale should be clear, too. The U.S. respects the right of all nations to make the best deals possible in world trade. But now that the Cold War is behind us, a new U.S. trade policy is needed. The U.S. has widespread unemployment, underemployment, and stubborn income inequalities. Poverty, drug abuse, and crime are serious problems. Americans must take care of their own people. Full employment must be achieved. And all nations must discipline their external accounts, and eliminate excessive trade and current account deficits. The U.S. must put its economic house in order.

New Realism Versus Holier Than Thou

An aspect of U.S. foreign policy that has been vexing, troubling, and alienating for many nations, including those well-disposed to Americans, is a tendency to self-righteous and self-centered moralism. All too frequently the U.S. proclaims a special wisdom and rightness in foreign policy, a superior commitment to democracy, human rights, and individual freedoms. "Be like us" is the implicit message. Accept U.S.-style free market institutions. Practice U.S.-style democratic politics. Observe U.S. social mores and conventions. Implement U.S. free trade policies, open your markets, and let MNCs into your markets on the same terms as domestic companies. Moreover, don't mistreat minorities, unions, workers, women, or child labor. And have free elections, with a free press (domestic and foreign) given access to everything. And, if you don't, well . . . you're uncivilized, mercantilist, or maybe even guilty of human rights violations.

Yet U.S. history hardly represents a clean slate on these issues. Slave labor came early in the British colonies (although already practiced by the Spanish, Portuguese, and French colonies, and elsewhere). Slavery in the U.S. continued into the Civil War (1861–65). It took another century for U.S. national policy to proclaim discrimination on the basis of national origin, race, religion, or sex unlawful. Unionization of workers began gradually, and was not clearly favored under U.S. law until the Wagner Act of 1935. Tariff protection in the U.S. was established policy from 1791 to 1945, although we moved toward reciprocal free trade after 1934. The U.S. has been a leader in democracy, but its practice has been imperfect. And the liberalism of U.S. social mores, recent fashions in family life, and outlooks on sexuality are controversial even among Americans. The Western press and media, while an inspiration to many in the world, are seen as licentious and corrupting by others.

Condemnation by the U.S. government, prominent senators or congressmen, elements of the American media, or special interest groups is often taken badly. Charges of hypocrisy are thrown back at Americans, based upon our own history or lack of consistency. To be sure, really brutal regimes, dictatorial and repressive governments, and extensive abuse and cruelties against peoples and minorities generally deserve international criticism. But the U.S. (like other countries) lacks consistency in applying these standards to trading partners, friendly nations, and allied states. And the failure to be consistent, evenhanded, and fair with other countries is often quite bitterly resented. If this hectoring persists, the results are often counter-productive, and frequently lead to political and economic alienation. Such pretentious, offensive moralism by the U.S. is bad, inept foreign policy.

Trading policies are better left to pragmatism and mutual interest among nations, at least for the most part. Certainly the overwhelming majority of states employ primarily mercantile, practical standards (commercial reliability, creditworthiness, and reciprocity) in their trade policies.[36] Rarely is there a strong consensus to sanction or outlaw a nation on moral or legal grounds (e.g., after Saddam Hussein's conquest of Kuwait, or during South Africa's apartheid regime). Sanctions may be needed, however, to deal with some dangerous adversaries or enemy powers (e.g., those sponsoring terrorism or responsible for acts of aggression). But U.S. trade sanctions normally should be confined to hostile regimes, governments that have earned broad and widespread condemnation among nations of the world, and countries with recent trade policies strongly in conflict with U.S. trade interests (such as large, disproportionate trade imbalances resulting from a lack of effective reciprocity).

A great advantage for a new, reciprocity-based U.S. trade policy is its lack of moral pretentiousness. Reciprocity-oriented trading policies are the traditional and realistic norms of international relations. Every nation has the right and expectation to be treated fairly and equally by others. Most of U.S. history, from the Revolutionary American Republic through the New Deal's proclaimed reciprocal trade policy, and into the post–World War II era, was dominated by this thinking. Treaties of Friendship, Commerce, and Navigation were sought with most states. But the U.S. took for granted its right to impose tariffs, industrial development, and growth policies as it saw fit. And, U.S. statesmen respected the rights of other states to do the same. Thus, in the new U.S. trade policy environment, the U.S. can and should seek common ground in mutually beneficial trade relationships with most nations. And within shrewd and effective limits, the U.S. should apply substantial pressures against allied and friendly states to achieve better balance and more effective reciprocity in import/export flows. But this is not a big deal morally. It is only common-sense, normal, and healthy business dealings. Realistic, sensible trading states understand that mutually beneficial, reciprocal trading, without disproportionate advantage to either side, is more satisfactory and sustainable over the long haul.

Teamwork: Labor, Environment, and Consumers

In healthy countries with good, realistic teamwork and pride in their general prosperity, engineering progress, and mutual achievements there is a harmony of interest between workers, industrial leaders, and consumers. And for our modern generation, an increasing awareness for shared enjoyment of the environment has become essential, too. But when major alienation and conflicts develop for industrial workers, labor organizations, environmental groups, and many consumer leaders with their own government officials responsible for trade policy, at the very least, it seems, there is troubling disharmony.[37] Sadly, U.S. trade negotiators (especially the USTR) chose a course of dealings between 1985 and 1998 that favored multinational corporations (MNCs), but neglected the interests of domestic workers, wage rates, and overall employment. MNCs were encouraged, increasingly after the early 1980s, to relocate their manufacturing operations in lower-wage countries, to achieve the lowest common denominators of cost and convenience.[38] This tended to undercut the standards for environmental protection that had been developed since the later 1960s. Communities and labor organizations, worried about losing their remaining industrial plants and employment, accepted lower wages and less favorable benefits, and became disinclined to support environmental safeguards that could limit industrial activity and jobs in their localities.

During much of the 1980s, however, many U.S. companies and industries did try to hang in there and get support from the U.S. government to limit disruptive imports and provide reasonable safeguard relief.[39] Steel products, machine tools, automobiles and trucks, textiles and clothing, shoes, and many other industries brought companies and working people together for efforts under U.S. trade laws. And, to some extent, the International Trade Administration (ITA) of the Commerce Department and the International Trade Commission (ITC) provided relief under U.S. trade laws. But the Uruguay GATT Round (1985–93) negotiation, with the USTR's "standstill" pledge against new trade "restrictions," undercut a lot of this industry–labor collaboration. And the final Uruguay Round outcome sadly weakened U.S. enforcement potential for countervailing duties against foreign subsidies, antidumping proceedings, Section 301 and Section 337 actions, and made it even more difficult to get effective safeguard relief.[40] Understandably, more American companies developed an "importer" mentality like many MNCs. Manufacturing jobs increasingly moved overseas to low-wage countries. This substantially weakened, over time, the teamwork of U.S. manufacturers with labor interests. By the early mid-1990s, the U.S. government's trade policies (NAFTA, GATT 1994 and the WTO) signaled a general lack of concern for U.S. workers, and a preference for investor–MNC interests.

What about consumer interests? Consumers share interests with business investors, producers, and working people. The incomes that consumers spend come from domestic industries, export sales, the service sector (including federal, state, and local government), and the overall share of the U.S. in world trading activities. Unfortunately, the U.S. share in global output has been declining for the last generation. In other words, combined incomes of American teamwork have been sagging. Thus, "U.S., Inc." has not done so well *in economic growth rates* as "Japan, Inc.," "Taiwan, Inc.," "South Korea, Inc.," and so forth (see Table 1.4). Also from low levels of income, China, India, and Southeast Asia were making rapid progress for their consumers from the mid-1980s to the mid-1990s. Thus, consumers for the American team have not done so well since the early 1970s.[41]

And what about shifting incomes among consumers? Data on U.S. worker wages, family incomes, and the redistribution of wealth showed a clear and troubling pattern. The average U.S. real wage declined between

1973 and the mid-1990s (see Table 1.6). The top 10 percent on the income and wealth scale improved their share, while middle and lower classes lost ground.[42] Some middle-income families held their own by working longer hours, and more women now work full-time. But single earner families fell back, for the most part, and lost real incomes. Industries like manufacturing, which used to employ a large portion of the higher-wage people, declined, with net losses in higher-wage jobs. Lower-paid service jobs cannot make up all of the difference. And some service sector expansion may be unsustainable, with big increases in the share of GNP going to health care, insurance, lawyering, and the criminal justice system. Even so-called "free trade" enthusiasts were conceding, by the mid- to late 1990s, that while the "global economy" brought some gains to "winners," substantial numbers of "losers" had accumulated. A majority of the American people are now doubtful about the benefits of free trade.[43]

Unease about the global trading "system" was spreading internationally in the late 1990s.[44] Europe was divided and troubled about high, chronic levels of unemployment. Europeans suffered overloads in their social welfare states, and increased inequalities like the United States. Many experts project more EU protectionism as a result. Eastern Europe, Russia, and the former USSR were struggling hard to create viable market economies from corrupt communist regimes.[45] Hopes were high, but progress slow. High incomes went to wheeler-dealer types (often former communist apparatchiks), with relative poverty for many. Most Islamic states suffer economic trouble, in one form or another, and there's a growing resurgence of anti-Western feeling as well. Southeast Asia's "New Tigers," especially Malaysia, Thailand, Indonesia, and the Philippines, were beneficiaries of global trade expansion for a decade and more, but recently suffered major speculative excesses, financial and stock market losses, and sharp currency declines. Japan had been the paragon of global growth and neomercantilism until a speculative bubble finally sagged in the early 1990s.[46] Japan's government thereafter attempted some liberalization measures, but became alarmed that a high yen in 1995 would cripple exports, and later brought the yen back down substantially. Africa remains greatly troubled, and has never fully trusted the global economy and foreign companies. Only Latin American nations, for the most part, retain faith in liberalizing their own internal economies; but Latin Americans never embraced a complete opening to foreign investors. Mexico's sad experience with a massive inflow of foreign investments, the disruptive peso crisis of 1994–95, and a 60 percent devaluation of the peso, taught sobering lessons.[47] Most of Latin America is learning a good lesson from Mexico. Overall, it seems clear that the widespread global market euphoria of 1991–94 was waning by 1996–98.

Most of the world is relearning, once again, the fundamental lessons of the Great Depression. We must be aware of the danger from speculative manias and the need to limit excessive swings in the business cycle (boom–bust scenarios with heavy unemployment and widespread distress).[48] Interestingly, OECD countries learned in the 1940s of the need for more sustained, reliable economic growth (the Keynesian revolution), and the advantages of a fuller employment society. Broad OECD prosperity in the 1940s–60s and on into the 1970s was the result. The GATT 1947 charter for *gradual* trade liberalization emphasized vital safeguards and limitations to prevent serious disruptions, for example, Article XII (Balance of Payments Relief), Article VI (Duties Against Foreign Subsidies and Dumping), and Article XIX (Safeguard or Escape Clause Relief). But the 1970s inflation and structural rigidities in the 1980s brought excesses in social welfare spending, health care waste, and the entrenchment of government deficits in many countries. Partly in response, multinational corporations (MNCs) began moving offshore to avoid higher wages and fringe benefits, which made the unions in Europe, the U.S., Canada, Australia, and New Zealand even more defensive. Japan avoided these difficulties until the early 1990s, because of their stronger resistance to manufactured imports (i.e., more effective safeguard relief through language, culture, marketing customs, and administrative guidance). Then GATT 1994 and the WTO Agreement distorted the ground rules (at least for the U.S.) by weakening national access to trade law relief, and by encouraging MNCs to break their national teamwork with labor, the environment, and low-middle-class consumers, and move their manufacturing and processing work to low-wage countries. Oddly, this opens up the industrialized OECD countries to greater import penetration, trade imbalances, and a renewed vulnerability to an "open market global capitalism" that has not really been seen since the 1920s. Greatly enlarged trade and current account deficits, of course, normally bring strong devaluation pressures to currencies.

Consumers lose again, through devaluations, higher living costs, economic slowdown, and increased unemployment. Overdependence on foreign imports and the global economy turns out to be a serious economic blunder. Many experts are worried now that most OECD countries are opening themselves up to global market imbalances and speculative disruptions, with a substantially weakened industrial-employment base, and a strained social safety net.[49] This resembles the late 1920s somewhat, although modern governments probably would print more money, increase budget deficits, and widen the safety net in the event of a broader recession and big unemployment increases.

But tragic dilemmas are built into the global economy now, because heavy Keynesian pump priming and budget deficits aggravate the external deficits problem. Thus, a vicious cycle of devaluations and excessive deficits may be hard to break. These vulnerabilities are the natural consequence of overdependence upon foreign goods, and the dangers that very large, speculative capital flows can turn quickly against a nation through events largely out of its own control.

Monitoring and Progress: Three- to Five-Year Transition Periods

Extensive monitoring is essential for a new, reciprocity-based trade policy that achieves an overall balance in U.S. exports/imports. Reasonably accurate data must be collected and maintained on industrial output, sales, costs, imports, exports, and services (especially those involving international transactions). Most of this data has been collected by the U.S. Census Bureau, Department of Commerce (with increasing care since the later 1930s.)[50] Statistical monitoring capabilities are greatly enhanced by computer age technology. Normal tabulations on standardized definitions are easy to maintain, provided that companies are required by law to report regularly their industrial activities on this basis.[51]

Any gaps that develop for new industries or products in this information base should be promptly closed. Appropriate up-dating is necessary to maintain adequate and reliable data collection. In this regard, special attention must be given to multinational corporations (MNCs), their affiliates, plants, intra-company transfers, prices, and costs. Obviously, MNCs could become a significant gap in the data, if they are not properly supervised and accounted for.

Our Department of Industry, Technology, and Trade (DITT) must have primary responsibility for maintaining a full set of current accounts for all domestic industrial and international trade-related transactions. Data from other agencies should be fed into the DITT data base, so that monitoring for all aspects of international trade is as complete and up-to-date as possible. In this way, DITT can be well informed about the details of changing trade flows between the U.S. and its many trading partners. Obviously, normal and prompt publication of these data should be continued by DITT, so that Congress, various industries, interest groups, and the public can be informed. DITT should work with other countries on a mutual, reciprocal basis to assure adequate transparency for all international sales, shipments, services, and trading activities.[52]

Progress in the U.S. balance of payments involving increased exports and (where needed) reduced imports is a crucial priority in the new, reciprocity-based trade policy. Data are presently tabulated on a monthly basis, but published after several months lag. Faster and more reliable data collection will be needed for all trade involving countries (and their companies) with large and/or disproportionate trade surpluses as against the United States. Remember that unconditional MFN will be discontinued against all such countries for so long as these large or disproportionate trade surpluses persist. Furthermore, 10 to 15 percent import fees will be charged for all shipments or services from these countries (*or traceable to them*) so long as large or disproportionate trade surpluses continue.

Collaboration in rapidly eliminating these large or disproportionate trade surpluses will be rewarded with kinder, easier treatment. A crucial dimension of collaboration will be working with U.S. companies to increase exports abroad, or to relocate foreign manufacturing, assembly, or component making back in the U.S. Companies from the U.S. and their foreign counterparts that cooperate in the new U.S. trade policy will be welcomed into the American Partner program and given special privileges and waivers from import fees, where substantial contributions to an improved U.S. balance of payments are being made.

By contrast, foreign companies or governments that refuse to cooperate, supply adequate data, or resist the new U.S. trade policy will be treated less favorably. Higher import fees, more extensive investigations under U.S. trade law (including antidumping, subsidy, Section 301, or Section 337 proceedings), and increased data reporting requirements will be imposed. The net result for non-collaborating countries or companies will be greater reductions in imports, substantially less trade with the U.S., and penalties for non-reporting.

Reasonable transition periods of three to five years must be allowed for large and disproportionate trade surpluses to be eliminated. Careful follow-through on improved trade balances will be required, so that "good performance" by foreign companies and countries can be rewarded. This means reasonably complete reporting for trade in goods and services with all countries is essential throughout, so that "good performance" (reasonably balanced trade) can be monitored. Backsliding must be promptly identified, along with desirable progress. And problems of new and growing imbalance with other countries (including possible diversion or evasive routings) must be promptly identified, too.

Another important part of DITT's trade monitoring responsibility would be current reporting on foreign industrial policies, tariffs, industrial subsidies, and targeting efforts for all U.S. trade partners. Foreign countries that refuse to cooperate in providing adequate information may be subject to import surcharges (or other U.S. trade law sanctions), at least for the sectors suspected of substantial non-reporting.

Additional trade monitoring expenses may be involved for DITT data gathering, surveillance, and oversight. These modest extra annual DITT costs should be prorated among all U.S. imports each year. A small monitoring and oversight fee will be charged each year. Discounts in these fees will be allowed for countries that actively collaborate with DITT in these efforts. Any country that resists these fees, however, or that tries to counter with penalty fees on the U.S. or its companies will be subjected to substantial further penalties in return.

Overall surveillance and reporting requirements for the new, reciprocity-based U.S. trade policy will be somewhat greater than present data collection. But for collaborating countries and companies these costs will be quite modest on the whole. On the other hand, for countries or companies that resist or obstruct the new data-gathering efforts, their conduct will be considered "trade hostile" to the U.S. Additional investigative efforts, data-gathering charges, and U.S. trade law enforcement efforts will be focused against such countries or companies. Continued obstruction or resistance may lead to the imposition of special import licenses for further exports or financial dealings with the U.S. Once again, the bottom line for the new reciprocity-based U.S. trade policy is that cooperation by foreign companies and governments will be rewarded, but obstruction, resistance, and a failure to cooperate must be discouraged and sanctioned—with reduced export access, higher import fees, oversight penalties, and, if necessary, special import licenses for continued trade and financial dealings.

Non-Action: Vulnerability and Decline

Damaging consequences follow if the U.S. takes no action to eliminate trade and current account deficits, restore trade reciprocity, and rejuvenate industries and technology. America has already lost ground in many industries; others are nearly abandoned. Recently U.S. imports exceeded U.S. exports by a margin of four to three. In 1996 this meant imports of $818 billion and exports of $622 billion out of $7,638 billion GNP. Since 1981 we have accumulated $2,000 billion in U.S. current trade deficits, and $1,500 billion in current account deficits. The U.S. transformed itself from the world's largest creditor nation (+$325 billion) to become the biggest debtor country (–$1,250 billion) in these years. The U.S. suffered a net loss of 10–12 million jobs, and reduced economic growth. Structural unemployment increased, poverty spread, and inequalities got worse. Morale is strained. Widespread unease exists about the economy, the reliability of Social Security reserves, and the future for our younger generation.

Although an upsurge in the U.S. stock market and a temporary upswing in the dollar provided a lift to the U.S. economy between 1995 and 1997, this is a fragile, and in many ways, false, prosperity. Many "fundamentals" are unsound: (1) unsustainable, excessive U.S. imports that greatly exceed exports; (2) dependence upon large inflows of foreign capital to sustain $150–200 billion in annual U.S. current account deficits; (3) long-term stagnation in U.S. real wages; (4) substantial and widespread underemployment (with *real* unemployment in the 9–10 percent range); (5) greatly enlarged U.S. federal debt loads since 1980 (from one-third to two-thirds of GNP); (6) continued large increases in federal debt ($200 billion annually); (7) stock market advances in the U.S. since 1990 that greatly exceed the increases in corporate earnings and profits; (8) an overvalued dollar resulting from heavy inflows of foreign investment (in spite of large U.S. trade and current account deficits); and (9) reduced economic growth due to large U.S. trade and current deficits (since the mid-1980s). In most countries these numbers would undermine economic confidence, especially when prosperity depends upon foreign capital inflows and speculative momentum.[53]

Already Federal Reserve Chairman Alan Greenspan warned that this speculative boom could be peaking out. Unfortunately, the more a speculative boom gets out of hand, the larger a corrective downsurge is likely. That is what happened in 1928–29 as a U.S. stock market boom galloped ahead to its rendezvous with destiny[54] (see Tables 5.1 and 5.2).

Failure by the United States to correct its external account deficits, restore trade reciprocity, and renew industrial vitality guarantees continued vulnerability to crises, and it assures relative stagnation and decline. Many other countries are expanding production and improving technology. The U.S. cannot afford to relax with passivity, letting its industries stagnate and decline. Unfortunately, recent stock market euphoria and unsustainable foreign investment into the U.S. (largely based on speculative impulses) cannot be relied upon by Americans to maintain their industrial base.

Good engineering, production operations, and marketing efforts require teamwork and continuity. In much of the American industrial scene there has been neglect. Thoughtful observers agree there has been a short-term, speculative, and stock market–oriented mentality. Entrepreneurial talent has been devoted in the U.S. to takeover games (both attack and defense). Not enough is devoted to building and maintaining first-class products, low-cost production, and responding to foreign competition (often subsidized, widely sheltered, and using marginal cost discounting into open markets like the U.S.). The U.S. government, at least for most manufacturing industries, has been a passive bystander.

The common response by apologists for one-way free trade, which ignores U.S. industrial decline and accumulated external deficits, is that currency

Table 5.1   Common Stock Prices and Yields, 1954–1998

| Year | Common Stock Prices [a] | | | | | | | Common Stock Yields | | |
| | New York Stock Exchange Indexes [b] (Dec. 31, 1965 = 50) | | | | | Dow Jones [b] Industrial Average | Standard & Poor's [b] Composite Index (1941-43=10) | (S&P)(in %) [d] | | (S&P) |
	Composite	Industrial	Transport. [c]	Utility [c]	Finance			Div./Price Ratio [e]	Earnings/Price Ratio [f]	P/E Ratio
1954	----	----	----	----	----	404.38	35.98	----	----	12.94
1955	21.54	----	----	----	----	442.72	45.48	4.08	7.95	12.71
1956	24.40	----	----	----	----	493.01	46.67	4.09	7.55	13.57
1957	23.67	----	----	----	----	475.71	39.99	4.35	7.89	11.78
1958	24.56	----	----	----	----	491.66	55.21	3.97	5.78	19.10
1959	30.73	----	----	----	----	632.12	59.89	3.23	5.78	17.63
1960	30.01	----	----	----	----	618.04	58.11	3.47	5.90	18.71
1961	35.37	----	----	----	----	691.55	71.55	2.98	4.62	21.25
1962	33.49	----	----	----	----	639.76	63.10	3.37	5.82	17.20
1963	37.51	----	----	----	----	714.81	75.02	3.17	5.50	18.16
1964	43.76	----	----	----	----	834.05	84.75	3.01	5.32	17.80
1965	47.39	----	----	----	----	910.88	92.43	3.00	5.59	17.45
1966	46.15	46.18	50.26	90.81	44.45	873.60	80.33	3.40	6.63	14.84
1967	50.77	51.97	53.51	90.86	49.82	879.12	96.47	3.20	5.73	17.67
1968	55.37	58.00	50.58	88.38	65.85	906.00	103.86	3.07	5.67	18.14
1969	54.67	57.44	46.96	85.60	70.49	876.72	92.06	3.24	6.08	15.08
1970	45.72	48.03	32.14	74.47	60.00	753.19	92.15	3.83	6.45	16.71
1971	54.22	57.92	44.35	79.05	70.38	884.76	102.09	3.14	5.41	18.31
1972	60.29	65.73	50.17	76.95	78.35	950.71	118.05	2.84	5.50	19.11
1973	57.42	63.08	37.74	75.38	70.12	923.88	97.55	3.06	7.12	12.25
1974	43.84	48.08	31.89	59.58	49.67	759.37	68.56	4.47	11.59	7.33

Table 5.1 (continued)

1975	45.73	50.52	31.10	63.00	47.14	802.49	90.19	4.31	9.15	11.70
1976	54.46	60.44	39.57	73.94	52.94	974.92	107.46	3.77	8.90	11.02
1977	53.69	57.86	41.09	81.84	55.25	894.63	95.10	4.62	10.79	8.75
1978	53.70	58.23	43.50	78.44	56.65	820.23	96.11	5.28	12.03	8.26
1979	58.32	64.76	47.34	76.41	61.42	844.40	107.94	5.47	13.46	7.42
1980	68.10	78.70	60.61	74.69	64.25	891.41	135.76	5.26	12.66	9.06
1981	74.02	85.44	72.61	77.81	73.52	932.92	122.55	5.20	11.96	8.07
1982	68.93	78.18	60.41	79.49	71.99	884.36	140.64	5.81	11.60	10.17
1983	92.63	107.45	89.36	93.99	95.34	1,190.34	164.93	4.40	8.03	12.41
1984	92.46	108.01	85.63	92.89	89.28	1,178.48	167.24	4.64	10.02	9.93
1985	108.09	123.79	104.11	113.49	114.21	1,328.23	211.28	4.25	8.12	13.47
1986	136.00	155.85	119.87	142.72	147.20	1,792.76	242.17	3.49	6.09	16.77
1987	161.70	195.31	140.39	148.57	146.48	2,275.99	247.08	3.08	5.48	15.41
1988	149.91	180.95	134.12	143.53	127.26	2,060.82	277.72	3.64	8.01	12.19
1989	180.02	216.23	175.28	174.87	151.88	2,508.91	353.40	3.45	7.41	14.70
1990	183.46	225.78	158.62	181.20	133.26	2,678.94	330.22	3.61	6.47	15.19
1991	206.33	258.14	173.99	185.32	150.82	2,929.33	417.09	3.24	4.79	21.85
1992	229.01	284.62	201.09	198.91	179.26	3,284.29	435.71	2.99	4.22	24.01
1993	249.58	299.99	242.49	228.90	216.42	3,522.06	466.45	2.78	4.46	23.55
1994	254.12	315.25	247.29	209.06	209.73	3,793.77	459.27	2.82	5.83	16.98
1995	291.15	367.34	269.41	220.30	238.45	4,493.76	615.93	2.56	6.09	17.41
1996	358.17	453.98	327.33	249.77	303.89	5,742.89	670.83	2.19	5.24	20.70
1997	456.54	574.52	414.60	283.82	424.48	7,441.15	872.72	1.77	——	24.53
1998 Peak[g]	——	——	——	——	——	9,162.27	1122.7	1.55	——	——
1998 Low[h]	——	——	——	——	——	7,580.42	927.69	1.62	——	——

Table 5.1 *(continued)*

Source: Columns corresponding to footnotes a–f (through 1996): Table B-93, "Common Stock Prices and Yields, 1955–1996," *Economic Report of the President,* February 1997. S&P PEs and 1997 data obtained from the Bloomberg Financial System and from <http://averages.dowjones.com>.

ªAverages of daily closing prices.

ᵇIncludes stocks as follows: for NYSE, all stocks listed (more than 2,000); for Dow Jones industrial average, 30 stocks; for S&P composite index, 500 stocks.

ᶜIn April 1993, the NYSE doubled the utility index value to facilitate options/futures trading. Annual indexes prior to 1993 reflect the doubling.

ᵈBased on 500 stocks in the S&P composite index.

ᵉAggregate cash dividends (based on latest annual rate) divided by the aggregate market value of closing prices. Annual figure from averages of monthly figures.

ᶠRatio of earnings (after taxes) for four quarters ending with quarter to price index for last day of that quarter. Annual figure based on average of quarterly ratios.

ᵍAs of April 17, 1998, the DJIA peaked on April 15, 1998; the S&P 500 peaked on April 3, 1998.

ʰAs of April 17, 1998, the DJIA reached its lowest point on January 9, 1998; the S&P 500 also reached its lowest point on January 9, 1998.

Table 5.2 NASDAQ Average Common Stock Prices, 1971–1998

Year	Composite	Industrial	Bank	Insurance	Other Finc.	Transport.	Telecom.	Utility	Biotech	Computer
1971	102.42	103.97	100.66	101.45	102.50	101.75	16.99	97.64	-----	-----
1972	128.52	133.20	109.75	136.52	136.38	122.68	16.60	95.40	-----	-----
1973	109.90	105.13	108.03	119.66	125.51	100.11	15.22	87.50	-----	-----
1974	76.29	72.84	81.77	84.10	84.39	78.68	10.85	62.38	-----	-----
1975	77.20	79.82	74.81	81.99	78.74	82.93	11.08	63.67	-----	-----
1976	89.90	94.70	83.59	91.92	91.02	98.40	13.22	76.01	-----	-----
1977	98.71	101.66	92.59	105.38	101.24	98.82	16.35	94.01	-----	-----
1978	117.52	126.36	103.30	123.75	114.88	106.44	18.43	105.91	-----	-----
1979	136.57	151.86	107.99	147.31	126.31	115.07	21.04	120.92	-----	-----
1980	168.61	206.48	109.42	160.78	137.09	138.78	24.39	140.17	-----	-----
1981	203.18	249.45	132.79	186.12	169.62	176.98	29.65	170.44	-----	-----
1982	188.97	216.81	139.91	194.52	174.96	165.64	36.31	208.70	-----	-----
1983	285.43	342.00	184.72	257.43	258.16	253.85	54.59	313.79	-----	-----
1984	248.88	277.55	206.78	256.52	273.81	229.24	38.53	221.50	-----	-----
1985	290.19	300.26	285.42	340.23	364.61	264.67	48.12	276.61	-----	-----
1986	366.96	367.27	410.17	430.57	492.74	336.24	57.31	329.42	-----	-----
1987	402.57	422.48	464.79	425.23	491.62	382.06	65.31	375.39	-----	-----
1988	374.43	379.49	444.14	408.17	457.16	365.30	75.87	436.10	-----	-----
1989	437.81	428.38	457.08	504.75	514.56	443.52	116.16	667.67	-----	-----
1990	409.17	430.56	318.90	471.27	419.29	445.78	99.66	572.83	-----	-----
1991	491.69	549.59	319.51	535.59	475.97	509.90	99.04	569.28	-----	-----
1992	599.26	654.61	438.50	660.49	662.39	584.33	112.47	646.46	-----	-----
1993	715.15	739.60	637.65	873.32	854.08	685.14	161.04	925.69	195.55	199.79
1994	751.65	769.28	723.22	909.65	908.43	721.92	163.69	940.89	166.81	209.43
1995	925.19	877.39	863.82	1,084.82	1,052.17	759.00	182.29	1,047.79	210.01	322.54
1996	1,164.96	1,061.49	1,100.17	1,314.50	1,348.54	862.37	215.49	1,238.65	301.16	430.78
1997	1,469.49	1,128.55	1,633.73	1,623.17	1,966.72	973.19	251.57	1,446.05	317.48	613.19
1998 [1]	1691.40	1,271.24	2,087.52	1,820.52	2,498.23	1141.79	343.86	1,976.52	315.56	703.71

Source: NASDAQ Daily Totals, <http://www.nasd.com>.
[1] 1998 average calculated form daily averages through March 31, 1998.

realignments solve any problems, effortlessly and smoothly. In other words, if world markets think U.S. external account deficits are excessive, the dollar gradually declines, and the mark, yen, pound, and euro increase in value. Thus, world markets, operating skillfully and efficiently, straighten out any disequilibria without any fuss or need for serious concern by the U.S. or any other governments.

But if this were so, why have there been recent, severe currency crises and financial disturbances? The big Japanese downfall in the Nikkei (late 1980s), the breakdown of the European Exchange Rate Mechanism in the early 1990s, the Mexican peso crisis of 1994, and Thai, Malaysian, Indonesian, and Philippine currency crises of 1997 illustrate that global financial markets are making really big miscalculations and costly blunders. Speculative booms and unrealistic euphoria were very significant in the 1990s. As Lester Thurow warned in 1996, the potential for the U.S. dollar to come down sharply in response to accumulated U.S. trade and current account deficits, and resurgent doubts about the U.S. industrial economy, is very great, indeed.[55] The U.S. economy and trade situation is like living on a great fault line for earthquakes. Pressures from accumulated distortions have been building up. A really "big one" could come anytime soon, or there could be a series of substantial, very disruptive shocks.

A big dollar devaluation could be quite damaging to the U.S., like Britain's 40 percent collapse of the pound in 1949 (when the pound was cut from $4.03 to $2.80).[56] Thereafter foreign investors no longer trusted the British pound as a serious place for liquidity. The role of the British pound as a reserve currency was undermined. Britain, like the United States today, was overextended, financially and militarily. Britain's trade and current account deficits in the late 1940s were large and could not be stopped by politically acceptable policies. Britain, like the U.S. today, was a large net debtor. Britain, like the U.S. today, suffered a weakened industrial base, and increasing challenge from foreign competitors.

How big a U.S. dollar downfall and correction in the U.S. stock market might occur? A 10–15 percent swing could be manageable and not that big a deal. But a 25–30 percent downfall would be seriously disruptive. Even more so a 40–60 percent downfall. Unfortunately, the bigger the downslide, the greater the potential for disruption. The growing U.S. dependence upon foreign capital makes its withdrawal, or need for much higher interest rates, very troublesome. Thus, with a bigger U.S. devaluation, great pressure will be exerted for increased U.S. interest rates (to compensate for risks of holding dollar financial assets). These tighter monetary pressures will be deflationary for the U.S. economy. But a sizable dollar devaluation brings inflationary pressures (increased prices for goods from abroad) to the U.S.

economy. Vicious, conflicting cross-currents will hit Americans as penalties for living beyond our means bear fruit. Economic slowdown, more unemployment, higher prices, and serious demoralization will follow.

Any presidential administration, whether Democratic or Republican, will be blamed for mismanagement of the economy. Unhappiness and cynicism will increase. Frustration will be directed at foreign governments, companies, and "profiteering speculators." Politicians will pass the buck to evil foreign influences.

What might trigger downfalls? Clearly the risk of downfall increases with higher dollar values and greater speculation in the stock markets. Sadly, these pressures feed each other in the final stages of a speculative bubble or euphoria. Specific triggers could come from many things: (1) An unexpected set of corporate, financial, or other economic losses (perhaps transmitted initially from abroad, e.g., Southeast Asia, Latin America, the Mideast, or Europe). (2) A costly military disaster (e.g., sinking U.S. carriers in the Persian Gulf, or surrender of sizable U.S. forces in Bosnia). (3) Major environmental disasters (e.g., earthquakes, big hurricanes, super-floods in the Mississippi valley, or crop failures traceable to El Niño). (4) Major riots and civil disturbances (in Los Angeles, Chicago, New York, Washington, D.C., and New York). In an overextended U.S. economy, with large and chronic external deficits, high stock market values (some say beyond justification), and an overvalued currency, bad things can happen.

Does it make sense to ignore warnings? To pretend bad things couldn't happen? Or even to avoid thinking of bad things, because it might trigger a correction or downfall? No! Responsible economic policy must take stock and implement corrective action. And the sooner, the better. Before things get worse, and we get more vulnerable.

Sadly, the U.S. neglected its economic fundamentals. Countries cannot live beyond their means. Heavy foreign borrowing to sustain a speculative boom is not healthy. U.S. imports must come back into balance with exports. To continue with big, unsustainable external deficits in these circumstances would be insanity, and grossly irresponsible mismanagement.

But to balance our trade accounts the U.S. must remedy its underlying structural asymmetries.[57] A patient, two-pronged effort must be made: (1) A new reciprocity-oriented U.S. trade policy must be implemented. This effort should be sustained for the next twenty years, a really long-term commitment. (2) U.S. industries must be renewed and brought up to speed with foreign competitors for the long haul. This effort should be sustained for the next twenty years. Engineering, product development, manufacturing, and international marketing take perseverance. U.S. companies, their American

Partners, and our government should work together for a new generation of U.S. industrial teamwork.

Does this mean the U.S. should withdraw from the world market? No, quite the contrary. But U.S. companies can only thrive and survive in tough world market competition with strong, uncompromising U.S. government support, a reciprocity-based trade policy, and a systematic renewal of America's industrial tradition, engineering, talent, and marketing success.

Sustainable Internationalism for Americans

American internationalism comes in three dimensions: (1) liberal democratic political ideology; (2) economic practices and trade policy; and (3) military power and alliance strategies.[58] From our beginning as a nation we felt the blessings of special democratic and liberal promise. But as a smaller, young country, we followed President Washington's advice not to get involved in foreign wars and European troubles. Instead, the United States focused mainly upon expansion to the West. Like most developing countries today, the U.S. used tariffs, infrastructure investment, and extensive educational efforts to promote industrial growth and prosperity.

The U.S. became a world power by the late 1890s, building a large navy and gathering colonies in the Philippines, Hawaii, Puerto Rico, and (for a while) Cuba. The U.S. began to compete more actively for exports. It sought an "open door" into restricted markets, although the American home market remained substantially protected. Being secure and separated by oceans from European and Asian conflicts, the U.S. was comfortable with a more independent, neutralist policy, with no need for significant alliances.

America's first major foreign intervention was World War I, crucial to Allied victory and Germany's defeat. President Wilson's creative idealism forged the League of Nations, but unwillingness to limit U.S. sovereignty defeated U.S. membership. Between the wars the U.S. receded into partial isolation, leaving world leadership mainly to Britain and France. This sufficed for the 1920s, a peaceful era, with reduced military budgets and few threats in the world.[59]

But the Great Depression changed all this. Hitler's German rearmament, Japanese invasions of Manchuria and China, and Italian conquest of Ethiopia undermined the peace. General rearmament followed. By the late 1930s British and French appeasement failed, and the Axis nations (Germany, Italy, and Japan) threatened further aggression. World War II followed (1939–45).

Initially the U.S. tried neutrality. But when Germany's blitzkrieg occupied France, the low countries, Denmark, and Norway (in addition to

Czechoslovakia and Poland), and later Yugoslavia and Greece, the Axis menace was too threatening. The U.S. heavily supported Britain, and later Russia, with Lend Lease Aid, and the U.S. cut off oil and other trade with Japan. Although Japan's attack at Pearl Harbor hurt the U.S. Navy temporarily, America's great industrial capacity allowed a massive mobilization. Within three years the U.S. created the world's biggest air force, the predominant navy and merchant marine, and more than 100 ground divisions. By 1944–45, at the Bretton Woods conference, the U.S. and Britain blocked out a post-war economic framework to promote free world prosperity.[60]

The United Nations organization was established in 1945–46 to promote a better, lasting world peace. Although the UN failed to bridge the Cold War conflict (1946–91) between the U.S. and the USSR, the multilateral institutions that complemented the UN have become very important. Some are now indispensable for the world economy. Most important is the International Monetary Fund (IMF). The IMF is a financial support system for countries troubled with balance of payments problems, and that need transitional help to ease crises. IMF support packages are linked, increasingly, to multinational banking loans, access to foreign direct investment, and trade finance flows. The World Bank provides more liberal, long-term infrastructure and development loans, above and beyond what market risks could absorb. World Bank loans, expertise, and assistance are very important for the poorest countries, and have been particularly productive in improving food supplies.

Happily, these multilateral financial institutions (IMF and World Bank), together with regional development banks in most parts of the world, are not tied to the policies of any particular country or regional bloc. They are multilateral, in a balanced, representative way. The IMF's Executive Board comprises twenty-four members (one for each major power), with a set of voting clusters that gives every part of the world a fair, but not excessive voice.[61] Neither the creditor countries nor the majority debtor countries can lord it over one or the other. The IMF binds them as marketplace partners, with supermajority requirements for any significant changes in IMF structure or policies (see Table 5.3).

Unfortunately, the new World Trade Organization (WTO) was together less carefully. EU countries have 15 votes, which together with 60 Lomé convention states (former European colonies) gives this grouping a voting majority. The U.S. received only one vote, a blatant imbalance problem. Furthermore, developing countries have a three-fourths voting majority in the WTO. Sadly, these imbalances combine with rigid, excessive preferences for developing countries in access to tariffs, trade restrictions, subsidies, and exchange controls. The result is entrenched trade asymmetries,

Table 5.3 IMF Executive Directors and Voting Power, September 3, 1997

Director Alternate	Casting Votes of	Total Votes	Percent of Fund Total[1]
APPOINTED			
Karin Lissakers *Barry S. Newman*	United States	265,518	17.78%
Bernd Esdar *Wolf-Dieter Donecker*	Germany	82,665	5.54%
Yukio Yoshimura *Hideaki Ono*	Japan	82,665	5.54%
Marc-Antoine Autheman *Ramon Fernandez*	France	74,396	4.98%
Gus O'Donnell *Jon Shields*	United Kingdom	74,396	4.98%
ELECTED			
Willy Kiekens (Belgium) *Johann Prader (Austria)*	Austria, Belarus, Belgium, Czech Republic, Hungary, Kazakhstan, Luxembourg, Slovak Republic, Slovenia, Turkey	75,983	5.09%
J. de Beaufort Wijnholds (Netherlands) *Yuriy G. Yakusha (Ukraine)*	Armenia, Bosnia and Herzegovina, Bulgaria, Croatia, Cyprus, Georgia, Israel, Macedonia, Moldova, Netherlands, Romania, Ukraine	74,276	4.97%
Juan Jose Toribio (Spain) *Javier Guzman-Calafell (Mexico)*	Costa Rica, El Salvador, Guatemala, Honduras, Mexico, Nicaragua, Spain, Venezuela	64,295	4.31%
Enzo R. Grilli (Italy) *Nikolaus Coumbis (Greece)*	Albania, Greece, Italy, Malta, Portugal, San Marino	59,987	4.02%
Thomas A. Bernes (Canada) *Charles X. O'Loghlin (Ireland)*	Antigua and Barbuda, The Bahamas, Barbados, Belize, Canada, Dominica, Grenada, Ireland, Jamaica, St. Kitts and Nevis, St. Lucia, St. Vincent and the Grenadines	55,500	3.72%
Eva Srejber (Sweden) *Benny Andersen (Denmark)*	Denmark, Estonia, Finland, Iceland, Latvia, Lithuania, Norway, Sweden	51,771	3.47%

Table 5.3 (continued)

Director Alternate	Casting Votes of	Total Votes	Percent of Fund Total [1]
ELECTED			
Abdulrahman A. Al-Tuwaijri (Saudi Arabia) Sulaiman M. Al-Turki (Saudi Arabia)	Saudi Arabia	51,556	3.45%
Dinah Z. Guti (Zimbabwe) Jose Pedro de Morais, Jr. (Angola)	Angola, Botswana, Burundi, Eritrea, Ethiopia, The Gambia, Kenya, Lesotho, Liberia, Malawi, Mozambique, Namibia, Nigeria, Sierra Leone, South Africa, Swaziland, Tanzania, Uganda, Zambia, Zimbabwe	51,292	3.43%
G.F. Taylor (Australia) Okyu Kwon (Korea)	Australia, Kiribati, Korea, Marshall Islands, Fed. States of Micronesia, Mongolia, New Zealand, Papua New Guinea, Philippines, Samoa, Seychelles, Solomon Islands, Vanuatu	49,182	3.29%
A. Shakour Shaalan (Egypt) Yacoob Yousef/Mohammed (Bahrain)	Bahrain, Egypt, Iraq, Jordan, Kuwait, Lebanon, Libya, Maldives, Oman, Qatar, Syrian Arab Rep., United Arab Emirates, Rep. of Yemen	47,646	3.19%
ZAMANI Abdul Ghani (Malaysia) Suharjo Joyosumarto (Indonesia)	Brunei Darussalam, Cambodia, Fiji, Indonesia, People's Dem. Rep. of Lao, Malaysia, Myanmar, Nepal, Singapore, Thailand, Tonga, Vietnam	43,505	2.91%
Aleksei V. Mozhin (Russia) Andrei Vernikov (Russia)	Russia	43,381	2.90%
Daniel Kaeser (Switzerland) Danuta Gotz-Kozierkiewicz (Poland)	Azerbaijan, Kyrgyz Rep., Poland, Switzerland, Tajikistan, Turkmenistan, Uzbekistan	41,229	2.76%
Abbas Mirakhor (Islamic Rep. of Iran) Mohammed Dairi (Morocco)	Afghanistan, Algeria, Ghana, Iran, Morocco, Pakistan, Tunisia	39,542	2.65%
Alexandre Kafka (Brazil) Hamid O'Brien (Trinidad & Tobago)	Brazil, Colombia, Dominican Republic, Ecuador, Guyana, Haiti, Panama, Suriname, Trinidad and Tobago	39,270	2.63%
M.R. Sivaraman (India) H.B. Disanayaka (Sri Lanka)	Bangladesh, Bhutan, India, Sri Lanka	38,561	2.58%
ZHANG Zhixiang (China) HAN Mingzhi (China)	China	34,102	2.28%

Table 5.3 *(continued)*

Director *Alternate*	Casting Votes of	Total Votes	Percent of Fund Total[1]
ELECTED			
A. Guillermo Zoccali (Argentina) *Nicolas Eyzaguirre (Chile)*	Argentina, Bolivia, Chile, Paraguay, Peru, Uruguay	31,985	2.14%
Koffi Yao (Cote d'Ivoire) *Alexandre Barro Chambrier (Gabon)*	Benin, Burkina Faso, Cameroon, Cape Verde, Central African Republic, Chad, Comoros, Congo, Cote d'Ivoire, Djibouti, Equatorial Guinea, Gabon, Guinea, Guinea-Bissau, Madagascar, Mali, Mauritania, Mauritius, Niger, Rwanda, São Tome and Principe, Senegal, Togo	19,936	1.34%
Total		1,492,639 [2,3]	99.95% [4]

Source: IMF Executive Directors and Voting Power, General Department and Special Drawing Rights Department, September 3, 1997, International Monetary Fund, <http://www.img.org/external/p/sec/ memdir/eds.htm>.

[1] Percentages of total votes (1,493,331) in the General Department and the Special Drawing Rights Department.

[2] This total does not include the votes of Somalia, which did not participate in the 1996 Regular Election of Executive Directors. The votes of this member are 692, or 0.05% of those in the General Department and Special Drawing Rights Department.

[3] This total does not include the votes of the Democratic Republic of the Congo and Sudan, which were suspended effective June 2, 1994, and August 9, 1993, respectively, pursuant to Article XXVI, Section 2(b) of the Articles of Agreement.

compounded by WTO voting imbalances that cannot be adjusted to meet the changing needs of countries like the United States (which now needs more offsets and relief against excessive imports). Thus, the U.S. is faced with an imminent need to withdraw from the WTO, because the new "international trade regime" is not sustainable for vital U.S. interests (eliminating large trade and current account deficits, and rejuvenating its industrial base). So, the WTO and GATT 1994 either need a major overhaul (rather unlikely), or the U.S. should give its six months' notice for WTO withdrawal.[62]

In the world's first euphoria over the collapse of communism, and Allied victory (of nearly all countries) against Iraq's conquest of Kuwait in 1990–91, many concluded that a new era of consensus and multinational peacekeeping had been established. The mood in the early 1990s was like the mid-1920s, after Allied forces had withdrawn from the USSR, and major powers in Europe had signed the Locarno Pact.[63] No significant international conflicts among major countries were on the world's horizon. Even the intractable Arab-Israeli conflict seemed resolved in 1993, when after negotiations between Arafat's PLO and Israel's government, a provisional peace accord was reached.

Unfortunately, the world now seems less peaceful again. U.S. economic, military, and political strength is no longer sufficient to allow us to act unilaterally as the world's policeman, or as primary guarantor of world peace. U.S. budget cuts (with bipartisan support in Congress) brought a 35–40 percent reduction in U.S. military forces.[64] Some in the U.S. even press for drastic unilateral reductions in U.S. nuclear weapons, even though the Russian Parliament is unwilling to ratify the Start II nuclear force reductions (and the deadline for Russian ratification is extended to the year 2005). Present U.S. conventional force levels might not be enough to refight the Gulf War victory over Saddam Hussein in Kuwait. U.S. carrier task forces are cut from 15 to 10, U.S. warships from 450 to less than 300, U.S. combat divisions from 21 to 13, and the U.S. Air Force was cut by nearly 50 percent.

A growing alienation of Islamic nations from the Western NATO bloc suggests a possible Islamic alliance.[65] Turkey is blocked from EU membership. Progress in Arab-Israeli peace talks has broken down. Economic conditions are troubled in many Islamic countries (Algeria, Egypt, Turkey, Pakistan, Malaysia, and Indonesia) while Saudi Arabia and other Gulf states remain shaky. Large numbers of North Africans and Turks in Europe are sources of friction in EU countries. And Greek-Turkish conflicts show no sign of resolution. Iranian antagonism against the U.S. is well entrenched, while friendly relations and trade have been improving among Iran, other Islamic states, France, Germany, China, Japan, and even Russia. When some Islamic states (Pakistan, Iran, Iraq, or Syria) acquire nuclear weapons, the prospects for trouble with the U.S. (and perhaps NATO) increase. It is not clear how much longer the U.S. can maintain naval ascendancy in the Persian Gulf.

The Russian government is not strong from the U.S. and NATO viewpoint.[66] While Yeltsin is friendly to the West, his health and economy remain shaky. Military officer cadres are alienated, and most want a Great Russia policy that renews military, industrial, and economic power. Many Russians are worried about NATO expansion, the menace of China, and want stronger influence in the near abroad and the Mideast. Russian arms sales, including missiles and nuclear technology, are a tool for Russian policy, and leakages occur through black market or non-governmental transactions. Changes in Russia's government could produce strongly anti-U.S. policies.

China is feeling more tension with the U.S.[67] Although the Chinese still need U.S. and Western markets, technology, and capital, they resent human rights criticism or other pressures from abroad. China wants Taiwan isolated and militarily weakened. Meanwhile, China has been willing to sell significant weapons technology to Middle Eastern countries. But China's trade with the U.S. is so unbalanced now that the U.S. enjoys substantial import leverage. Another complication for China is growing unease among its Asian neighbors.

Relations between Japan and the U.S. are strained and need correction.[68] The Japan–U.S. trade deficit is the biggest and longest imbalance problem (lasting more than fifteen years). Frictions over continued U.S. bases in Japan are a problem, too. Many Japanese want a stronger military to offset China's growing strength, although whether Japan needs its own nuclear deterrent is an awkward question.

Although the U.S. regards EU countries as allies, frictions in U.S.–EU relations are a problem.[69] The EU naturally seeks consensus within Europe. But many experts see increased EU protectionism against outsiders. Trade conflicts from agriculture to airlines, commercial aircraft, banking and finance, fisheries, shipbuilding, telecommunications, and trade with Cuba, Libya, Iran, and Iraq are prickly. NATO expansion and EU enlargement are tough issues within Europe itself, and American views complicate the game. Few predict any fundamental demarche, but continued friction seems likely.

For most other countries in the world—India, the rest of Asia, Australia–New Zealand, the Americas and Africa—U.S. relations had been relatively comfortable. India has a federal democracy like that of the U.S. in many ways, although they insisted upon their own nuclear deterrent (against

China, Pakistan, and other dangers). Korea, Taiwan, and Southeast Asia have been good trading partners for the U.S., except that the U.S. allowed them to accumulate excessive trade surpluses, which need to be corrected. Australia and New Zealand are friendly democracies and good trading partners. In Latin America and the Caribbean, after a decade of economic slump from the debt overload crisis, market-oriented reforms are unleashing substantial economic growth. But Latin America is not ready for completely open trade with the United States. Africa has been widely troubled in recent years, although the new South African Republic shows promise as a multiracial society. The biggest problems in Africa have been weak, irresponsible military governments. Reliable property rights and incentives need to be established in many areas, but most of Africa can be more successful with internal reforms that create stable, productive teamwork.

In this world scene, three conclusions should be drawn. First, the United States lacks the economic, military, and political strength to enforce American-style institutions, marching orders, or policy prescriptions.[70] This means the U.S. cannot dictate what other countries should do in trade and industrial policy. Most countries want to decide these things themselves, and use selectively the best lessons from British, U.S., French, German, Swiss, Scandinavian, Japanese, Korean, Taiwanese, or Singaporean success. Each country tries to learn from the most productive, rapidly growing nations, and how that experience can be adapted most productively in their own cultures. To be sure, experts and scholars from the U.S. and other nations are welcome in this work, along with teams from the IMF and World Bank. Certainly world market forces, access to capital, loans, and investment affect what countries and governments can afford. Countries that default on loans, confiscate investments, or become unreliable trade partners pay penalties in the global marketplace. Access to trade, financing, and capital is valuable, and should not lightly be sacrificed. But the mix of responsible compromises, for good or ill, is a challenge for the relevant local authorities, national governments, or regional decision-makers (for trading areas like the EU, NAFTA, ASEAN, CIS, Mercosur, Andean Pact, Central American Common Market, Caribbean Basin Association, or Organization of African States).

Second, the U.S. must rely mainly upon its own efforts to eliminate excessive trade and current account deficits, renew industries, and strengthen technology. Other countries cannot assume responsibility for past U.S. self-neglect, and they will not volunteer concessions to rebalance U.S. trade flows. Other countries (and groupings like the EU, NAFTA, ASEAN, a revitalized CIS, or an Islamic bloc) naturally focus on their own needs, and internal political constituencies, and they will try to cut the best deal they can with the global marketplace. The U.S. must do likewise, and switch to a new, reciprocity-based trade policy. No longer can the U.S. afford to be the global banker, creditor, importer, and concessionaire of last resort. The U.S. suffers from a generation of stagnant real wages. Inequalities, poverty, and structural unemployment have increased. Americans must first take care of their own people. U.S. domestic politics enforce this priority. *For many purposes,* the global economy, international bankers, IMF, MNCs, and World Bank can take care of themselves. But the U.S. *can, should, and must* concentrate on getting a better, fair share of global industry, technology, trade, work, and profits. Other countries and regional blocs watch out for themselves. The U.S. should do no less. A strong, new Department of Industry, Technology, and Trade (DITT) must be established immediately by the U.S. to implement the new American trade policy.

Unfortunately, the GATT 1994 and WTO Agreement were deeply flawed from the standpoint of U.S. interests.[71] The WTO voting regime is badly unbalanced and should be replaced with an IMF-like Executive Board, GDP-weighted voting, and better balanced representation (Table 5.3). The WTO's excessive, rigid, and unsustainable preferences for developing countries needs correction. And the GATT 1994's weakening of national safeguard, unfair trade practice, and balance of payments relief measures should be corrected as well. The U.S. must press immediately for prompt solutions to these WTO problems, or give six months' notice of U.S. withdrawal to the UN Secretary General and the WTO Director General.

Third, the U.S. must implement a more realistic, overall foreign policy for the twenty-first century. A naïve faith in U.S. hegemony, U.S. predominance as the world's policeman, and the U.S. as beneficent law-giver to all is unworkable. Reality is more subtle, nuanced, and complex. The twenty-first century world is multipolar, with at least six or seven major power blocs (in economic, military, nuclear, and political terms). The U.S.–NAFTA, EU, Russia, China, Japan, India, and possibly an Islamic Alliance, are the world's major powers at 2000 (See Figure 5.1). An expanded ASEAN or some South American grouping might also be added to the major power listing.[72]

Clearly, none of these big six or seven regional powers (or blocs) is strong enough to dominate the others. But all the major powers are strong enough to enforce substantial deference and independence for themselves. Fortunately, most of the major world powers today understand their interdependence in a global economy and the fragile ecosphere of our planet earth. This means that regular IMF meetings, economic summit conferences among the major powers, and a broader UN Security Council will be the principal world forums for accommodation in the world economy. In this

Figure 5.1. **Major World Power Balances, 1550–2000**

At 1550

France	Hapsburg			China
Portugal	Spain-Austria	Turkey	India	

At 1650

Britain	Dutch	Sweden	Russia		China	
Spain		France	Austria	Turkey	India	Japan

At 1750

Britain	Prussia	Russia	China	
Spain	France	Austria	Turkey	Japan

At 1900

Britain	Germany		Russia	Japan
U.S.	France	Italy	Austria	China

At 1940

Britain	Germany	Russia	Japan
U.S.	France	Italy	China

At 2000

U.S.	E.U.		Russia	China
	(?) Islamic Alliance		India	Japan

multipolar system strong incentives will operate for the smaller, isolated states to affiliate with one or another of the major power blocs. This inner logic is evident already in political competition for memberships in the EU, NAFTA, and ASEAN expansion. This momentum could be influential in shaping possible economic-political blocs among Islamic states, and in South America. In a global economy of powerful regional blocs, smaller nations can be isolated, lonely, and marginalized in competition for export markets, fair treatment, and economic well-being.

We should not be alarmed at these regional developments. This does not mean the world is drifting toward increasing conflict, rivalry, or war. It does mean, however, that the twenty-first-century world is more complex than the bi-polar world of the late 1940s–91.[73] The successful blocs (those who get along with others) will accept realistically the logic of mutual self-restraint, and avoid excessive claims or interventions in other parts of the world. If the U.S. does not promptly adjust to the new reality, and instead tries to assert hegemonic priority over others, the reactions of other blocs will be unfriendly, hostile, and involve likely counter-measures. But collaboration among blocs for their joint advantage will be encouraged. And each major power, the United States, EU, Russia, China, Japan, India, and any others, must assure their own vital interests. Each major power will nurture and safeguard its own industries, technology, prosperity, and military strength.

Notes and References

All references to Chapters 1 and 5 are set forth after the Notes to Chapter 5. Notes and references are provided after Chapters 3 and 4 also, but sources for Chapter 2 are contained only in the Notes to Chapter 2.

Notes to Chapter 1

1. Lovett, *World Trade Rivalry,* 1987, provides many sources on British economic development, industrial and trade policies. But special emphasis should be given to Kitson and Solomou, *Protectionism and Economic Revival* (about the 1920s-30s), 1990; and Middlemas and Barnes, *Baldwin* (about the 1920s-30s), 1969. See also, Feis, *Europe: The World's Banker,* 1930. And see Aldcroft 1970, Cairncross and Eichengreen 1983. Finally, Kindleberger, *Financial History of Western Europe,* 2nd ed., 1993, is helpful for general background.

2. See Kindleberger 1993, generally, along with Cairncross 1983, James 1996, Kenen 1994, Funabashi 1989, Bergsten 1991, Dobson 1991, Volcker and Gyohten 1992, Root 1994, Bergsten 1996, and Blecker 1996.

3. For the significance of safeguard and unfair trade practice relief under GATT 1947, see Lovett, "Current World Trade Agenda: GATT, Regionalism and Unresolved Asymmetry Problems," 1994a; Lovett, Testimony before House Ways and Means Committee, 1994b; Jerome, *World Trade at the Crossroads: The Uruguay Round, GATT, and Beyond,* Economic Strategy Institute, 1992; and Mastel, *American Trade Laws After the Uruguay Round,* 1996. See also, Schott, *The World Trading System,* 1996; Jackson, *Antidumping Law and Practice,* 1989; Hufbauer and Erb, *Subsidies in International Trade,* 1984; and Jackson, *The World Trading Systems,* 2nd ed., 1997.

4. See, for example, Stein, *Fiscal Revolution in America,* 1990; and standard texts like Peterson and Estenson, *Income, Employment and Economic Growth,* 1992; Kidwell, *Financial Institutions Markets, and Money,* 1997, or Lovett, *Banking and Financial Institutions Law,* 1997.

5. See Thurow, *Future of Capitalism,* 1996; Blecker, *Beyond the Twin Deficits,* 1992; Godley, *A Critical Imbalance in U.S. Trade,* 1995; McKinnon, *Rules of the Game,* 1996; James, *International Monetary Cooperation Since Bretton Woods,* 1996; Erdman, *Tug of War,* 1996; Eichengreen, *International Monetary Arrangements for the Twenty-first Century,* 1994; and Dornbusch, *Exchange Rates and Inflation,* 1988.

In this connection, we should remember the fundamental importance of the overall "balance of produce and consumption" in Adam Smith, *Wealth of Nations,* at 464

(Modern Library, 1937). Smith explains that this overall balance determines whether a nation prospers or decays, pp. 81 and 464.

6. See this text, Tables 1.1 and 1.2. Also, Blecker 1992, Thurow 1996, Godley 1995, and Beinert 1997. Some foreign policy writers recognize the U.S. "twin deficits" as a problem. See Brzezinski 1993 (p. 109); Paul Kennedy's thesis of imperial over-stretch is illustrated by U.S. deficits in the 1980s-90s. See Kennedy, *Rise and Fall of Great Powers,* 1987.

7. A rough estimate of the shifting capital position for the U.S. can be suggested from its accumulated current account deficits. Thus, because the net creditor position of the U.S. was estimated in 1980 to be around +$141 billion and the accumulated current deficits between 1981 and 1997 totaled some $1,650 billion as of end 1997, the U.S. stands roughly –$1,500 billion in debt as of end 1997. Between the years 1981 and 1988, the U.S. net position went from +$141 billion to –$532 billion—a swing of –$671 billion in a period with about –$700 billion in current account deficits. *Survey of Current Business* (June issues). If the same valuation estimates were extended (based largely on historical costs), the net U.S. debtor position would have reached around –$1,500 billion by the end of 1997. Since June 1990, however, a different valuation procedure, based more upon contrasting stock market indexes, has been utilized by the *Survey of Current Business.* (June issues for most years, except October 1997). This new procedure yields a creditor position for the U.S. of +$374 billion in 1981 versus –$870 billion at end 1996. Either way, the U.S. net international investment position has suffered a major deterioration between 1981 and 1997, anywhere from –$1,250 to –$1,500 billion, depending upon the valuation procedure.

Recently, Michael R. Sesit, writing the Foreign Exchange column for the *Wall Street Journal,* November 4, 1997, at C1 and C26, estimated "America's net external debt—that Americans owe foreigners—of $1.2 trillion is roughly 15% of its total output. By contrast, the rest of the world owes Switzerland 130% of its gross national product, Japan about 23% and Germany 9%."

William Burke, a former Federal Reserve economist, estimated in mid-1995 that the U.S. net external debt was then $1,048 billion. See Burke 1995. We estimate that the net U.S. investment position is, *at the end of 1997,* at least –$1,250 billion, and it could be somewhat worse. Unfortunately for the *Survey of Current Business,* contrasting stock market indexes are complicated by major declines in Asian stock market values for 1997.

Finally, according to Muriel Seibert and Co., Inc., *Behind the Numbers,* April 1997, at p. 2, Foreign Ownership of the U.S. federal government's debt has risen to 27.61 percent in 1997. Thus, the willingness of foreign investors and governments to continue investing in U.S. debt *(or not)* has become a major factor in U.S. interest rates, economic growth prospects, and prosperity.

8. See Bergsten, "The Dollar and the Euro," 1997; together with Lovett, "World Trade Policies: Limits on Economic Integration," 1996; and Eichengreen, *European Monetary Unification,* 1997; Feldstein, "EMU and International Conflict," 1997; Templeton, *The European Monetary Crisis,* 1993; and Kenen, *EMU After Maastricht,* 1992.

9. A very large literature has developed since the early 1980s on the U.S. economic slowdown, job losses, industrial competitiveness problems, wage and earnings squeeze, growing inequality, and weakness in U.S. trade policies. See Choate and Schwartz 1980, Bluestone and Harrison 1982, Peterson and Estenson 1982, Reich and Magaziner 1982, Kuttner 1983, Zysman and Tyson 1983, Eckstein 1984, Lovett 1984, Culbertson 1985, Adams and Klein 1983, Phillips 1984, Johnson 1984, Shepherd 1983, Reich and Donahue 1985, President's Commission on Competitiveness 1985, Shutt 1985, Lamont 1986, Lodge and Vogel 1987, Cohen and Zysman 1987, Lovett 1987, Porter 1986,

Prestowitz 1988, Kaden and Lee 1988, Mishel and Simon 1988, Starr 1988, Kuttner 1989, Culbertson 1989, Fallows 1989a, 1989b, Van Wolferen 1989, McCraw 1989, Krugman 1990, Dertouzos 1990, Frieden and Lake 1991, Florida and Kenney 1990, Porter 1990, Derian 1990, Lodge 1990, Holbrooke 1991, Mishel and Frankel 1991, Reich 1991a, 1991b, Kuttner 1991, Graham 1992, Thurow 1992, Jerome 1992, Vargish 1992, Marshall and Tucker 1992, Kaden and Smith 1992, Kearns 1992, Wood 1992, Coote 1992, Lovett 1993, Newman 1993, Batra 1993, Perot and Choate 1993, Bergsten 1997, Tolchin 1993, Bernstein and Adler 1994, Goldsmith 1994, Fallows 1994, Layard 1994, Lovett 1994a, 1994b, Phillips 1994, Korten 1995, Godley 1995, Dryden 1995, Eckes 1995, Madrick 1995, Mishel and Bernstein 1995, Faux and Schafer 1996, Pozo 1996, Thurow 1996, Beinart 1997, Bernstein and Monro 1997, Greider 1997, Faux 1997, Mastel 1997, Wallach 1997, and Wolman and Colamosca 1997.

10. Most of the media-highlighted trade debate focused upon the NAFTA controversy. See, for example, Hufbauer and Schott, *NAFTA: An Assessment,* 1993, versus Perot and Choate, *Save Your Job, Save Our Country: Why NAFTA Must Be Stopped— Now,* 1993. Later, of course, after the Mexican peso collapsed in value by 60 percent in 1994–95, most of the U.S. export gains slumped, and a large U.S. trade deficit developed with Mexico. See Lovett, "Lessons from the Peso Crisis," 1996. Also, see Table 1.2, this text.

But the Uruguay GATT Round deal of 1991–94 led to controversy as well. See, for example, Jerome, *World Trade at the Cross-roads,* 1992; Lawrence and Schultze, *An American Trade Strategy,* 1990; Kuttner, *Managed Trade and Economic Sovereignty,* 1989; Blecker, *Beyond the Twin Deficits,* 1992; Prestowitz, *Trading Places: How We Allowed Japan to Take the Lead,* 1988; Lovett, *World Trade Rivalry,* 1987; Culbertson, *The Trade Threat,* 1989; Lovett, "Rethinking U.S. Trade Policy in the Post–Cold War Era," 1993; Lovett, "Current World Trade Agenda: GATT Regionalism, and Unresolved Asymmetry Problems," 1994a; Godley, *A Critical Imbalance in U.S. Trade,* 1995; Schott, *The World Trading System,* 1996; Jackson, *The World Trading System,* 2nd ed., 1997; Thurow, *The Future of Capitalism,* 1996; Lovett, "World Trade Policies: Limits on Economic Integration," 1996; and Blecker, *U.S. Trade Policy and Global Growth,* 1996.

Unfortunately, the only open debate on the final Uruguay Round GATT deal was held in a half day hearing before the House Ways and Means Committee, *Hearing,* "The World Trade Organization," June 10, 1994. Favoring the GATT deal were Mickey Kantor (USTR), Jeff Lang, Julius Katz, Bill Frenzel, and Willard Workman (U.S. Chamber of Commerce). Opposing were Pat Choate, Bruce Fein, and William Lovett. Hardly any media coverage was devoted to GATT 1994–WTO issues. (It seemed too complicated for most of the media and their reporters to cover.)

11. The GATT 1994–WTO deal needs careful review of its lengthy text to fully understand it.

Most of the text is set forth in the documentary supplements to two international trade law casebooks: Jackson, *International Economic Relations,* 3rd ed., 1995; and Bhala, *International Trade Law,* 1996. Limited selections of material relating to these issues is provided in the Jackson and Bhala casebooks. Remarkably, most U.S. economists and lawyers remain poorly informed on the Uruguay Round deal, i.e., GATT 1994 and the WTO. Favorable reviews are given by Schott, *The Uruguay Round: An Assessment,* 1994; Schott, *The World Trading System,* 1996; and Jackson, *The World Trading System,* 2nd ed., 1997. Critical evaluations and emphasis on the shortcomings are provided by Jerome, *World Trade at the Cross-roads,* 1992; Lovett, "Current World Trade Agenda: GATT, Regionalism, and Unresolved Asymmetry Problems," 1994a; and Mastel, *American Trade Laws After the Uruguay Round,* 1996.

12. The extent of job losses (or gains) from expanding world trade is an emotional issue. Divergent claims are offered by free trade enthusiasts versus labor-oriented and other critics. Unfortunately, the data have not been properly tabulated or disclosed, so that only "rough" estimates can be offered. An estimate of U.S. job flows and turnover between 1972 and 1988 was offered recently, but major ambiguities remain about its underlying data. See Stephen J. Davis et al., *Job Creation and Destruction.* 1997.

We must be clear about the crucial questions in estimating trade-related job losses and creation. The real problem for trade policy is to decide *by how much* U.S. manufacturing jobs (and collateral employment in communities) *would have grown faster, and not declined so much,* if a stronger, reciprocity-based U.S. trade policy had been enforced. Experts should agree that the U.S. opened up industrial markets substantially more than most of its trade partners, so that industrial growth, exports, and net jobs expansion were greater (in varying degrees) elsewhere. We concede that improved productivity and "fair trade" expansion probably required some U.S. downsizing and job relocation. But stronger U.S. trade policy that enforced effective reciprocity, greatly limited asymmetries, and used rationalization measures to keep more manufacturing in the U.S. would have "saved" a substantial number of U.S. jobs from the late 1960s through 1997. This author estimates that 8–9 million U.S. industrial jobs (and another 2–3 million collateral jobs in the affected communities) would have been "saved" by a stronger policy that used more systematic rationalization measures. This means that more U.S. economic growth, exports, and employment would have resulted on a cumulative, mutually reinforcing basis. Why were such measures not taken? Overly partisan politics, lack of interest by MNCs, rigid job-saving attitudes by unions, and a lack of concern and imagination by top U.S. leaders responsible for trade-industrial policies.

This is how the job losses played out by presidential administrations. Truman–Eisenhower: 300,000–500,000 job losses; U.S. economy growing substantially, still competitive, and only limited asymmetries. Kennedy–Johnson: 200,000–400,000 job losses; U.S. economy growing well, largely competitive, and only somewhat greater asymmetries. Nixon–Ford: 400,000–800,000 job losses; U.S. growth slowing, foreign competition increasing, and asymmetries accumulating (especially in NICs). Carter: 800,000–1 million job losses; increased foreign competition, more asymmetries, and U.S. trade policy encourages more job relocation abroad. Reagan: 2–3 million job losses; greater foreign competition pressures, major recession, and increased job relocation. Bush: 2–3 million job losses; more explicit U.S. job relocation policies with slowed domestic growth. Clinton: 2–3 million job losses; somewhat better growth, but continued U.S. job relocation policies. NAFTA 1993 and GATT 1994 trade deals entrench MNC influence and sustain job relocation trends. Note that until recent years no adequate U.S. government data were provided on jobs displacement. But some effort at disclosing these job losses was made in the *U.S. Statistical Abstract,* 1996, Table No. 635. Displaced Workers, by Selected Characteristics. These data reveal 10 million displaced workers between 1987 and 1993 (about half were involved in plant closings). These job loss estimates are consistent with the foregoing analysis, except that not all displaced workers in 1987–93 were trade related (and the job growth *foregone* by weakened U.S. manufacturing was not counted as displaced workers). A special problem, widely neglected, involves rural workers. See Podgursky, *Job Displacement and the Rural Worker,* 1989.

U.S. trade and current account deficits grew increasingly large and chronic since the mid-1970s, with U.S. imports exceeding exports. This should have been prevented by stronger U.S. trade and rationalization measures. U.S. imports should have been capped each year at U.S. export levels. U.S. manufacturing, exports, and balanced trade would have been somewhat larger since the mid-1970s, when serious asymmetries began to bite into U.S. industrial growth prospects. At each stage no drastic net increase in U.S. jobs, manufactures, and exports would have resulted, but the cumulative benefits for U.S. employment, economic growth, and industrial progress would have been substantial. These data are consistent with estimates provided in Chapter 2 that the U.S. economy probably lost around 1 percent per annum in real economic growth in recent years as a result of U.S. trade policy. See note 96, Chapter 2.

13. In other words, the U.S. must reemphasize its overall balance of production and consumption. See Adam Smith, *Wealth of Nations,* at 464 (Modern Library, 1937).

Notes to Chapter 2

1. John J. McCusker and Russell R. Menard, *The Economy of British America, 1607–1789* (Chapel Hill: University of North Carolina Press, 1985), p. 86.

2. On cotton diplomacy, see Frank L. Owsley, *King Cotton Diplomacy: Foreign Relations of the Confederate States of America* (Chicago, 1931); on oil see Daniel Yergin, *The Prize* (New York: Simon & Schuster, 1991), pp. 178, 183; Alfred E. Eckes, *The United States and the Global Struggle for Minerals* (Austin: University of Texas Press, 1979), pp. 15, 51.

3. U.S. Bureau of the Census, *Historical Statistics of the United States, Bicentennial Edition* (Washington: GPO, 1975), II; *Statistical Abstract of the United States* (various issues); and *Survey of Current Business* (June 1992 and July 1997).

4. McCusker and Menard, *Economy of British North America,* p. 357; Gerald Stourzh, *Benjamin Franklin and American Foreign Policy,* 2d ed. (Chicago: University of Chicago Press, 1969).

5. Alfred E. Eckes, Jr., *Opening America's Market: U.S. Foreign Trade Policy since 1776* (Chapel Hill: University of North Carolina Press, 1995), pp. 2–3; John Adams to John Jay, February 26, 1786, in Mary A. Giunta, ed., *The Emerging Nation: A Documentary History of the Foreign Relations of the United States under the Articles of Confederation, 1780–1789* (National Historical Records Commission) (Washington, DC: GPO, 1996), III:108–109. On Franklin's free trade vision, see Drew R. McCoy, "Benjamin Franklin's Vision of a Republican Political Economy for America," *William and Mary Quarterly* 35, no. 4 (October 1978): 605.

6. Eckes, *Opening America's Market,* pp. 5–6.

7. On problems in implementing the Franco-American commercial treaty, see Giunta, *Emerging Nation,* II:261–268, 844–846, 883, 917, 954, 958.

8. Samuel Shaw to John Jay, May 19, 1785, in Giunta, ed. *Emerging Nation,* II: 637–641; Foster Rhea Dulles, *The Old China Trade* (New York: AMS, 1970, reprint of 1930 ed.), p. 26; Elizabeth M. Nuzoll and Mary A. Gallagher, *The Papers of Robert Morris* (Pittsburgh: University of Pittsburgh Press, 1995), 8:857–865.

9. John Adams to John Jay, August 30, 1785, in Giunta, ed. *Emerging Nation,* II:785.

10. *Brown v. Maryland,* 25 U.S. 420 (1827).

11. Eckes, *Opening America's Market,* pp. 13–14.

12. Harold C. Syrett, ed., *The Papers of Alexander Hamilton* vol. 1, (New York: Columbia University Press, 1961–.), pp. 262, 285–286, 297.

13. Arthur H. Vandenberg, *The Greatest American: Alexander Hamilton* (New York: G.P. Putnam's Sons, 1921), p. 200; James D. Richardson, comp., *A Compilation of the Messages and Papers of the Presidents* (New York: Bureau of National Literature, 1917), 1:470.

14. Emory R. Johnson, T.W. Van Metre, G.G. Huebner, and D.S. Hanchett, *History*

of Domestic and Foreign Commerce of the United States (Washington, DC: Carnegie Institute, 1915), 2:3, 5. Jefferson also favored bilateral free trade agreements, but he insisted on strict reciprocity and enforcement. See Eckes, *Opening America's Market,* pp. 12–13.

15. Tariff data from Bureau of the Census, Historical Statistics of the United States, II:888. On Clay's system, Robert V. Remini, *Henry Clay: Statesman for the Union* (New York: Norton, 1991), pp. 225–233.

16. Hong Kong and Singapore may have relied more on free trade, but they are small city trading states. The former prospered on account of proximity and access to the large, but restricted, Chinese market. A strategic location and a development-minded government benefited the latter. Of course, not every nation that practiced protectionism pursued successful development policies. David Landes, *The Wealth and Poverty of Nations* (New York: Norton, 1998), pp. 265–268.

17. Kirk H. Porter and Donald Bruce Johnson, *National Party Platforms* (Urbana: University of Illinois Press, 1956), pp. 107, 123.

18. Elizabeth Feaster Baker, *Henry Wheaton, 1785–1848* (1937. Reprint, New York: Da Capo Press, 1971), pp. 235–253.

19. Naomi C. Miller, ed., *The Political Writings of Richard Cobden* (1903. Reprint, New York: Garland, 1973), 1:36; *Economist,* August 1843, pp. 14–15.

20. Edward Stanwood, *American Tariff Controversies in the 19th Century* (New York: Russell and Russell, 1903), pp. 2:41–45.

21. William Belmont Parker, *Life and Public Services of Justin Smith Morrill* (Boston: Houghton Mifflin, 1924), p. 320; *Congressional Globe,* February 5, 1857 (app., p. 226), April 23, 1860 (p. 1832).

22. Charles W. Calhoun, "Political Economy in the Gilded Age: The Republican Party's Industrial Policy," *Journal of Policy History* 8, no. 3 (1996): 304.

23. In 1932, cotton and tobacco amounted to 26 percent. U.S. Bureau of the Census, *Historical Statistics of the United States: Bicentennial Edition,* 2:889–898.

24. Ida M. Tarbell, *The Tariff in Our Times* (New York: Macmillan, 1911); Arthur Link, ed., *The Papers of Woodrow Wilson* (Princeton: Princeton University Press, 1982): 40:343, 372, 384.

25. Eckes, *Opening America's Market,* pp. 37–42.

26. National Association of Manufacturers, "Chronological Documents of NAM Positions on the Tariff and Reciprocity Agreements since 1895," April 1947, NAM Papers, Hagley Library, Box 196.

27. Eckes, *Opening America's Market,* pp. 82–84.

28. Richardson, *Messages,* 18:8939.

29. U.S. Tariff Commission, *Information Concerning Dumping and Other Unfair Foreign Competition in the United States and Canada's Anti-Dumping Law* (Washington, DC: GPO, 1919), pp. 22–23.

30. U.S. Census Bureau, *Statistical Abstract of the United States, 1929* (Washington, DC: GPO, 1930), p. 469.

31. Alfred E. Eckes, "Smoot–Hawley and the Stock Market Crash, 1929–1930," *International Trade Journal* 12, no. 1 (Spring 1998).

32. U.S. Bureau of the Census, *Historical Statistics,* II:888.

33. Eckes, *Opening America's Market,* pp. 100–139.

34. Ibid., pp. 44–45.

35. U.S. Senate, Committee on Finance, *Hearings on H.R. 8687,* 73d Cong., 2d sess., April–May 1934, pp. 1, 7; Edgar B. Nixon, ed., *Franklin D. Roosevelt and Foreign Affairs* (Cambridge: Harvard University Press, 1969): 2:1–3.

36. Fowler and Hawkins memo, February 13, 1935, Committee on Trade Agreements, RG 353, National Archives.

37. Eckes, *Opening America's Market,* pp. 145–146. On Roosevelt's views, see William Phillips Papers, February 14, 16, 1935, Houghton Library, Harvard University.

38. Emphasis added. U.S. House of Representatives, Committee on Ways and Means, *Report to Accompany H.J. Res. 96,* 75th Cong., 1st sess., H. Rept. 166, pp. 1–2.

39. William Diebold, Jr., *The End of the I.T.O., Essays in International Finance,* No. 16, (Princeton: Princeton University, Department of Economics, 1952), p. 4.

40. See generally David Broscious, "One World into Two Worlds: The Evolution of U.S. Grand Strategy, 1947–1950," doctoral diss., Ohio University, 1997, pp. 196–202.

41. Philip Cortney, "Havana ITO Charter: A Dishonest Document," *Vital Speeches,* June 1, 1949, pages 490–493.

42. American Tariff League, *The Story Behind GATT,* (New York: American Tariff League, 1955), p. 19; Diebold, *End of the I.T.O.*

43. George Bronz, "An International Trade Organization: The Second Attempt," *Harvard Law Review* 69, no. 3 (1956): 440–482.

44. U.S. House of Representatives, Ways and Means Committee, *The Agreement on the Organization for Trade Cooperation,* H.R. 5550, 84th Cong., 2d sess., House Report 2007, 1956, page 47.

45. U.S. Tariff Commission, *Operation of the Trade Agreements Program* [OTAP] (19th Report, 1967), (Washington, DC: U.S. Tariff Commission, 1969): 240–241; Reginald Maudling to Prime Minister Macmillan, October 27, 1959, BT 11/5771, Public Record Office, Kew, England. See also Alan S. Milward and George Brennan, *Britain's Place in the World: A Historical Enquiry into Import Controls 1945–1960* (London: Routledge, 1996).

46. Unpublished pages from "memoirs," Truman Library, Independence, MO.

47. Ferrell, *Eisenhower Diaries* (New York: Norton, 1981), p. 242; Dwight D. Eisenhower, *Public Papers of the Presidents,* 1957, pp. 460–462.

48. Truman, *Public Papers of the Presidents,* 1947: 167–172.

49. U.S. President, *Public Papers of the Presidents: Dwight Eisenhower,* 1954, pp. 585–590.

50. Minutes of meetings on February 22, March 27, and April 18, 1955, International Trade File, box 234, RG 43.

51. Minutes, March 26, 1955, International Trade Files, RG 43, NA.

52. Quotes from various meetings February 22 to April 18, 1955, box 234, International Trade Files, RG 43, NA.

53. U.S. President, *Public Papers . . . Johnson,* 1968, p. 199; 1967, pp. 1073, 1148; U.S. Tariff Commission, *Operation of the Trade Agreements Program,* 19th Report, 1967, TC Pub. 287, pp. 170–174.

54. Gilbert to Nixon, June 15, 1969, WHCF, RMN; Public Law 93–618, 93d Cong., H.R. 10710, January 3, 1975.

55. U.S. Tariff Commission, *Trade Barriers* (Invs. 332–66 and 332–67) (TC Pub. 665) (Washington, DC: U.S. Tariff Commission, 1974), 8:113.

56. Data from John W. Evans, *The Kennedy Round in American Trade Policy: The Twilight of the GATT?* (Cambridge: Harvard University Press, 1971), p. 253; U.S. Tariff Commission, *Operation of the Trade Agreements Program, 1967* (Washington, DC: U.S. Tariff Commission, 1967), p. 172.

57. Steve Dryden, *Trade Warriors: USTR and the American Crusade for Free Trade* (New York: Oxford University Press, 1995), pp. 107–109.

58. U.S. Department of State, *Bulletin,* July 31, 1967, pp. 127–29.

59. Author's interview with Eugene Stewart, trade lawyer representing domestic industries, September 18, 1996.

60. Tun Razak quote from Mohd Ariffin, "A Fantasy Theme Analysis of Selected

Speeches of Tun Abdul Razak Hussein on the Issues of New Economic Policy in Malaysia 1971–1975," M.A. thesis, Ohio University, Athens, Ohio, 1989. Rajah Rasiah, "Free Trade Zones and Industrial Development in Malaysia," in Jomo, *Industrializing Malaysia,* pp. 118–146.

61. U.S. International Trade Commission, *Year in Trade 1995: Operations of the Trade Agreements Program* (Washington, DC: GPO, 1996), p. 79. U.S. Trade Representative, Annual Report on National Trade Estimates (Foreign Trade Barriers) (1985–).

62. U.S. Senate, Committee on Finance, *Trade Reform Act of 1974,* 93d Cong., 2d sess., November 26, 1974, report no. 93–1298, pp. 11, 94.

63. I.M. Destler, *Making Foreign Economic Policy* (Washington, DC: Brookings Institution, 1980), pp. 151–190.

64. Committee on Finance, *Trade Reform Act of 1974,* pp. 94–95; Pub. Law 93–   , secs. 103–104.

65. U.S. International Trade Commission, *Operation of the Trade Agreements Program,* 31st Report 1979, pp. 29–56.

66. Thomas R. Graham, "Results of the Tokyo Round," *Georgia Journal of International and Comparative Law* 9 (1979): 153–179; Leslie Alan Glick, *Multilateral Trade Negotiations: World Trade after the Tokyo Round* (Totowa, NJ: Rowman and Allanheld, 1984); Gilbert R. Winham, *International Trade and the Tokyo Round Negotiation* (Princeton: Princeton University Press, 1985), pp. 164–167; Strauss to Carter, June 5, 1979, Jimmy Carter Library; R. Michael Gadbaw, "Reciprocity and its Implications for U.S. Trade Policy," *Law & Policy in International Business* 14 (1982): 718–720.

67. Susan C. Schwab, *Trade Offs: Negotiating the Omnibus Trade and Competitiveness Act* (Boston: Harvard Business School Press, 1994), p. 45; U.S. House of Representatives, Committee on Ways and Means, *Multilateral Trade Negotiations,* 96th Cong., 1st sess., April 27, 1979, pp. 498–502; U.S. President, *Public Papers of the President: Jimmy Carter,* 1979, I:944.

68. Ibid., 4–10, 415–438.

69. U.S. Senate, Committee on Finance, *Trade Agreements Act of 1979,* 96th Cong., 1st sess., Report No. 96–249, July 17, 1979, pp. 234–236. But see Thomas O. Bayard and Kimberly Ann Elliott, *Reciprocity and Retaliation in U.S. Trade Policy* (Washington, DC: Institute for International Economics, 1994), pp. 26–27.

70. U.S. Senate, Committee on Finance, *MTN and the Legal Institutions of International Trade,* 96th Cong., 1st sess., 1979, CP 96–14, p. 14; Glick, *Multilateral Trade Negotiations,* p. 174.

71. U.S. International Trade Commission, *Operation of the Trade Agreements Program* (42nd Repoɪ .990) (USITC pub. 2403, July 1991), pp. 53–54.

72. U.S. House of Representatives, Committee on Government Operations, *Buy America Act of 1987, Hearings,* in H.R. 1750, 100th Cong., 1st sess., March 25, 1987, pp. 2, 15; AFL-CIO, "States Should Keep Their 'Buy America' Laws Intact," (1990?).

73. Finance Committee, *Trade Agreements Act of 1979,* pp. 162–165. U.S. Census Bureau, *Statistical Abstract of the United States,* 1986, pp. 809–817; 1990, pp. 804–815; *Survey of Current Business,* June 1992, pp. 90–92; July 1997, pp. 64–65.

74. U.S. House of Representatives, Committee on Energy and Commerce, Subcommittee on Oversight and Investigations, *Unfair Foreign Trade Practices: Barriers to U.S. Exports,* 99th Cong., 2d sess., committee print 99–BB, May 1986, p. 2; U.S. Senate, Committee on Finance, *Omnibus Trade Act of 1987,* Report on S. 490, 100th Cʌng., 1st sess., June 12, 1987, Report 100–71, pp. 2–3.

75. Trade data from *Survey of Current Business,* June 1992, pp. 90–91. Exchange rate from *Economic Report of the President, 1997,* p. 422. Data on debt from U.S. Treasury *Bulletin,* various issues; and *Survey of Current Business,* July 1997, p. 64.

76. Congressional Research Service, *Protectionist Policies of Major U.S. Trading Partners* (April 30, 1986), in House Commerce Subcommittee, *Unfair Trade Practices,* p. 33–34; President's Export Council, *Coping with the Dynamics of World Trade in the 1980's* (Washington, DC: December 1984), pp. 165–173.

77. William A. Niskanen, *Reaganomics: An Insider's Account of the Policies and the People* (New York: Oxford University Press, 1988), p. 137.

78. U.S. President, *Public Papers of the President: Ronald Reagan,* 1987, pp. 476–478.

79. U.S. International Trade Commission, Operations of the Trade Agreements Program, 36th Report, 1984 (Washington, DC: June, 1986) (USITC pub. 1725), pp. 26–33. B.R. Mitchell, *International Historical Statistics: Africa, Asia & Oceania, 1750–1988* (New York: Stockton Press, 1995), p. 585; *Washington Post,* April 23, 1985, p. C-4; Israel, Central Bureau of Statistics, worldwide web [http://cbs.gov.il/shnaton/ st08–05.gif]; U.S. Trade Representative, *Foreign Trade Barriers,* 1997, pp. 178–180.

80. Data from World Bank, *World Tables 1991;* Mitchell, *International Historical Statistics: The Americas, 1750–1988,* pp. 431, 446; Mitchell, *International Historical Statistics: Africa, Asia & Oceania, 1750–1988,* pp. 530, 585.

81. U.S. International Trade Commission, *Operation of the Trade Agreements Program,* 39th Report 1987, pp. 1-5 to 1-12.

82. *Survey of Current Business,* July 1997, p. 94.

83. For a summary of the NAFTA agreement, see U.S. International Trade Commission, *The Year in Trade, 1992: Operation of the Trade Agreements Program* (44th report) (USITC Pub. 2640), July 1993, pp. 1–13.

84. U.S. International Trade Commission, *The Year in Trade 1993: Operation of the Trade Agreements Program* (45th report)(USITC Pub. 2769), June 1994, pp. 55–63.

85. U.S. Senate, Committee on Finance, *NAFTA and Related Side Agreements, Hearing,* 103d Cong., 1st sess., September 15, 1993, pp. 25–33.

86. *Washington Post,* July 20,1993; *Business Week,* November 22, 1993, pp. 32–42; *Washington Post,* July 1, 1993.

87. Robert C. Shelburne, "U.S.–Mexico Trade Under NAFTA: Two Different Years, Two Different Stories," in Denise Dimon, Irene Gutierrez Tomlinson, and Susan E.W. Nichols, eds., *Competitiveness in International Business and Trade* (Laredo: Texas A&M International University, May 1996), III:670–671.

88. See dissenting opinion of Judge Malcolm Wilkey in Softwood Lumber Products from Canada, ECC-94–1904–01USA

89. Paul Volcker and Toyoo Gyohten, *Changing Fortunes: The World's Money and the Threat to American Leadership* (New York: Times Books, 1992), p. 189.

90. U.S. Senate, *Uruguay Round Agreements Act,* Joint Report of the Committee on Finance, Committee on Agriculture, Nutrition and Forestry, and Committee on Governmental Affairs, 103d Cong., 2d sess., Report 103–412, pp. 3–12.

91. U.S. House of Representatives, Committee on Ways and Means, *Uruguay Round Trade Agreements, Texts of Agreements, Implementing Bill, Statement of Administrative Action, and Required Supporting Statements,* 103d Cong., 2d sess., Sept. 27, 1994, pp. 1–2.

92. *Wall Street Journal,* November 2, 1994; Roll Call, May 2, 1994.

93. National Association of Manufacturers, draft no. 4, Jan. 21, 1994.

94. Patti Goldman and Richard Wiles, *Trading Away U.S Food Safety,* Washington, DC: Public Citizen, April 1994.

95. "Online Original: A Deeper Look at the Numbers," *Business Week,* September 16, 1997; "Freer Trade Gets an Unfriendly Reception," *Business Week,* September 22, 1997, p. 34.

96. J. Steven Landefeld and Robert P. Parker, "BEA's Chain Indexes, Time Series,

and Measures of Long-Term Economic Growth," *Survey of Current Business* 77, no. 5 (May 1997): 56–68. For other analysis of this data, Pat Choate and Charles McMillion, *The Mysterious U.S. Trade Deficit* (Washington, DC: Manufacturing Policy Project, May 1997).

In most discussions of the monthly trade data, pundits and economists devote little attention to the relationship between the persistent deficit and economic growth. Elementary textbooks usually offer a flow-of-expenditures approach to national income accounting. It explains that total expenditures in the economy on final goods and services (GNP) are composed of four basic items: private consumption expenditures (C), private domestic investment expenditures by businesses (I), government expenditures (G), and net exports of goods and services ($X - M$, that is foreign purchases of U.S. goods and services minus U.S. purchases of foreign goods and services). The equation is GNP = $C + I + G + (X - M)$. Simply stated, it follows from the above that if imports exceed exports, and other items on the right side of the equation remain constant, trade deficits suppress the growth of GNP. And, when GNP is reduced, the flow of earnings to workers, corporations, and the government are negatively impacted.

Using gross domestic product (GDP), a concept virtually identical with GNP, the Department of Commerce's Bureau of Economic Analysis recalculated the economic measures of long-term growth, and reported data assessing the component contributions of real GDP growth over decades since 1930. This data, which the bureau says is more reliable for periods close to 1992, show that the trade deficits in the period from 1980 have exerted a significant drag on economic growth in every year since 1982. See J. Steven Landefeld and Robert P. Parker, "BEA's Chain Indexes, Time Series, and Measures of Long-Term Economic Growth," *Survey of Current Business* 77, no. 5 (May 1997): 58–68. For 1996, for example, balance in exports and imports, rather than a deficit of $113.6 billion in chained 1992 dollars, would have increased the rate of growth from 2.4 percent to 4.1 percent, other items remaining equal. This would have increased U.S. jobs appreciably.

Economist Peter Morici, an adjunct senior fellow at the Economic Strategy Institute, recently concluded that "persistent trade deficits have lowered the growth of labor productivity and potential real GDP in the Unites States by about 0.5 to 0.6 percentage points per year." See Peter Morici, "Trade Deficits Reconsidered," *Journal of Commerce,* October 21, 1997, at 8A; and Morici, *The Trade Deficit: Where Does It Come From and What Does It Do?* (Washington, DC: Economic Strategy Institute, October 1977).

Notes to Chapter 3
(References to Chapter 3 follow.)

1. Some argue that "Ricardo never made use of the comparative cost idea in his criticism of the Corn Laws but relied instead on absolute cost differences" (Gomes 1990, 5); to argue that the free trade movement was based on science, note Cunningham 1904, or on politics, Condliffe 1950, 203–236.

2. For a sampling of a large literature that exists relevant to the view of American long-term economic decline and the need to change policy and economic structure: Bernstein and Adler 1994; Blecker 1996; Cuomo Commission 1992; Dertouzos, Lester and Solow 1989; Madrick 1995; Mishel, Bernstein, and Schmitt 1997; Peterson 1994; and Schafer and Faux 1996. The issue is, of course, debated; many disagree (Nau 1991).

3. Though diverse in nature, the most frequently noted cultural lag occurs when material culture manifests maladjustment in need of institutional adjustment; see Brinkman and Brinkman 1997.

4. Although there were predecessors, the origination of free trade theory is credited to Adam Smith, Viner 1965, pp. 91–92, and on the history: Bhagwati 1964; Chipman 1965; and Gomes 1990.

5. Whereas Viner 1965, 437–526; and Gomes 1990, 8–9; referred to Ricardo's matrix of comparative costs as a "Doctrine," some in the literature refer to the "Law" (Deardorff 1980). "This is one of the most important and still unchallenged laws of economics, with many practical applications" (Salvatore 1998, 30); and Paul Samuelson in Levisohn, Deardorff, and Stern 1995, p. 22.

6. "[A]lmost a quarter of the whole Wealth of Nations, is devoted to an exposition or scathing criticism of that which Adam Smith conceived mercantilism to be" (Heckscher 1934, vol. 1, p. 29). And on mercantilism, Heckscher 1955, and Viner 1968.

7. Myrdal 1957, 46, 39–49, draws a distinction between that of an "oppressor state" characteristic of mercantilism and that of a "welfare state" characterizing the twentieth century.

8. Marshall apparently conceded that mercantilism was "consistent with a national organization of external trade" and the advent of industrialism (1927, 41–51).

9. Kindleberger's work (1973) has resulted in many discussions concerning the relevancy of global hegemony, be it British or American, to the successful operation of the global economy; note also, Blecker 1996, 12–19.

10. Viner, in dealing with "The Emergence of Free-Trade and Laissez-Faire Doctrine," states that "The history of free-trade doctrine is largely a history of a phase of laissez-faire doctrine" in Irwin 1991, 54–62, 85–113, and 200–225; see also Condliffe 1950, 135–168. Viner notes, however, that Adam Smith was not that doctrinaire in his conception of the policy of laissez faire.

11. Kindleberger 1996, 134; "Moreover, in this supposedly laissez-faire period, India, far from being evacuated, was subjected to intensive development as an economic colony along the best mercantilist lines." Gallagher and Robinson 1953, 4; and Semmel 1970.

12. Bhagwati 1964; ". . . not under any obligations to make foreign payments excepting those arising from trade, so that in equilibrium the exports of each country exchange for her imports" (Marshall 1949, 1).

13. Meier 1968, 22, 216; and, "[S]uch development has to be pictured as an outward movement in the production possibility curve" (Haberler 1968, 107).

14. Free trade served as an "Engine of Development" for Britain but an "Engine of Growth" for the LDC world. The important distinction between growth and development will be dealt with in the next chapter.

15. H. Flam and M.J. Flanders in Heckscher and Ohlin 1991, 1, 25, 30.

16. "Now it is true that the theory of comparative costs is static" (Haberler 1968, 106); "the trade theory discussed thus far is completely static in nature" (Salvatore 1998, 185). Heckscher also draws attention to the fact of the static nature of the classical laissez-faire world view, but the mercantilists were equally guilty (1934, vol. 1, pp. 23–26).

17. Knight 1921, xix; and Klein 1977, 13–14; the conception of a dynamic economics offered by Kuznets (1930) is noteworthy. On general discussions of the static versus dynamic issue: Baumol 1968; Blatt 1983; Klein 1977; Kuznets 1930; and Machlup 1963.

References, Chapter 3

Baumol, William J. 1951. *Economic Dynamics.* New York: Macmillan.

———. 1968. "Statics and Dynamics in Economics." Vol. 15: 169–77, in D.L. Sills, ed., *International Encyclopedia of the Social Sciences.* New York: Macmillan, The Free Press.

Bernstein, Michael, and David E. Adler, eds., 1994. *Understanding American Economic Decline.* New York: Cambridge University Press.

Bhagwati, J.N. 1964. "The Pure Theory of Trade." *Economic Journal* 74 (March): 1–84

Blatt, John M. 1983. *Dynamic Economic Systems: A Post Keynesian Approach.* Armonk, NY: M.E. Sharpe.

Blecker, Robert A. 1996. *U.S. Trade Policy and Global Growth.* Armonk, NY: M.E. Sharpe.

Bloomfield, Arthur I. 1994. *Essays in the History of International Trade Theory.* Brookfield, VT: Edward Elgar.

Brinkman, June E., and Richard L. Brinkman. 1997. "Cultural Lag: Conception and Theory." *International Journal of Social Economics* 26, no. 4: 609–627.

Chipman, John. 1965. "A Survey of the Theory of International Trade: Part 2, The Neo-Classical Theory." *Econometrica* 33 (October): 685–761.

Condliffe, J.B. 1950. *The Commerce of Nations.* New York: W.W. Norton.

Cunningham, W. 1904. *The Rise and Decline of the Free Trade Movement.* London: C.J. Clay.

Cuomo Commission on Competitiveness Staff. 1992. *America's Agenda: Rebuilding America's Strength.* Armonk, NY: M.E. Sharpe.

Deardorff, Alan V. 1980. "The General Validity of the Law of Comparative Advantage." *Journal of Political Economy* 88 (October): 941–957.

Dertouzos, Michael L., Richard K. Lester, and Robert M. Solow. 1989. *Made in America.* Cambridge, MA: MIT Press.

Dosi, Giovanni, Keith Pavitt, and Luc Soete, eds., 1990. *Economics of Technical Change and International Trade.* New York: New York University Press.

Dosi, Giovanni, Laura D'Andrea Tyson, and John Zysman. 1989. "Trade Technologies and Development: A Framework for Discussing Japan" pp. 3–38. In Chalmers Johnson, Laura D'Andrea Tyson, and John Zysman, eds., *Politics and Productivity.* New York: Harper Business.

Dowd, Douglas. 1993. *U.S. Capitalist Development since 1776.* Armonk, NY: M.E. Sharpe.

Ellsworth, P.T. 1969. *The International Economy.* New York: Macmillan.

Gallagher, John, and Ronald Robinson. 1953. "The Imperialism of Free Trade." *Economic History Review,* 2nd Series, 6: 1–15.

Gomes, Leonard. 1990. *Neoclassical International Economics: An Historical Survey.* New York: St. Martin's Press.

Haberler, Gottfried. 1968. "International Trade and Economic Development," pp. 103–112. In James D. Theberge, ed., *Economics of Trade and Development.* New York: John Wiley.

———. 1979. "The Present Economic Malaise," pp. 261–90. In William Fellner, ed., *Contemporary Economic Problems.* Washington, DC: American Enterprise Institute.

Heaton, Herbert. 1948. *Economic History of Europe.* New York: Harper and Row.

Heckscher, Eli. 1955. *Mercantilism.* 2 vols. New York: Macmillan.

Heckscher, Eli, and Bertil Ohlin. 1991. *Heckscher–Ohlin Trade Theory.* Cambridge, MA: MIT Press.

Irwin, Douglas A., ed., 1991. *Jacob Viner: Essays on the Intellectual History of Economics.* Princeton: Princeton University Press.

Jones, Ronald W., and Peter B. Kenen, eds., 1984. *Handbook of International Economics,* vol. 1. Amsterdam: Elsevier, North Holland.

Kindleberger, Charles P. 1973. *The World in Depression.* Berkeley: University of California Press.

———. 1996. *World Economic Primacy: 1500–1990.* Oxford: Oxford University Press.

Klein, Burton. 1977. *Dynamic Economics*. Cambridge, MA: Harvard University Press.

Knight, Frank H. 1921. *Risk Uncertainty and Profit*. Boston: Houghton Mifflin.

———. 1951. "Statics and Dynamics," pp. 161–186. In *The Ethics of Competition and Other Essays*. New York: Augustus M. Kelley.

Kuznets, Simon. 1930. "Static and Dynamic Economics." *American Economic Review* 20 (September): 426–441.

———. 1973. "Modern Economic Growth: Findings and Reflections,"[Nobel laureate address] *American Economic Review* 63 (June): 247–258.

Levinsohn, Jim, Alan V. Deardorff, and Robert M. Stern, eds., 1995. *New Directions in Trade Theory*. Ann Arbor: University of Michigan Press.

MacDonald, Glenn M., and James R. Markussen. 1985. "A Rehabilitation of Absolute Advantage." *Journal of Political Economy* 93 (April): 277–297.

Machlup, Fritz. 1963. "Static and Dynamics: Kaleidoscopic Words," pp. 9–41. In *Essays on Economic Semantics*. Englewood Cliffs, NJ: Prentice-Hall.

Madrick, Jeffrey. 1995. *The End of Affluence*. New York: Random House.

Marshall, Alfred. 1927. *Industry and Trade*. London: Macmillan.

———. 1949. *The Pure Theory of Foreign Trade: The Pure Theory of Domestic Values*. London: The London School of Economics and Political Science.

Meier, Gerald M. 1968. *The International Economics of Development*. New York: Harper and Row.

Mill, John S. 1911. *The Principles of Political Economy*. London: Longmans.

Mishel, Lawrence, Jared Bernstein, and John Schmitt. 1997. *The State of Working America, 1996–1997*. Armonk, NY: M.E. Sharpe.

Myint, H. 1958. "The 'Classical Theory' of International Trade and Underdeveloped Countries." *Economic Journal* 68 (June): 317–337.

Myrdal, Gunnar. 1957. *Rich Lands and Poor*. New York: Harper.

Nau, Henry R. 1990. *The Myth of America's Decline*. New York: Oxford University Press.

Packard, Laurence B. 1948. *The Commercial Revolution: 1400–1776*. New York: H. Holt.

Peterson, Wallace C. 1994. *The Silent Depression*. New York: W.W. Norton.

Robinson, Joan. 1980. "Reflections on the Theory of International Trade," pp. 130–145. In *Collected Economic Papers*, vol. 5. Cambridge, MA: MIT Press.

Rostow, Walt W. 1968. *The Stages of Economic Growth*. Cambridge: Cambridge University Press.

Salvatore, Dominick. 1998. *International Economics*. New York: Macmillan.

Samuelson, Paul. 1939. "The Gains from International Trade." *Canadian Journal of Economics and Political Science* 5 (May): 195–205.

———. 1970. *Economics*. New York: McGraw-Hill.

Schafer, Todd, and Jeff Faux, eds., 1996. *Reclaiming Prosperity*. Armonk, NY: M.E. Sharpe.

Schumpeter, Joseph A. 1954. *History of Economic Analysis*. New York: Oxford University Press.

———. 1983. *The Theory of Economic Development*. New Brunswick: Transaction Books.

Smith, Adam. 1937. *The Wealth of Nations*. New York: Random House.

Thurow, Lester. 1992. *Head to Head*. New York: William Morrow.

———. 1996. *The Future of Capitalism*. New York: William Morrow.

Viner, Jacob. [1937] 1965. *Studies in the Theory of International Trade*. New York: Augustus M. Kelley.

———. 1952. *International Trade and Economic Development*. Glencoe, IL: The Free Press.

—————. 1968. "Mercantilism." Vol. 4, pp. 435–443. In the *International Encyclopedia of the Social Sciences*. New York: Macmillan, The Free Press.

Notes to Chapter 4

(References to Chapter 4 follow.)

1. The problem addressed by Ricardo was not absolute costs, but the "ratios between costs," and that "imports could be profitable even though the commodity imported could be produced at less cost at home than abroad" (Viner 1965, 338–341).

2. "The most opulent nations, indeed, generally excel all their neighbours in agriculture as well as manufactures; but they are commonly more distinguished by their superiority in the latter than in the former" (Smith 1937, 6).

3. "[T]he nineteenth-century theory of international division of labor . . . is hardly tenable" (Kuznets 1968, 3, 80).

4. For the sequential pattern of "logistical surges" relevant to transportation technology and general culture evolution, see Brinkman 1995, 1181.

5. The "Principle of Similitude," Bell 1974, 163–174, provides a framework from which to combine Hart's "logistic surges" and Schumpeter's "creative destruction."

6. Mill 1911, 351. "Mill's hypothetical history of economic development through international trade now strikes us as roseate, naïve" (Hughes 1970, 6–7).

7. In his Nobel address, Kuznets (1973) draws attention to these basic characteristics of modern economic growth.

8. On the conception of social technology, Kuznets 1968, 2, 17, and 35; and, "The social sciences are increasingly called upon to develop a new social technology" (Myrdal 1958, 14); also see Brinkman 1997.

9. Given the "Dichotomy of Useful Knowledge," to change technology is to change culture (civilization), in that culture is made up of the technics of technology, not all of culture but, rather, the "core of culture" (Brinkman 1995, 1183).

10. "The new growth theory, while advertising its break from traditions, in fact has stayed very close to the status quo ante," but there is a need to pioneer into the domain of "cultural and institutional factors" (Nelson 1997, 35, 39); also Bernstein and Adler 1994, 379, 383.

11. In numerous instances Grossman and Helpman endorse the traditional trade theory and the Heckscher–Ohlin model (1991, 187, 191, and 204), and are further supported by Baldwin 1992.

12. Consequently it is through a larger market size and the division of labor that a nation improves upon Schumpeterian innovation and absolute advantages embodied in machines of manufacturing, such as the "fire engine" (steam engine) (Smith 1937, 9, 1–12); also Young 1928.

13. Certainly, enough has been written on the paradigmatic blinders and lack of relevancy of orthodox economic analysis: Kindleberger 1982; Bernstein and Adler 1994, 361–393; Whalen 1996.

14. On a central issue, jobs and wages, the orthodox view—'This volume offers strong skepticism concerning the evidence in support of the fear that freer trade has been pushing down the wages of the unskilled" (Bhagwati and Kosters 1994, xii), also see Levy and Murnane 1992—is challenged, among others, by Mishel, Bernstein, and Schmitt 1997; Belman and Lee 1996; and Wood 1994.

15. And while many nations give lip service to free trade, which nations really practice or want it? Batra 1993; and Shutt 1985.

16. While Adam Smith (1937, 31) felt that wealth is translated into economic power, but not necessarily political, a large and growing literature argues the converse, espe-

cially relevant to the MNC: Greider 1997; Bowman 1996; Korten 1996; Harrison 1994; and Dugger 1989.

17. Madrick 1995; Bernstein and Adler 1994; Peterson 1994; Cuomo Commission 1992; and, "I think the changes are in favor of sclerosis and decline" (Kindleberger 1996, 190).

18. In international economics, the Swan diagram (Salvatore 1998, 576) offers a model devoid of structural transformation and comprised of three basic macroeconomic policy options: exchange rate manipulation, plus both monetary and fiscal policy. Dertouzos, Lester, and Solow (1989, 38), among others, argue that macroeconomic policy, alone, is not enough.

References, Chapter 4

Abramowitz, Moses. 1993. "The Search for Sources of Growth: Areas of Ignorance, Old and New." *Journal of Economic History* 53 (June): 217–243.

Arndt, H.W. 1981. "Economic Development: A Semantic History." *Economic Development and Cultural Change* 29 (April): 457–466.

Atlantic Institute. 1970. *The Technology Gap: U.S. and Europe.* New York: Praeger.

Baldwin, Robert E. 1992. "Are Economists' Trade Policy Views Still Valid?" *Journal of Economic Literature* 30 (June): 804–809.

Batra, Ravi. 1993. *The Myth of Free Trade.* New York: Charles Scribner's Sons.

Baumol, William J. 1951. *Economic Dynamics.* New York: Macmillan.

Bell, Daniel. 1973. *The Coming Post Industrial Society.* New York: Basic Books.

Belman, Dale, and Thea M. Lee. "International Trade and the Performance of U.S. Labor Markets," pp. 61–107. In R.A. Blecker, ed., 1996.

Bernstein, Michael A., and David E. Adler, eds., 1994. *Understanding American Economic Decline.* New York: Cambridge University Press.

Bhagwati, Jagdish, and Marvin H. Kosters, eds., 1994. *Trade and Wages: Leveling Wages Down?* Washington, DC: AEI Press.

Blecker, Robert A. ed., 1996. *U.S. Trade Policy and Global Growth.* Armonk, NY: M.E. Sharpe.

Bloomfield, Arthur I. 1994. *Essays in the History of International Trade Theory.* Brookfield, VT: Edward Elgar.

Bowman, Scott R. 1996. *The American Corporation and American Political Thought: Law Power and Ideology.* University Park: Pennsylvania State University Press.

Brinkman, Richard E. 1992. "Culture Evolution and the Process of Economic Evolution." *The International Journal of Social Economics* 19: 248–267.

———. 1995. "Economic Growth versus Economic Development: Toward a Conceptual Clarification." *Journal of Economic Issues* 29 (December): 1171–1188.

———. 1997. "Toward a Culture-Conception of Technology." *Journal of Economic Issues* 31 (December): 1027–1038.

Clower, Robert, George Dalton, Mitchell Hawitz, and A.A. Walters. 1966. *Growth Without Development: An Economic Survey of Liberia.* Evanston, IL: Northwestern University Press, 1966.

Crystal, Graef S. 1991. *In Search of Excess: The Overcompensation of American Executives.* New York: W.W. Norton.

Culbertson, John M. 1989. *The Trade Threat and U.S. Trade Policy.* Madison, WI: 21st Century Press.

Cuomo Commission on Competitiveness. 1992. *America's Agenda: Rebuilding America's Strength.* Armonk, NY: M.E. Sharpe.

Dertouzos, Michael L., Richard L. Lester, and, Robert M. Solow. 1989. *Made in America.* Cambridge: MIT Press.

Dosi, Giovanni, Keith Pavitt, and Luc Soete. 1990. *The Economics of Technological Change and International Trade.* New York: New York University Press.

Dosi, Giovanni, Laura D'Andrea Tyson, and John Zysman. 1989. "Trade Technologies and Development: A Framework for Discussing Japan," pp. 3–38. In C. Johnson, L. Tyson, and J. Zysman, eds., *Politics and Productivity.* New York: Harper Business.

Dugger, William M. 1989. *Corporate Hegemony.* Westport, CT: Greenwood Press.

Easterlin, Richard A. 1996. *A Growth Triumphant: The Twenty-first Century in Historical Perspective.* Ann Arbor: University of Michigan Press.

Findlay, Ronald. 1984. "Growth and Development in Trade Models," pp. 185–236. In R.W. Jones and P. Kenen, eds., *Handbook of International Economics,* vol. 1. Amsterdam: Elsevier, North Holland.

Friedman, Milton, and Rose D. Friedman. 1980. *Free to Choose.* Newark: Harcourt Brace Jovanovich.

Galbraith, John Kenneth. 1994. *A Journey Through Economic Time.* Boston: Houghton Mifflin.

Gillis, Malcolm, Dwight H. Perkins, Michael Roemer, and Donald R. Snodgrass. 1992, 1996. *Economics of Development.* New York: W.W. Norton.

Greider, William. 1997. *One World, Ready or Not: The Manic Logic of Global Capitalism.* New York: Simon & Schuster.

Griffin, Keith, and Terry McKinley. 1994. *Implementing a Human Development Strategy.* New York: St. Martin's Press.

Grossman, Gene M., and Elhanen Helpman. 1991. *Innovation and Growth in the Global Economy.* Cambridge: MIT Press.

Hammonds, Keith H. 1997. "Freer Trade Gets an Unfriendly Reception." *Business Week* (September 22): 34.

Harrison, Bennet. 1994. *Lean and Mean.* New York: Basic Books.

Hart, Hornell. 1946. "Technological Acceleration and the Atomic Bomb" *American Sociological Review* 11 (June): 277–293.

Hughes, Jonathan. 1970. *Industrialization and Economic History.* New York: McGraw-Hill.

Johnson, Chalmers. 1995. *Japan: Who Governs?* New York: W.W. Norton.

Johnson, Chalmers, Laura D'Andrea Tyson, and John Zysman, eds. 1989. *Politics and Productivity.* New York: Harper Business.

Kindleberger, Charles P. 1982. "Assets and Liabilities of International Economics: The Postwar Bankruptcy of Theory and Policy," pp. 47–64. In F. Caffe, ed., *Experiences and Problems of the International Monetary System.* Siena, Italy: Monte Dei Paschi Di Siena.

———. 1996. *World Economic Primacy: 1500–1990.* New York: Oxford University Press.

Korten, David C. 1996. *When Corporations Rule the World.* West Hartford, CT: Kumarian Press.

Kreinen, Mordechai E. 1998. *International Trade: A Policy Approach.* Fort Worth, TX: The Dryden Press.

Kroeber, Alfred A., and Clyde Kluckholm. 1952. *Culture: A Critical Review of Concepts and Definitions.* Cambridge, MA: Peabody Museum.

Krugman, Paul. 1986. *Strategic Trade Policy and the New International Economics.* Cambridge: MIT Press.

———. 1997. "What Should Trade Negotiators Negotiate About?" *Journal of Economic Literature* 35 (March): 113–120.

Kuznets, Simon. 1959. *Six Lectures on Economic Growth.* New York: Macmillan.

———. 1966. *Modern Economic Growth.* New Haven: Yale University Press.

————. 1968. *Toward a Theory of Economic Growth: With Reflections on the Economic Growth of Modern Nations.* New York: W.W. Norton.

————. 1989. *Economic Development, the Family, and Income Distribution.* New York: Cambridge University Press.

————. 1973. "Modern Economic Growth: Findings and Reflections" [Nobel laureate address]. *American Economics Review* 63 (June): 247–258.

Levinsohn, Jim, Alan V. Deardorff, and Robert M. Stern, eds., 1995. *New Directions in Trade Theory.* Ann Arbor: University of Michigan Press.

Levy, Frank, and Richard J. Murnane. 1992. "U.S. Earnings Levels and Earnings Inequality: A Review of Recent Trends and Proposed Explanations." *Journal of Economic Literature* 30 (September): 1333–1381.

Lucas, Robert E. 1988. "On the Mechanisms of Economic Development." *Journal of Monetary Economics* 22 (July): 3–42.

McClintock, Brent. 1996. "International Trade and the Governance of Global Markets," pp. 225–255. In C.J. Whalen, ed., 1996.

McCord, Norman. 1970. *Free Trade: Theory and Practice from Adam Smith to Keynes.* Newton Abbot, UK: David and Charles.

Madrick, Jeffrey. 1995. *The End of Affluence.* New York: Random House.

Marshall, Alfred. 1927. *Industry and Trade.* London: Macmillan.

Meier, Gerald M. 1968. *The International Economics of Development.* New York: Harper and Row.

Meier, Gerald M., and Robert E. Baldwin. 1959. *Economic Development.* New York: John Wiley and Sons.

Mill, John S. 1911. *The Principles of Political Economy.* London: Longmans.

Mishel, Lawrence, Jared Bernstein, and John Schmitt. 1997. *The State of Working America 1996–97.* Armonk, NY: M.E. Sharpe.

Myrdal, Gunnar. 1957. *Rich Lands and Poor.* New York: Harper.

————. 1974. "What Is Development?" *Journal of Economic Issues* 8 (December): 729–736.

Nelson, Richard. 1997. "How New Is New Growth Theory?" *Challenge* 40 (September–October): 29–58.

New York Times. 1996. *The Downsizing of America.* New York: Times Books.

North, Douglas C. 1961. *The Economic Growth of the United States 1790–1860.* Englewood Cliffs, NJ: Prentice-Hall.

————. 1990. *Institutions, Institutional Change and Economic Performance.* New York: Cambridge University Press.

Peterson, Wallace C. 1994. *Silent Depression.* New York: W.W. Norton.

Porter, Michael E. 1990. *The Competitive Advantage of Nations.* New York: The Free Press.

President's Commission on Industrial Competitiveness. 1985. *Global Competition. The New Reality,* vol. 1. Washington, DC: Government Printing Office.

Ricardo, David. 1912. *The Principles of Political Economy and Taxation.* London: J.M. Dent.

Schafer, Todd, and Jeff Faux, eds. 1996. *Reclaiming Prosperity.* Armonk, NY: M.E. Sharpe.

Scott, Maurice Fitzgerald. 1989. *A New View of Economic Growth.* New York: Oxford University Press.

Schumpeter, Joseph A. 1947. *Capitalism, Socialism and Democracy.* New York: Harper and Brothers.

————. 1983. *The Theory of Economic Development.* New Brunswick, NJ: Transaction Books.

Shutt, Harry. 1985. *The Myth of Free Trade.* Oxford: Oxford University Press.

Solow, Robert F. 1957. "Technological Change and Aggregate Production Function." *The Review of Economics and Statistics* 39 (August): 312–320.

Soros, George. 1997. "The Capitalist Threat" *The Atlantic* 329 (February): 45–70.

Thurow, Lester. 1996. *The Future of Capitalism.* New York: William Morrow.

Todaro, Michael P. 1989. *Economic Development in the Third World.* New York: Longman.

Viner, Jacob. 1952. *International Trade and Economic Development.* Glencoe, IL: The Free Press.

———. 1965. *Studies in the Theory of International Trade.* New York: Augustus M. Kelley.

Whalen, Charles J., ed., 1996. *Political Economy for the 21st Century.* Armonk, NY: M.E. Sharpe.

Wood, Adrian. 1994. *North-South Trade, Employment and Inequality.* Oxford: Clarendon Press.

Young, Allyn A. 1928. "Increasing Returns and Economic Progress." *Economic Journal* 38 (December): 527–542.

Notes to Chapter 5

1. In note 12 of Chapter 1 we considered the net job losses from a weaker U.S. trade-industrial policy that failed to enforce reciprocity and overall balance in U.S. trading activities. Since the mid-1970s the U.S. lost about 10–12 million U.S. jobs from "weaker" trade policy, and perhaps another 1.5 million jobs were lost between 1945 and 1975. But if the U.S. had retained these jobs, and nurtured more export manufacturing (without allowing trade deficits since the mid-1970s), the cumulative U.S. economic growth would have been stronger. In the end, U.S. GNP by 1997 would have been at least 10 percent larger, and perhaps even 20 percent higher. Obviously, these estimates assume that U.S. industry, manufacturing, and economic growth would have benefited from a more level playing field, stronger export nurturing, industrial rationalization measures, and the elimination of significant U.S. trade deficits.

2. In the 1997 debates over expanded fast-track authority, to allow more trade deals like NAFTA, critics emphasized the dangers of weakened environmental standards, reduced food, drug, and other consumer protection and safety standards, and an erosion of import surveillance that would bring even larger volumes of illegal drug trafficking. See, for example, Matt Witt and Steve Trossman, "NAFTA, Round Two," *Working USA,* September–October 1997.

3. See Table 1.1, Chapter 1.

4. Only a few allies (e.g., De Gaulle's France) grumbled about U.S. profits from "seigniorage," but it was clear that no other U.S. ally could afford to maintain a reserve currency comparable to the dollar area. After the British pound was heavily devalued in 1949 and 1967, no other currency but the dollar was strong enough to assume major reserve currency responsibilities. In September 1997, the dollar constituted almost 60 percent of currency reserves ($423 billion out of a global total of $762 billion in government currency reserves were held in dollars), while 14 percent were in German marks and 6 percent in Japanese yen. David Wessel, "Dollar's Share of World Reserves Grows," *Wall Street Journal,* September 10, 1997, at A2.

5. For the impact of trade deficits see Culbertson 1989, Blecker 1992, Godley 1995, Lovett 1996a,1996b,1996c, Blecker 1996, Thurow 1996, Thomas 1997, Choate and McMillion 1997, Morici 1997, and Aliber 1997. With respect to globalization and

MNCs see Lodge 1990, Kuttner 1991, Vargish 1992, Newman 1993, Graham 1992, Coote 1992, Goldsmith 1994, Fallows 1994, Adler and Bernstein 1994, Peterson 1994, Madrick 1995, Korten 1995, Hirst 1996, Lovett "Limits on Integration" 1996c, Greider 1997, and Wolman and Colamosca 1997.

6. Macroeconomic adjustment cannot be avoided. Sooner or later, and for most countries sooner, current account deficits must be eliminated. See Cairncross and Eichengreen 1983, Dornbusch 1988, Kenen 1994, Helleiner 1994, Godley 1995, McKinnon 1996, James 1996, Lovett 1996c, Erdman 1996, and Murphy 1997. Of special importance was Adam Smith's emphasis upon the *overall balance* of "produce and consumption," *Wealth of Nations,* at 464 (Modern Library, 1937). Although Smith urged that less attention be paid to some bilateral trading imbalances, as part of his overall case for *laissez faire* internally, Smith recognized three exceptions to freer trade internationally: (i) national defense and the maritime industry (pp. 429–431); (ii) retaliation against restrictions or distortions by other nations (pp. 434–435); and (iii) easing displacement costs (pp. 435–436). But Smith also stressed the special productivity of manufactures and public works (pp. 410–414 and 651–716). Only a modest extension of Smith's reasoning explains the protective tariff and national development policies of Alexander Hamilton, Friedrich List, and Henry Clay, especially for countries like the U.S. and Germany that needed to catch up with British industrial progress.

7. The unique, long sustained "boom" in U.S. stock prices from the early 1980s to 1998 also helps explain continuing capital inflows into the U.S. But some argue that U.S. increases of stock prices, recently at least, constitute a speculative "bubble." Accordingly, many fear a substantial downward correction, as bad as or worse than the October 1987 correction or downslide in U.S. stock prices. Experts differ, however, on how much, if any correction, is "required" for the next several years (Tables 5.1 and 5.2).

8. See Table 1.2 (Chapter 1) for bilateral trade balances. And see Lovett, "Lessons from the Recent Peso Crisis in Mexico," 1996a; Witt and Trossman, "NAFTA, Round Two," 1997; Faux, "NAFTA'S Rules Don't Work," 1997.

9. See "Rescuing Asia," *Business Week,* November 4, 1997, pp. 116–132. South Korea and Japan also suffered financial stresses. Fortunately, the Fifty-Second Annual Meetings of the IMF (Hong Kong, 1997) concluded with an agreement to increase quotas (IMF capitalization) by 45 percent, and a doubling of SDR allocations. This will greatly increase IMF liquidity resources at a crisis period for global financial markets (with strains in Asia and another emerging markets, and a stressful challenge from the euro against the dollar). See *IMF Survey* 26:18; 289–292. October 6, 1997.

10. See Cohen and Zysman 1987, Prestowitz 1988, Vargish 1988, Fallows "Containing Japan" 1989a, Culbertson 1989, Kuttner 1989, Lodge 1990, Dertouzos 1990, Kearns 1992, Thurow 1992, Jerome 1992, Blecker 1992, Graham 1992, Perot and Choate 1993, Lovett "Current World Trade Agenda" 1994a, Phillips 1994, Godley 1995, Thurow 1996, Blecker 1996, and Beinart 1997.

11. OECD, *The New World Trading System, Readings,* Paris: OECD, 1994, Tables 1 and 4 (at pp. 47, 50), summarizes the trade-weighted tariff averages pre-Uruguay (post-Uruguay) for many countries. Thus, trade weighted average tariffs were for the U.S. 5.4 (3.5) percent, E.C. 5.7 (3.6), Japan 3.9 (1.7), Canada 9.0 (4.8), Australia 20.1 (12.2), New Zealand 23.8 (11.9), South Africa 24.6 (17.3), Argentina 38.2 (30.9), Brazil 40.7 (27.0), Chile 34.9 (24.9), Colombia 44.3 (35.3), Costa Rica 54.9 (44.1), India 71.4 (32.4), Indonesia 20.4 (36.9), S. Korea 18.0 (8.3), Malaysia 10.0 (9.1), Romania 11.7 (33.9), Senegal 13.7 (13.8), Sri Lanka 28.6 (28.1), Thailand 35.8 (28.1), Tunisia 28.3 (40.3), Turkey 25.1 (22.3), Uruguay 20.9 (30.9), Venezuela 50.0 (31.1). Thus, net tariff reductions for most NICs are not drastic, which leaves significantly protective tariffs in place.

12. See Paul Kennedy, *Rise and Fall of Great Powers,* 1987. And see Huntington 1996, Brzezinski 1997, Mahbubani 1994, Bodansky 1993, Miller 1995, Kohout 1995, Lehman 1988, Myers 1997, and Bernstein and Munro 1997. In "America's Defense Policy," *Economist,* November 15, 1997, at pp. 26–27, we see that U.S. defense spending has come down from $400 billion to $250 billion (in 1998 dollars) between 1991 and 1998, a 40 percent reduction. See also, IISS, *Strategic Balance, 1997–98,* 1997, for a breakdown in U.S. force reductions.

13. See Peterson, *Silent Depression,* 1994. Also, see Mishel and co-authors, *The State of Working America,* 1989, 1991, 1993, 1995, and 1997. And see Adler and Bernstein 1994; Kuttner 1989, 1991, and 1997; Newman 1993; Layard 1994; Phillips 1994; Madrick 1995; and Wolman and Colamosca 1997. (Also, from this text Chapter 1, *supra,* see Tables 1.1–1.6).

14. Most countries do not have large or disproportionate trade surpluses with the United States.

15. A few EU countries have developed fairly large trade surpluses with the U.S., most notably Germany ($16 billion), Italy ($10 billion), France ($4.5 billion), and Sweden ($4 billion) in 1996. But Western Europe as a whole has only a moderate trade surplus, i.e., $20 billion on exports to the U.S. of $147 billion and imports from the U.S. of $127 billion in 1996.

16. Some historical perspective is interesting. In 1980 only Japan had a "serious" trade imbalance problem (exports to the U.S. of $33 billion and imports from the U.S. of $21 billion). By 1987 Western Europe had a $24 billion trade surplus (on exports to the U.S. of $85 billion and imports from the U.S. of $61 billion), and West Germany accounted for $16 billion of Europe's trade surplus. But in 1987 Japan had a $60 billion trade surplus with the U.S. (on exports to the U.S. of $88 billion and imports from U.S. of $28 billion), Taiwan had a $21 billion trade surplus, and South Korea a $10 billion trade surplus. By 1996 the European imbalance was not that disproportionate, but large Mexican, Chinese, and other Asian country trade surpluses had developed—except that South Korea had a modest trade *deficit* with the U.S. of –$3 billion (see Table 1.2).

17. Some might say a tougher U.S. trade policy could provoke a "trade war." The best response is—"Hah, get real. Everybody knows there's been a trade war going on for twenty years. But the U.S. has been losing badly. Americans can no longer afford neglect, industrial erosion, and national decline. We must put our house in order, and rejuvenate the American economy."

18. The U.S. should be impartial, of course, in enforcing reciprocity-based trade policy. Corrective import fees should be imposed against any country (in any part of the world) with large, disproportionate trade surpluses in manufactured goods that is not equally open to U.S. manufactures and exports. However, a few large raw materials suppliers (e.g., Saudi Arabia or Venezuela) do not fit this characterization although the U.S. imports a lot from them. Trade imbalances with raw materials suppliers result merely from disproportionate natural resource endowments among countries.

19. For comparative industrial policy appraisals, see Reich and Magaziner 1982, Zysman and Tyson 1983, Adams and Klein 1983, Shepherd 1983, Johnson 1984, Lovett 1984, Eckstein 1984, Phillips 1984, Nelson 1984, Shutt 1985, Reich and Donahue 1985, Culbertson 1985, President's Commission 1985, Porter 1986, Cohen and Zysman 1987, Lodge and Vogel 1987, Lovett 1987, Rubner 1987, Kaden and Lee 1988, Prestowitz 1988, Kuttner 1989, Porter 1990, Lodge 1990, Derian 1990, Dertouzos 1990, Kaden and Smith 1992, Thurow 1992, Graham 1992, Hart 1994, OECD 1994, Faux and Schafer 1996, Forrant 1997, Japan Commission on Industrial Performance 1998.

20. For macroeconomic policy that incorporates industrial trade concerns, see Peterson and Estenson 1982, Lovett 1987, Kaden and Lee 1988, Kaden and Smith 1992,

Peterson 1992, Thurow 1992, Adler and Bernstein 1994, Faux and Schafer 1996, and Thurow 1996.

21. For the growing economic stress on U.S. politics, see Phillips 1984, Lodge and Vogel 1987, Prestowitz 1988, Friedman 1988, Fallows "More Like Us" 1989b, Stabile and Cantor 1991, Kuttner 1991, Thurow 1992, Calleo 1992, Peterson 1993, Phillips 1994, Drew 1994, Woodward 1994, Fukuyama 1995, Greenburg 1995, Walker 1996, Thurow 1996, Darman 1996, Johnson and Broder 1996, and Beinart 1997. See Adam Smith, *Wealth of Nations,* p. 81 (Modern Library).

22. See, particularly, with respect to deficits, Lovett 1987, Friedman 1988, Stein 1990, Stabile and Cantor 1991, Peterson 1993, Woodward 1994, Drew 1994, Phillips 1994, Greenburg 1995, and Darman 1996. For trade policy concerns, see Bluestone and Harrison 1982, Kuttner 1993, Phillips 1989, Johnson 1984, Culbertson 1985, President's Commission 1985, Lodge 1987, Lovett 1987, Kaden and Smith1988, Prestowitz 1988, Culbertson 1989, Kuttner 1989, Fallows 1989a, 1989b, Detourzos 1990, Lodge 1990, Kuttner 1991, Kearns 1992, Graham 1992, Thurow 1992, Blecker 1992, Lovett 1987, Adler and Bernstein 1994, Peterson 1994, Faux and Schafer 1996, and Thurow 1996.

23. See Haynes Johnson and Davis S. Broder, *The System: The American Way of Politics at the Breaking Point,* Boston: Little Brown, 1996.

24. Both the Dunkel draft Uruguay GATT Round agreement, and the final Uruguay GATT Round World Trade Organization Agreement had many hundreds of text pages. The legal language was highly technical, for the most part, and required extensive background understanding of the seven previous GATT round deals (1947–79), together with some familiarity with the massive accumulation of prior national trade concessions, reservations, and tariff rates.

25. The best books by far on post–World War II trade history were Alfred Eckes, *Opening America's Market,* 1995; and Steve Dryden, *Trade Warriors,* 1995. 1995. Both were published *after* Congress accepted GATT 1994 and the WTO Agreement.

26. For the House and Senate votes, see *Congressional Quarterly Weekly,* December 3, 1994, at 3469–71. Clearly, the NAFTA opposition would have been more successful in challenging GATT 1994 and the WTO Agreement. The Uruguay Round deal was full of asymmetries, non-reciprocity, and vulnerable to challenge on many details. If seriously attacked, GATT 1994 and the WTO would have been a much harder "sell" with Congress, and a solid majority could have been mobilized against it.

27. See, for example, Zysman and Tyson 1983, Nelson 1984, Eckstein 1984, Johnson 1984, Porter 1986, Lodge and Vogel 1987, Eckstein 1984, Prestowitz 1988, Porter 1990, Derian 1990, Lodge 1990, Dertouzos 1990, Graham 1992, Thurow 1992, Thurow 1996, and Forrant 1997.

28. See Eckes, *Opening America's Market,* 1995; and Dryden, *Trade Warriors,* 1995.

29. For the mission and style of the new agency, see Lodge and Vogel 1987 and Lodge 1990. The newly established DITT should take over the functions of the Office of the U.S. Trade Representative, together with most of the Commerce Department, including Office of the Secretary, Economics and Statistics Administration, Bureau of Economic Analysis, Census Bureau, Bureau of Export Administration, and Technology Administration. The domestic Economic Development Administration, Minority Business Development Agency, and Small Business Administration might be consolidated into a Domestic Business Promotion Agency. The National Oceanic and Atmospheric Administration (Weather Bureau) should become an independent scientific agency.

30. Among the most dramatic areas of U.S. industrial decline are the shipping and shipbuilding industries. The U.S. came out of World War II with the biggest shipbuilding effort in history, and nearly 60 percent of ocean-going tonnage. But through neglect,

kindness to allies (needing balance of payments revenues), and favors to flags of convenience vessels, the U.S. maritime sector became marginalized. By 1998 the U.S. accounts for less than 4 percent of world merchant tonnage (ranking fourth behind the EU, Japan, and China), and only 1.3 percent of world merchant shipbuilding. Japan, South Korea, China, and Taiwan now make nearly 75 percent of the world's merchant shipbuilding tonnage. And three-fourths of U.S. tonnage does not fly the U.S. flag; it sails under convenience registry. An emergency U.S. maritime revival effort is needed now. Only a cabinet-level Maritime Department can give the heft and visibility required. Its mandate must be to greatly enlarge the U.S. merchant marine, its share of world commerce, and U.S. shipbuilding. The Maritime Department must work hand-in-hand with DITT to expand U.S. exports, enlarge U.S. balance of payments earnings, and where appropriate, reduce U.S. imports and dependence upon foreign suppliers. For background, see Lovett, *United States Shipping Policies and the World Market,* 1996b.

31. On tax haven complications, see Tanzi, *Taxation in an Integrating World,* 1995; Jorgenson and Landau, eds., *Tax Reform and the Cost of Capital,* 1993; Hufbauer, *U.S. Taxation of International Income,* 1992; and Richards, "Offshore Financial Centers and Tax Havens," 1996. For these reasons it is easier, relatively speaking, to enforce adequate data on merchandise trade, real products, raw materials, components, and finished manufactured products, than on financial flows and services. This is especially so if a nominal import fee (say 1 percent) is imposed upon all merchandise imports. (See the section on monitoring and targets later in the chapter.)

32. See Report of the President's Commission on Industrial Competitiveness, *Global Competition: The New Reality,* Washington, DC, at pp. 41–42. Also, see Lovett, *World Trade Rivalry,* 1987, at pp. 89–90.

33. See Jackson 1995, Bhala 1996, Lovett 1994a, 1996c.

34. In Section 102 of the Uruguay Round Agreements Act of 1994 (codified as Title 19, 3512 of the U.S. Code), Congress provided that: "(1) U.S. LAW TO PREVAIL IN CONFLICT. No provision of any of the Uruguay Round Agreements, nor the application of any such provision to any person or circumstance, that is inconsistent with any law of the United States shall have effect. (2) CONSTRUCTION.—Nothing in this Act shall be construed—(A) to amend or modify any law of the United States, including any law relating to—(i) the protection of human, animal, or plant life or health, (ii) the protection of the environment, or (iii) worker safety, or (B) to limit any authority conferred under any law of the United States, including section 301 of the Trade Act of 1974, unless specifically provided for in this Act."

Yet the Agreement establishing the World Trade Organization, Article XVI, Miscellaneous Provisions, provided that: "4. Each member shall ensure the conformity of its laws, regulations and administrative procedures with its obligations as provided in the annexed agreements." Under U.S. implementing law, therefore, Congress clearly intended that U.S. law prevails over GATT 1994 and the WTO agreement.

35. WTO withdrawal is allowed for any member after six months' notice to the Director General. See Agreement Establishing the World Organization, Article XV (1994).

36. Extensive use by the U.S. of "trade sanctions," often to please splinter groups in politics, has become a problem for U.S. export competitiveness. See, for example, Haass, "Sanctioning Madness," 1997; Bernstein and Munro, *The Coming Conflict with China,* 1997; and Carter, *International Economic Sanctions: Improving the Haphazard U.S. Legal Regime,* 1988. Sanctions by one or only a few countries tend to be ineffectual. On the other hand, when a broader consensus among many nations supports sanctions, they can be more effective politically and economically.

37. During the mid-1980s increasing disharmony developed over U.S. trade policy, which continues through the later 1990s. Most of the AFL-CIO, their Congressional

supporters, most environmental organizations, and the leading consumer advocate (Ralph Nader) became strong critics of U.S. negotiators. This contrasts greatly with the general U.S. harmony and agreement over U.S. trade policy that prevailed in the late 1890s until 1913, a major growth and prosperity era, the roaring 1920s, and even 1940–early 1970s, a strong growth period, before heavier job losses and displacement affected Americans. The recent era, mid-1970s to 1998, illustrates a breakdown in effective teamwork and industrial collaboration in America. See, also, sources cited in notes 13, 19, 21, and 22 above.

38. Ibid.

39. See Eckes 1995, Dryden 1995, Lovett 1987, Lovett 1994a, and many unfair trade practice cases and safeguard proceedings brought under the U.S. trade laws (cited by Jackson et al., *International Economic Law,* 3d ed., 1995, or Bhala, *International Trade Law,* 1996).

40. See Jerome 1992, Lovett 1994a, and Mastel 1996.

41. There is some evidence, however, that a further acceleration of the U.S. stock market boom in 1996–98 combined with a transitory surge in the dollar's value, between the summer of 1995 into spring 1998, to lift real U.S. incomes for the past couple of years. Clearly, more foreign investment shifted medium-term into U.S. dollar investments as the yen and mark sagged, and as euphoria in emerging markets ebbed. Thus, a special short-term inflow of foreign liquidity added strength to what may be the "final" stages of a U.S. stock market bubble or speculative boom. This spilled over into a temporary up-surge in "U.S., Inc.," consumer incomes as against other countries. But, rather ominously, U.S. current account deficits grew even larger, U.S. export expansion stalled, and signs of dollar overvaluation were noticeable.

In the summer–fall of 1997 a series of financial strains, stock market slumps, and currency devaluations spread from Southeast Asia into South Korea, Japan, and other emerging markets. In the fall of 1997 the U.S. stock market suffered a moderate downward correction, with experts divided among bears, bulls, and the uneasy about future prospects. For good analysis of speculative mania and slumps, see Minsky 1982, Minsky 1986, Kindleberger 1993, Kindelberger 1997, Balder 1997, and Miller 1997. See also note 9 above.

42. See Peterson 1994, Phillips 1994, Marshall and Tucker 1992, Batra 1993, Vargish 1992, Newman 1993, Layard 1994, Madrick 1995, Korten 1995, Kuttner 1997, Galbraith 1997, Briggs 1992, Wolman and Colamosca 1997, Coote 1992, Greider 1997, Hirst and Thompson 1996, and Beinart 1997. And special attention has been focused upon these issues by Mishel and co-authors, *The State of Working America,* 1988, 1991, 1993, 1995, and 1997. Worth emphasizing is the substantial understatement of real unemployment (and underemployment) by the U.S. official unemployment statistics, which, broadly speaking, require unemployment compensation recipients to be actively seeking employment. Many of the unemployed are no longer eligible, are lost track of, drift into marginal unreported work, or become discouraged. Mishel and his co-authors consistently report a large understatement of real unemployment. This affects rural workers, urban workers, and especially blacks in the labor force. Many believe that real U.S. unemployment rates have been more like 9–10 percent (or more) in recent years, which helps explain the limited inflation pressure in recent years. These *real* U.S. unemployment rates are more like Western and Northern European structural unemployment rates.

43. In the fall of 1997, when Clinton failed to get expanded "fast-track" trade negotiation authority approved by the House of Representatives, polls were showing a public majority opposed. Too many families experienced wage stagnation, and feared job losses among friends or relatives. See John Harwood and Jackie Calmes, "Gephardt,

Fresh from Victory in Trade Scrap, Flexes His Muscles with Clinton," *Wall Street Journal,* November 12, 1997, at A24; "A *Wall Street Journal*/NBC News Poll last month, for example, shows 56% of Americans strongly or somewhat opposed to fast track, compared to 35% somewhat or strongly in favor."

44. Many European countries would have rejected Maastricht 1992 and the EMU if popular referenda had been held in every country. High structural unemployment and worries about job prospects for younger workers are widespread. And as financial strains, stock market slumps, and devaluations spread in Asia and other emerging markets during 1997, confidence in the global marketplace was eroding.

45. The public in Russia and Eastern Europe strongly felt that market progress, increased incomes, and broad prosperity were needed. The older Communist ways were discredited, but until solid improvements became entrenched there is widespread dissatisfaction.

46. See Wood 1992, McKinnon and Ohno 1997, Murphy 1997, and Japan Commission on Industrial Performance 1998. Also, see Burke 1995.

47. See Lovett 1996a.

48. See sources cited in notes 6, 9, and 41. And see Tables 5.1 and 5.2.

49. See, for example, Culbertson 1989, Kuttner 1991 and 1997, Goldsmith 1994, Mishel and others 1989–97, Godley 1995, Thurow 1992 and 1996, Faux and Schafer 1996, Phillips 1994, Choate and McMillion 1997, Thomas 1997, Beinart 1997, Lovett 1996c, Wolman and Colamosca 1997, and Greider 1997.

50. Other industrial data have been collected by the Department of Interior, Maritime Administration, Department of Agriculture, Treasury Department (Internal Revenue Service), the Federal Reserve system, U.S. International Trade Commission (formerly the U.S. Tariff Commission), and the U.S. Federal Trade Commission. This data base has spread internationally through more or less comparable information in the standardized industrial classification (the SITC) system.

51. Confidentiality of industrial reports by particular companies is safeguarded by government statistics-gathering agencies.

52. Transparency has been a legitimate goal of the IMF for many years, and this principle should be extended into trade activities (at least for summary data) as well.

53. In Mexico, Thailand, Malaysia, Indonesia, and the Philippines, it only took several years for this kind of a speculative boom to collapse with a major, costly, and inevitable correction. How much longer can the U.S. import, high dollar, and speculative boom sustain itself? Another "fundamental" problem with the U.S. economy has been low productivity growth since 1973. Annual U.S. productivity growth (non-farm) was only 1.3 percent between 1973 and 1980, 1.1 percent between 1981 and 1990, 1.1 percent between 1981 and 1990, and 1.1 percent between 1990 and 1997. *Business Week,* November 17, 1997, at p. 40. See also, Paul Krugman, *The Age of Diminished Expectations,* 1990, at pp. 12–13.

54. See John Kenneth Galbraith, *The Great Crash* (50th Anniversary Edition) 1979a; and Kindleberger 1993. Also, see sources cited note 41 above. Why had the U.S. boom surged so far in 1995–98? It was the conjunction of recent slowdowns and worries in the European and Japanese economies combined with a rather surprising turnabout in U.S. fiscal deficits. During 1995–97 Europe was troubled about meeting EMU convergence criteria, trying to cut budget deficits, and suffering the blues. Japan's yen went too far up in 1994–95, with its economy not recovered fully from the big downslide of the early 1990s. Accordingly, Japanese and German interest rates were reduced. Meanwhile, in the U.S. there was bitter partisan conflict over how to cut excessive budget deficits in 1994–95, which helped to bring the dollar to a record post-war low. But then in 1996–97 U.S. budget discipline actually improved, and the U.S. economy recovered somewhat. Meanwhile, the mood was sour in most of Europe and Japan. The 1996 U.S. election, in

an odd way, provided reassurance. After the re-election of Clinton with a Republican Congress, U.S. spending was constrained, moderate tax cuts were enacted, and reasonable ease could continue in monetary policy. In these circumstances, a further surge in the U.S. stock market occurred in 1997. Interestingly, financial crises in Southeast Asia (Thailand, Malaysia, Indonesia, and Philippines) in the summer–fall of 1997 cooled enthusiasm for many emerging markets, so that investment favor for the U.S. was actually accentuated, at least for the short-term.

55. Thurow, *The Future of Capitalism,* 1996. This book deserves much more professional and public attention than it has received so far. And see Tables 1.1–1.6, 5.1, and 5.2 of this text.

56. See Cairncross and Eichengreen, *Sterling in Decline: The Devaluations of 1931, 1949 and 1967,* 1983.

57. See Lovett 1987, Peterson 1994, Goldsmith 1994, Thurow 1996, and Beinart 1997, among many other works cited thus far. Also, for the urgency of industrial rejuvenation, see Choate and Schwartz 1980, Choate and McMillion 1997, Eckstein 1984, Cohen and Zysman 1987, Culbertson 1989, Dertouzos 1990, Prestowitz 1988, Kuttner 1991, and Graham 1992.

58. See the following: Kennedy, *Rise and Fall of Great Powers,* 1987; Huntington, *The Clash of Civilizations,* 1996; Crankshaw, *Bismarck,* 1981; Morganthau, *Politics among Nations,* 1954; Kissinger, *Diplomacy,* 1994; Crockatt, *The Fifty Years War,* 1996; Lehman, *Command of the Sea,* 1988; Lovett 1996b; Perry, *Four Stars,* 1989; Kohout, "Alternative Grand Strategy Options," 1995; Miller, "International Systems and Regional Security," 1995; Sheehan, *The Balance of Power,* 1995; Brzezinski, *Out of Control,* 1993; Allison and Treverton, *Rethinking America's Security,* 1992; Johnston, *Foreign Policy into the 21st Century,* 1996; Ruggie, *Winning the Peace,* 1996; Kennedy, *Preparing for the 21st Century,* 1993; Mandelbaum, *The Dawn of Peace in Europe,* 1996; Kennan, *At a Century's Ending,* 1996; "America's Defense Policy," *Economist,* 1997; Myers, "U.S. and Russians Put Off Deadline on Arms," 1997; IISS, *Military Balance, 1996–97 and 1997–98;* Joffee, "How American Does It," 1997; Huntington, "The Erosion of American National Interests," 1997; Beinart, "An Illusion for Our Time," 1997; Mahbubani, "Asia and a U.S. in Decline," 1994; Lewis, *China's Strategic Seapower,* 1994; Bernstein and Munro, *The Coming Conflict with China,* 1997; Dunlop, "Aleksandr Lebed and Russian Foreign Policy," 1997; Brzezinski, "Geostrategy for Eurasia," 1997; Nye, "What New World Order?" 1992; Bodansky, "The Grand Strategy of Iran," 1993; Esposito and Voll, *Islam and Democracy,* 1996; and Viorst, "Algeria's Long Night," 1997.

59. The Washington Naval Treaty of 1921 was a major British–U.S. arms control initiative to prevent a post-war naval arms race. Britain and the U.S. each were limited to 15 battleships, Japan could have 10 battleships, and soon after France and Italy each could have 5 battleships.

60. See Mikesell, *The Bretton Woods Debates: A Memoir,* 1994. And see Kindleberger 1993, Bordo with Eichengreen 1993, James 1996, Helleiner 1994, and the Bretton Woods Commission 1994. But see Solomon 1995, Dominguez and Frankel 1993, Cavanaugh 1994, and George and Sabelli 1994 for more critical views.

61. See Table 5.3.

62. This is a pity, because an IMF-style voting regime combined with stronger WTO safeguards, unfair trade practice remedies, and balance of payments relief (the original GATT 1947) would have allowed the U.S. to remain within the WTO. *Note:* Some WTO supporters (e.g., John Jackson) claim that WTO dispute settlement proceedings are a blessing of the new system. By August 1997, 100 trade disputes had been filed— 34 complaints by the U S and 21 by the EC, with 20 against the U.S. and 21 against the

EC. But most disputes involve only relatively narrow, minor issues. Hardly any impact on U.S. trade deficits, asymmetries, and unequal access is likely to result from these proceedings. Unfortunately, the major U.S. trade imbalance problems result from accumulated U.S. neglect of its industrial and trade interests over the past 20–25 years, a failure to assert rights under GATT and U.S. trade laws, and prior trade concessions by the U.S. In fact, WTO dispute settlement panels have their greatest impact as inhibiting the vigorous assertion of U.S. interests under U.S. trade laws. For recent tabulations on these dispute settlement proceedings, see *WTO Focus-Newsletter,* no. 20 and no. 21, June/July and August 1997.

63. See Donald Kagan, "Locarno's Lessons for NATO," 1997; Middlemas and Barnes, *Baldwin,* 1969.

64. See International Institute of Strategic Studies, *The Military Balance, 1996–97 and 1997–98,* 1997; "America's Defense Policy," *Economist,* 1997; James Schlesinger, "Nukes: Test Them or Lose Them," *Wall Street Journal,* November 19, 1997, at 22; and Report, National Academy of Sciences, "The Future of U.S. Nuclear Weapons Policy," *Arms Control Today,* May 1997, pp. 14–18. And see Myers, "U.S. and Russia Put Off Deadline on Arms," 1997.

65. See Bodansky, "The Grand Strategy of Iran," 1993; Esposito and Voll, *Islam and Democracy,* 1996; Viorst, "Algeria's Long Night," 1997. Also see Douglas Jehl, "Gulf Alliance: A Falling Out," *New York Times,* November 13, 1997, at A1, 6; Michael Gordon, "Russia and Iraq Draft Plan for Ending Gulf Crisis," *New Orleans, Times-Picayune,* November 19, 1997, at A14. And see Figure 5.1.

66. See Myers 1997, IISS 1997, Mandelbaum 1996, and Dunlop, 1997.

67. See Lewis and Xue 1994, Bernstein and Munro 1997, Mastel 1997, Jones 1992, Hwang 1991, and Wei 1994.

68. See Murphy 1997, MacKinnon and Ohno 1997, Wood 1992, Tsuru 1995, Funabashi 1994, Van Wolferen 1989, Prestowitz 1988, Burke 1995, and Judis 1997.

69. See Bergsten 1997, Livingston 1997, Eichengreen 1997, Feldstein 1997, and Erdman 1996.

70. See sources cited in notes 53–55 and 63–69, above; Tables 1.1–1.5, 5.1, and 5.2, and Figure 5.1.

71. See previous text, at pp. 148–151, 155–156, 164–172, and 172.

72. Conceivably, Taiwan, Korea, Australia, New Zealand, Sri Lanka, and Burma could join ASEAN. Meanwhile, Mercosur and an Andean Grouping might link most of South America. Or, NAFTA could expand into the Americas. Russia and other CIS members could be reconstituted (minus a few republics) as an economic-military bloc. Islamic states could form an Alliance (from among Iran, Egypt, Turkey, Syria, Jordan, Saudia Arabia, the Gulf States, Tunisia, Algeria, Morrocco, the Turkestans, Pakistan, and others).

73. The Cold War's predominance of only two giant super-powers, the U.S. and USSR, was really a short-lived (1946–91) historical anomaly. It was based upon unusual concentrations of nuclear weapons and other military power that proved unsustainable for the long term. See Kennedy 1987, Gaddis 1997, Crockatt 1996, Brzezinski 1993, Thurow 1992, Huntington 1996, Matlock 1995, and Thurow 1996.

References, Chapters 1 and 5

Adams, F. Gerard, and Lawrence R. Klein. 1983. *Industrial Policies for Growth and Competitiveness.* Lexington, MA: D.C. Heath, Lexington Books.
Aldcroft, Derek M. 1970. *The Inter-War Economy: Britain, 1919–1939.* New York: Columbia University Press.

Aliber, Robert Z. 1997. "The U.S. Trade Deficits Revisited." *Jobs and Capital* 6, no. 2 (Spring 1997): 7–13.

Allison, Graham and Gregory F. Treverton. 1992. *Rethinking America's Security: Beyond Cold War to New World Order.* American Assembly and Council on Foreign Relations. New York: W.W. Norton.

"America's Defence Policy: Absence of 2020 Vision," *Economist,* November 15, 1997, at 26–27.

Amsden, Alice. 1989. *Asia's Next Giant: South Korea and Late Industrialization.* New York: Oxford University Press.

Balder, John M., Jr. 1997. "Financial Market Volatility and Monetary Policy." *Challenge* 40, no. 6 (November–December 1997): 32–52.

Batra, Ravi, 1993. *The Pooring of America: Competition and the Myth of Free Trade.* New York: Collier Books, Macmillan.

Beck, Roy. 1996. *The Case Against Immigration: The Moral, Economic, Social and Environmental Reasons for Reducing U.S. Immigration Back to Traditional Levels.* New York: W.W. Norton.

Beinert, Peter. 1997. "An Illusion for Our Time: The False Promise of Globalization." *New Republic,* October 20, 1997, at 20–24.

Bergsten, C. Fred, ed. 1991. *International Adjustment Financing: The Lessons of 1985–1991.* Washington, DC: Institute for International Economics.

———. 1996. *Dilemmas of the Dollar: The Economics and Politics of United States Economic Policy.* 2d ed. Council on Foreign Relations. Armonk, NY: M.E. Sharpe,

———. 1997. "The Dollar and the Euro." *Foreign Affairs* 76, no. 4 (July/August): 83–95.

Bernstein, Michael A., and David E. Adler. 1994. *Understanding American Economic Decline.* New York: Cambridge University Press.

Bernstein, Richard, and Ross Munro. 1997. *The Coming Conflict with China.* New York: Alfred A. Knopf.

Bhala, Raj. 1996. *International Trade Law.* Charlottesville, VA: Michie.

Blecker, Robert A. 1992. *Beyond the Twin Deficits: A Trade Strategy for the 1990s.* Economic Policy Institute. Armonk, NY: M.E. Sharpe.

———. 1996. *U.S. Trade Policy and Global Growth: New Directions in the International Economy.* Economic Policy Institute. Armonk, NY: M.E. Sharpe.

Bluestone, Barry, and Bennett Harrison. 1982. *The Deindustrialization of America: Plant Closings, Community Abandonment, and the Dismantling of Basic Industry.* New York: Basic Books.

Bodansky, Yossef. 1993. "The Grand Strategy of Iran." *Global Affairs: The American Journal of Geopolitics* (Fall 1993): 19–36.

Bordo, Michael, with Barry Eichengreen. 1993. *A Retrospective on the Bretton Woods System: Lessons for International Monetary Reform.* Chicago: University Chicago Press.

Bretton Woods Commission. 1994. *Bretton Woods: Looking to the Future.* Washington, DC: Bretton Woods Committee.

Briggs, Vernon M., Jr. 1992. *Mass Immigration and the National Interest.* Armonk, NY: M.E. Sharpe.

Brittan, Samuel. 1995. *Capitalism with a Human Face.* Cambridge, MA: Harvard University Press.

Brzezinski, Zbigniew. 1993. *Out of Control: Global Turmoil on the Eve of the 21st Century.* New York, NY: Charles Scribner.

———. 1997. "A Geostrategy for Eurasia." *Foreign Affairs* 76, no. 5 (September–October): 50–64.

Burke, William M. 1995. "Rising Sun . . . Falling Dollar." *Challenge* 38, no. 4 (July–August): 46–51.

Cairncross, Alec, and Barry Eichengreen. 1983. *Sterling in Decline: The Devaluations of 1931, 1949 and 1967.* Oxford: Basil Blackwell.

Calleo, David P. 1992. *The Bankrupting of America: How the Federal Budget Is Impoverishing the Nation.* New York: William Morrow.

Carter, Barry. 1988. *International Economic Sanctions: Improving the Haphazard U.S. Legal Regime.* Cambridge: Cambridge University Press.

Cavanaugh, John, et al. 1994. *Beyond Bretton Woods: Alternatives to the Global Economic Order.* Institute for Policy Studies and Transnational Institute. London: Pluto Press.

Choate, Pat, and Charles McMillion. 1997. *The Mysterious U.S. Trade Deficit.* Occasional Paper. Washington, DC: Manufacturing Policy Project, May 1997.

Choate, Pat, and Gail Garfield Schwartz. 1980. *Being Number One: Rebuilding the U.S. Economy.* Lexington, MA: D.C. Heath, Lexington Books.

Cline, William R. 1984. *Exports of Manufactures from Developing Countries.* Washington, DC: Brookings Institution.

Cohen, Stephen, and John Zysman. 1987. *Manufacturing Matters: The Myth of the Post-Industrial Economy.* Council on Foreign Relations. New York: Basic Books.

Committee on Ways and Means. 1994. "The World Trade Organization." *Hearings,* U.S. House of Representatives, 103rd Congress, 2nd Session, June 10, 1994. Washington, DC: U.S. Government Printing Office, 1994.

Coote, Belinda. 1992. *The Trade Trap: Poverty and the Global Commodity Markets.* Oxford: Oxfam.

Crandall, Robert W. 1993. *Manufacturing on the Move.* Washington, DC: Brookings Institution.

Crankshaw, Edward. 1981. *Bismarck.* New York: Viking Press.

Crockatt, Richard. 1996. *The Fifty Years War: The U.S. and the Soviet Union in World Politics, 1941–1991.* London: Routledge.

Culbertson, John M. 1985. *The Trade Threat.* Madison, WI: 21st Century Press.

———. 1989. *The Trade Threat: And U.S. Trade Policy.* Madison, WI: 21st Century Press.

Darman, Richard. 1996. *Who's in Control: Polar Politics and the Sensible Center.* New York: Simon & Schuster.

Davis, Steven J., et al. 1996. *Job Creation and Destruction.* Cambridge, MA: MIT Press.

Derian, Jean-Claude. 1990. *America's Struggle for Leadership in Technology.* Cambridge, MA: MIT Press.

Dertouzos, Michael L., et al. 1990. *Made in America: Regaining the Productive Edge.* The MIT Commission on Industrial Productivity. Cambridge, MA: MIT Press.

Dobson, John M. 1976. *Two Centuries of Tariffs: The Background and Emergence of the United States International Trade Commission.* Washington, DC: U.S. International Trade Commission.

Dobson, Wendy. April 1991. *Economic Policy Coordination: Requiem or Prologue?* Washington, DC: Institute for International Economics.

Dominguez, Kathryn M., and Jeffrey A. Frankel. 1993. *Does Foreign Exchange Intervention Work?* Washington, DC: Institute for International Economics.

Dornbusch, Rudiger. 1988. *Exchange Rates and Inflation.* Cambridge, MA: MIT Press.

Drew, Elizabeth, 1994. *On the Edge: The Clinton Presidency.* New York: Simon & Schuster.

Dryden, Steve. 1995. *Trade Warriors: USTR and the American Crusade for Free Trade.* New York: Oxford University Press.

Dunlop, John B. 1997. "Aleksandr Lebed and Russian Foreign Policy." *SAIS Review* 17, no. 1 (Winter–Spring 1997): 47–72.

Eckes, Alfred E., Jr. 1995. *Opening America's Market: U.S. Foreign Trade Policy since 1776.* Chapel Hill: University of North Carolina Press.

———. 1997. "Evaluating the Fast-Track Debate." Speech, The Miller Center, University of Virginia, Charlottesville, October 28, 1997.

Eckley, Robert S. 1991. *Global Competition in Capital Goods: An American Prospective.* Westport, CT: Quorum Books.

Eckstein, Otto, et al. 1984. *The DRI Report on U.S. Manufacturing Industries.* Data Resources, Inc. New York: McGraw Hill.

Eichengreen, Barry. 1994. *International Monetary Arrangements for the 21st Century.* Washington, DC: Brookings Institution.

———. 1997. *European Monetary Unification.* Cambridge, MA: MIT Press.

Erdman, Paul. 1996. *Tug of War: Today's Global Currency Crisis.* New York: St. Martin's Press.

Esposito, John L., and John O. Voll. 1996. *Islam and Democracy.* New York: Oxford University Press.

Evans, John W. 1971. *The Kennedy Round in American Trade Policy: The Twilight of the GATT?* Cambridge, MA: Harvard University Press.

Fallows, James. 1989a. "Containing Japan." *Atlantic,* May 1989.

———. 1989b. *More Like Us: Making American Great Again.* Boston: Houghton Mifflin.

———. 1994. *Looking at the Sun: The Rise of New East Asian Economic and Political System.* New York: Pantheon Books.

Faux, Jeff. 1997. "NAFTA's Rules Don't Work: So Why Rush Down a Track to Extend Them to All of Latin America?" *EPI Journal* (Fall 1997): 1, 6. Washington, DC: Economic Policy Institute.

Faux, Jeff, and Todd Schafer, eds. 1996. *Reclaiming Prosperity: A Blueprint for Progressive Economic Reform.* Economic Policy Institute. Armonk, NY: M.E. Sharpe.

Feis, Herbert. 1930. *Europe: The World's Banker, 1870–1914.* Council on Foreign Relations. New Haven: Yale University Press.

Feldstein, Martin. 1992. "Europe's Monetary Union: The Case Against EMU," *Economist,* June 13.

———. 1997. "EMU and International Conflict." *Foreign Affairs* 76, no. 6 (November–December): 60–64.

Florida, Richard, and Martin Kenney. 1990. *The Breakthrough Illusion: Corporate America's Failure to Move from Innovation to Mass Production.* New York: Basic Books.

Forrant, Robert. 1997. *Good Jobs and the Cutting Edge: The U.S. Machine Tool Industry and Sustainable Prosperity.* Working Paper No. 199. Annadale on Hudson, NY: Jerome Levy Institute of Bard College.

Frieden, Jeffrey A., and David A. Lake, 1991. *International Political Economy: Perspectives on Global Power and Wealth.* 2d ed. New York: St. Martin's Press.

Friedman, Benjamin, 1988. *Day of Reckoning: The Consequences of American Economic Policy Under Reagan and After.* New York: Random House.

Fukao, Mitsuhiro. 1995. *Financial Integration, Corporate Governance, and the Performance of Multinational Companies.* Washington, DC: Brookings Institution.

Fukuyama, Francis. 1995. *Trust: The Social Virtues and the Creation of Prosperity.* New York: The Free Press.

Funabashi, Yoichi. 1989. *Managing the Dollar: From the Plaza to the Louvre.* 2d ed. Washington, DC: Institute for International Economics.

————. 1994. *Japan's International Agenda.* Japan Center for International Exchange. New York: New York University Press.

Gaddis, John Lewis. 1997. *We Now Know: Rethinking Cold War History.* Council on Foreign Relations. Oxford: Clarendon Press.

Galbraith, James K. 1997. *Dangerous Metaphor: The Fiction of the Labor Market: Unemployment, Inflation, and the Job Structure.* Public Policy Brief No. 3G. Annandale-on-Hudson, NY: Jerome Levy Institute of Bard College.

Galbraith, John Kenneth. 1979a. "The Founding Faith: Adam Smith's Wealth of Nations." Chapter 7. In *Annals of an Abiding Liberal.* Boston: Houghton Mifflin.

————. 1979b. *The Great Crash.* 50th Anniversary ed. New York: Avon and Houghton Mifflin.

George, Susan, and Fabrizio Sabelli. 1994. *Faith and Credit: The World Bank's Secular Empire.* Boulder, CO: Westview Press.

Godley, Wynne, 1995. *A Critical Imbalance in U.S. Trade.* Public Policy Brief No. 23. Annandale-on-Hudson, NY: Jerome Levy Institute of Bard College..

Goldsmith, Sir James. 1994. *The Trap.* New York: Carroll and Graf.

Graham, Edward M. 1996. *Global Corporations and National Governments.* Washington, DC: Institute for International Economics.

Graham, Otis L., Jr. 1992. *Losing Time: The Industrial Policy Debate.* Cambridge, MA: Harvard University Press.

Greenberg, Stanley B. 1995. *Middle Class Dreams: The Politics and Power of the New American Majority.* New York: Times Books, Random House.

Greider, William. 1997. *One World, Ready or Not: The Manic Logic of Global Capitalism.* New York: Simon & Schuster.

Grunwald, Joseph, and Kenneth Flamm. 1985. *The Global Factory: Foreign Assembly in International Trade.* Washington, DC: Brookings Institution.

Haass, Richard N. 1997. "Sanctioning Madness." *Foreign Affairs* 76, no. 6 (November–December): 74–85.

Hamilton, Alexander. 1791. *Report on the Subject of Manufactures.* Secretary of the Treasury. Philadelphia: William Brown, 1827.

Hart, Jeffrey A. 1994. "A Comparative Analysis of the Sources of America's Relative Economic Decline." Chapter 6. In Michael Bernstein and David Adler, eds., 1994.

————. 1992. *Rival Capitalists: International Competitiveness in the United States.* Ithaca, NY: Cornell University Press.

Helleiner, Eric. 1994. *States and the Reemergence of Global Finance: From Bretton Woods to the 1990s.* Ithaca, NY: Cornell University Press.

Henderson, W.O. 1983. *Friedrich List: Economist and Visionary, 1789–1846.* London: Frank Cass.

Hirst, Paul, and Grahame Thompson. 1996. *Globalization in Question: The International Economy and the Possibilities of Governance.* Cambridge: Polity Press.

Holbrooke, Richard. 1991. "Japan and the U.S.: The Unequal Partnership." *Foreign Affairs* 70, no. 5 (Winter 1991/92): 41–57.

Hossein-Zadeh, Esmail. 1995. "Rethinking the Trade–Currency Relationship." *Challenge* 38, no. 4 (July–August): 55–56.

Hufbauer, Gary Clyde, 1992. *U.S. Taxation of International Income.* Washington, DC: Institute for International Economics.

Hufbauer, Gary Clyde, and Joana Shelton Erb. 1984. *Subsidies in International Trade.* Institute for International Economics. Cambridge, MA: MIT Press.

Hufbauer, Gary Clyde, and Jeffrey J. Schott. 1993 *NAFTA: An Assessment.* Rev. ed. Washington, DC: Institute for International Economics.

Huntington, Samuel P. 1996. *The Clash of Civilizations and the Remaking of World Order.* New York: Simon & Schuster.

———. 1997. "The Erosion of American National Interests." *Foreign Affairs* 76, no. 5 (September–October): 28–49.

Hwang, Y. Dolly. 1991. *The Rise of a New World Economic Power: Postwar Taiwan.* Westport, CT: Greenwood Press.

International Institute for Strategic Studies. 1997. *The Military Balance, 1996–97 and 1997–98.* IISS. Oxford: Oxford University Press.

Jackson, John, ed. 1989. *Antidumping Law and Practice: A Comparative Study.* Ann Arbor: University of Michigan Press.

———. 1997. *The World Trading System: Law and Policy of International Economic Relations.* 2d ed. Cambridge, MA: MIT Press.

Jackson, John, et al. 1995. *International Economic Relations.* St. Paul: West.

James, Harold. 1996. *International Monetary Cooperation since Bretton Woods.* Washington, DC: International Monetary Fund; Oxford: Oxford University Press.

Japan Commission on Industrial Performance. 1998. *Made in Japan: A Guide to Restructuring Japanese Manufacturing.* Cambridge, MA: MIT Press.

Jerome, Robert W. 1992. *World Trade at the Cross-roads: The Uruguay Round, GATT, and Beyond.* Economic Strategy Institute. Washington, DC: University Press of America.

Joffee, Josef. 1997. "How America Does It." *Foreign Affairs* 76, no. 5 (September–October): 13–27.

Johnson, Chalmers, ed. 1984. *The Industrial Policy Debate.* San Francisco: Institute for Contemporary Studies.

Johnson, Haynes, and David Broder. 1996. *The System: The American Way of Politics at the Breaking Point.* Boston: Little, Brown.

Johnston, Douglas, ed. 1996. *Foreign Policy into the 21st Century: The U.S. Leadership Challenge.* Washington, DC: Center for Strategic and International Studies.

Jones, Randall. 1992. *The Chinese Economic Area: Economic Integration Without a Free Trade Agreement.* Paris: OECD, Department of Economics and Statistics.

Jorgenson, Dale, and Ralph Landau, eds. 1993. *Tax Reform and the Cost of Capital: An International Comparison.* Washington, DC: Brookings Institution.

Judis, John B. 1997. "The Sun also Rises: The Myth of Japan's Decline." *New Republic,* November 3, 1997, pp. 22–26.

Kaden, Lewis B., and Lee Smith. 1988. *The Cuomo Commission Report: A New American Formula for a Strong Economy.* New York: Simon & Schuster, Touchstone.

———. 1992. *America's Agenda: Rebuilding America's Strength.* Armonk, NY: M.E. Sharpe.

Kagan, Donald. 1997. "Locarno's Lessons for NATO." *Wall Street Journal,* October 28, 1997, A22.

Kearns, Robert. 1992. *Zaibatu America: How Japanese Firms Are Colonizing Vital U.S. Industries.* New York: Macmillan, The Free Press.

Kenen, Peter B. 1992. *EMU after Maastricht.* Washington, DC: Group of Thirty.

———, ed. 1994. *Managing the World Economy: Fifty Years after Bretton Woods.* Washington, DC: Institute for International Economics.

Kennan, George. 1996. *At a Century's Ending: Reflections, 1982–1995.* New York: W.W. Norton.

Kennedy, Paul. 1987. *The Rise and Fall of the Great Powers.* New York: Random House, Vintage.

———. 1993. *Preparing for the 21st Century.* New York: Random House.

Kidwell, David S., et al. 1997. *Financial Institutions, Markets, and Money.* 6th ed. Fort Worth, TX: Harcourt Brace, Dryden Press.

Kindleberger, Charles P. 1993. *A Financial History of Western Europe.* 2d ed. New York: Oxford University Press.

———. 1997. "Mania and How to Prevent Them." Interview. *Challenge* 40, no. 6 (November–December): 21–31.

Kissinger, Henry. 1994. *Diplomacy.* New York: Simon & Schuster.

Kitson, Michael, and Solomos Solomou. 1990. *Protectionism and Economic Revival: The British Interwar Economy.* Cambridge: Cambridge University Press.

Kohout, John J. III, et al. 1995. "Alternative Grand Strategy Options for the United States." *Comparative Strategy* 14: 361–420.

Korten, David C. 1995. *When Corporations Rule the World.* San Francisco: Berret-Koehler; West Hartford, CT: Kumarian Press.

Kosai, Yutaka. Translated by Jacqueline Kaminski. 1986. *The Era of High-Speed Growth: Notes on the Post War Japanese Economy.* Tokyo: University of Tokyo Press.

Krugman, Paul, ed. 1986. *Strategic Trade Policy and the New International Economics.* Cambridge, MA: MIT Press.

———. 1990. *The Age of Diminished Expectations: U.S. Economic Policy in the 1990s.* Cambridge, MA: MIT Press.

Kuo, Chich-Heng. 1991. *International Capital Movements and the Developing World: The Case of Taiwan.* New York: Praeger.

Kuttner, Robert. 1983. "The Free Trade Fallacy." *New Republic,* March 28, 1983, pp. 16–21.

———. 1989. *Managed Trade and Economic Sovereignty.* Washington, DC: Economic Policy Institute.

———. 1991. *The End of Laissez-Faire: National Purpose and the Global Economy after the Cold War.* New York: Alfred A. Knopf.

———. 1997. "Workers on the Auction Block: Is Labor Just a Market?" *Working USA* (May–June 1997).

Lamont, Douglas F. 1986. *Forcing Our Hand: America's Trade Wars in the 1980s.* Lexington, MA: Lexington Books.

Lawrence, Robert Z., and Schultze, eds. 1990. *An American Trade Strategy: Options for the 1990s.* Washington, DC: Brookings Institution.

Layard, Richard, et al. 1994. *The Unemployment Crisis.* Oxford: Oxford University Press.

Lehman, John F. 1988. *Command of the Sea.* New York: Scribner's.

Leigh, Duane E. 1990. *Does Training Work for Displaced Workers: A Survey of Existing Experience.* Kalamazoo, MI: W.E. Upjohn Institute for Industrial Research.

Lewis, John Wilson, and Litai Xue. 1994. *China's Strategic Seapower: The Politics of Force Modernization in the Nuclear Age.* Stanford: Stanford University Press.

List, Friedrich. Translated by Sampson S. Lloyd. 1841. *The National System of Political Economy.* Reprint. Fairfield, NJ: Augustus M. Kelley, 1991.

Livingston, Robert Gerald. 1997. "Life after Kohl?" *Foreign Affairs* 76, no. 6 (November–December): 2–7.

Lockwood, William W., ed. 1965. *The State and Economic Enterprise in Japan: Essays in the Political Economy of Growth.* Princeton: Princeton University Press.

Lodge, George C. 1990. *Perestroika for America: Restructuring Business–Government Relations for World Competitiveness.* Boston: Harvard Business School Press.

Lodge, George C. and Ezra F. Vogel, eds. 1987. *Ideology and National Competitiveness: An Analysis of Nine Countries.* Boston: Harvard Business School Press.

Lovett, William A. 1982. *Inflation and Politics: Fiscal, Monetary, and Wage–Price Discipline.* Lexington, MA: Lexington Books, D.C. Heath.

———. 1984. "Competitive Industrial Policies and the World Bazaar." Subcommitee on Economic Stabilization, Committee on Banking, Finance, and Urban Affairs, U.S. House of Representatives, 98th Congress, 2d Session. Washington, DC: U.S. Government Printing Office, November 1984.

———. 1984, 1988, 1992, and 1997. *Banking and Financial Institutions Law.* 1st ed. 1984, 2d ed. 1988, 3rd ed. 1992, and 4th ed. 1997. St. Paul: West.

———. 1987. *World Trade Rivalry: Trade Equity and Competing Industrial Policies.* Lexington, MA: D.C. Heath, Lexington Books.

———. 1993. "Rethinking U.S. Industrial-Trade Policy in the Post–Cold War Era." *Tulane Journal of International and Comparative Law* 1 (Spring 1993): 135–189.

———. 1994a. "Current World Trade Agenda: GATT, Regionalism, and Unresolved Asymmetry Problems." *Fordham Law Review* 52, no. 7 (May 1994): 2001–2045.

———. 1994b. Testimony and Statement. "The World Trade Organization." *Hearings,* Committee on Ways, and Means, U.S. House of Representatives, 103rd Congress, 2nd Session, June 10, 1994. Washington, DC: U.S. Government Printing Office.

———. 1996a. "Lessons from the Recent Peso Crisis in Mexico." *Tulane Journal of International and Comparative Law* 4, no. 2 (Summer 1996): 143–159.

———, ed. 1996b. *United States Shipping Policies and the World Market.* Westport, CT: Greenwood Press, Quorum Books.

———. 1996c. "World Trade Policies: Limits on Economic Integration." In *International Market Change and the Law.* Ed. Jukka Mähönen; Vol. 2, No. 1: 151–193. Turku, Finland: Turku Law School.

McCraw, Thomas K., ed. 1989. *America Versus Japan: A Comparative Study.* Boston: Harvard Business School Press.

McKinnon, Ronald I. 1996. *The Rules of the Game. International Money and Exchange Rates.* Cambridge, MA: MIT Press.

McKinnon, Ronald, and Kenichi Ohno. 1997. *Dollar and Yen. Resolving Economic Conflict Between the United States and Japan.* Cambridge, MA: MIT Press.

Madrick, Jeffrey. 1995. *The End of Affluence: The Causes and Consequences of America's Economic Dilemma.* New York: Random House.

Mahbubani, Kishore. 1994. "Asia and a United States in Decline." *Washington Quarterly* 17, no. 2 (Spring 1994): 5–23. Washington, DC: Center for Strategic and International Studies.

Mandelbaum, Michael. 1996. *The Dawn of Peace in Europe.* New York: Twentieth Century Fund Press.

Markusen, Ann, and Catherine Hill. 1992. *Converting the Cold War Economy: Investing in Industries, Workers, and Communities.* Washington, DC: Economic Policy Institute.

Marshall, Alfred. 1923. *Money, Credit, and Commerce.* London: Macmillan. See Ch. XI (Infant Industry Tariffs), pp. 210–224.

Marshall, Ray, and Marc Tucker. 1992. *Thinking for a Living: Education and the Wealth of Nations.* New York: Basic Books.

Mastel, Greg. 1996. *American Trade Laws after The Uruguay Round.* Armonk, NY: M.E. Sharpe, Inc.

———. 1997. *The Rise of the Chinese Economy: The Middle Kingdom Emerges.* Economic Strategy Institute. Armonk, NY: M.E. Sharpe.

Matlock, Jack F. 1995. *Autopsy of an Empire: The American Ambassador's Account of the Collapse of the Soviet Union.* New York: Random House.

Middlemas, Keith, and John Barnes. 1969. *Baldwin: A Biography.* London: Weidenfeld and Nicolson, and later, Macmillan.

Mikesell, Raymond F. 1994. *The Bretton Woods Debates: A Memoir.* No. 192. Princeton: International Finance Section.

Miller, Benjamin. 1995. "International Systems and Regional Security: From Competition to Cooperation, Dominance or Disengagement?" *Journal of Strategic Studies* 18, no. 2 (June): 52–100.

Miller, James P. 1997. "Buffet Sounds Cautious Note About Stocks," "Heard on the Street." *Wall Street Journal,* May 6, 1997, at C1, 2.

Minsky, Hyman P. 1982. *Can "It" Happen Again? Essays on Instability and Finance.* Armonk, NY: M.E. Sharpe.

———. 1986. *Stabilizing an Unstable Economy.* New Haven: Yale University Press.

Mishel, Lawrence, and Jared Bernstein. 1993. *The State of Working America, 1992–93.* Economic Policy Institute. Armonk, NY: M.E. Sharpe.

———. 1995. *The State of Working America, 1994–95.* Economic Policy Institute. Armonk, NY: M.E. Sharpe.

Mishel, Lawrence, and David M. Frankel. 1991. *The State of Working America, 1990–91.* Economic Policy Institute. Armonk, NY: M.E. Sharpe.

Mishel, Lawrence and Jacqueline Simon. 1988. *The State of Working America.* Washington, DC: Economic Policy Institute.

Mishel, Lawrence, Jared Bernstein, and John Schmitt 1997. *The State of Working America, 1996–97.* Economic Policy Institute. Armonk, NY: M.E. Sharpe.

Morganthau, Hans J. 1954. *Politics among Nations: The Struggle for Power and Peace.* New York: Alfred A. Knopf.

Morici, Peter. 1997. *The Trade Deficit: Where Does It Come From and What Does It Do?* Washington, DC: Economic Strategy Institute, October.

Murphy, R. Taggart. 1997. *The Weight of the Yen.* New York: W.W. Norton.

Myers, Steven Lee. 1997. "U.S. and Russians Agree to Put Off Deadline on Arms—New Accords Give Moscow until 2007 to Dismantle Its Launch Systems." *New York Times,* September 27, 1997, at A1, 5.

Nelson, Richard R. 1984. *High-Technology Policies: A Five-Nation Comparison.* Washington, DC: American Enterprise Institute.

Newman, Katherine S. 1993. *Declining Fortunes: The Withering of the American Dream.* New York: Basic Books.

Nye, Joseph S. 1992. "What New World Order?" *Foreign Affairs* 71, no. 2. (Spring 1992): 83–96.

Organization for Economic Cooperation and Development. 1994. *Industrial Policy in OECD Countries: Annual Review 1994.* Paris: OECD.

———. 1997. *Implementing the OECD Jobs Strategy: Member Countries Experience.* Paris: OECD.

Perot, Ross, with Pat Choate. 1993. *Save Your Job, Save Our Country: Why NAFTA Must Be Stopped—Now!* New York: Hyperion.

Perry, Mark. 1989. *Four Stars: The Inside Story of the Forty-Year Battle Between the Joint Chiefs of Staff and America's Civilian Leaders.* Boston: Houghton Mifflin.

Peterson, Peter G. 1993. *Facing Up: How to Rescue the Economy from Crushing Debt and Restore the American Dream.* New York: Simon & Schuster.

Peterson, Wallace C. 1982. *Our Overloaded Economy: Inflation, Unemployment, and the Crisis in American Capitalism.* Armonk, NY: M.E. Sharpe.

———. 1994. *Silent Depression: The Fate of the American Dream.* New York: W.W. Norton.

Peterson, Wallace C., and Paul Estenson. 1992. *Income, Employment, and Economic Growth.* 7th ed. New York: W.W. Norton.

Phillips, Kevin. 1984. *Staying on Top: The Business Case for a National Industrial Strategy.* New York: Random House.

———. 1994. *The Arrogant Capital: Washington, Wall Street and the Frustrations of American Politics.* Boston: Little, Brown.

Podgursky, Michael. 1989. *Job Displacement and the Rural Worker.* Washington, DC: Economic Policy Institute.

Porter, Michael E., ed. 1986. *Competition in Global Industries.* Boston: Harvard Business School.

Porter, Michael E. 1990. *The Competitive Advantage of Nations.* New York: Macmillan, The Free Press.

Pozo, Susan, ed. 1996. *Exploring the Underground Economy: Studies of Unreported and Illegal Activity.* Kalamazoo, MI: Upjohn Institute for Employment Research.

President's Commission on Industrial Competitiveness. January. 1985. *Global Competition: The New Reality, Vol. I and II.* Report of the President's Commission on Industrial Competitiveness. Washington, DC: U.S. Government Printing Office.

Prestowitz, Clyde V. 1988. *Trading Places: How We Allowed Japan to Take the Lead.* New York: Basic Books.

Radelet, Steven and Jeffrey Sachs. 1997. "Asia's Re-emergence." *Foreign Affairs* 76, no. 6 (November–December): 44–49.

Reich, Robert B. 1991a. "The Real Economy." *Atlantic Monthly,* February 1991.

———. 1991b. *The Work of Nations: Preparing Ourselves for 21st Century Capitalism.* New York: Alfred A. Knopf.

Reich, Robert B., and John D. Donahue. 1985. *New Ideas: The Chrysler Revival and the American System.* New York: Times Books, Random House.

Reich, Robert B., and Ira Magaziner. 1982. *Minding America's Business: The Decline and Rise of the American Economy.* New York: Harcourt Brace Jovanovich.

Richards, William Le Gro, Jr. 1996. "Offshore Financial Centers and Tax Havens." Unpublished doctoral dissertation for S.J.D. Program. New Orleans, LA: Tulane Law School.

Root, Franklin R. 1994. *International Trade and Investment.* 7th ed. Cincinnati: South-Western.

Rubner, Alex. 1987. *The Export Cult: A Global Display of Economic Distortions.* Boulder, CO: Westview Press.

Ruggie, John Gerard. 1996. *Winning the Peace: America and World Order in the New Era.* Twentieth Century Fund. New York: Columbia University Press.

Scherer, F.M. 1992. *International High-Technology Competition.* Cambridge, MA: Harvard University Press.

Schott, Jeffrey J. 1990. *Completing the Uruguay Round: A Results-Oriented Approach to the GATT Trade Negotiations.* Washington, DC: Institute for International Economics.

———. 1994. *The Uruguay Round: An Assessment.* Washington, DC: Institute for International Economics.

———, ed. 1996. *The World Trading System: Challenges Ahead.* Washington, DC: Institute for International Economics.

Sheehan, Michael. 1995. *The Balance of Power: History and Theory.* London: Routledge.

Shepherd, Geoffrey. 1983. *Europe's Industries: Public and Private Strategies for Change.* Ithaca: Cornell University Press.

Shutt, Harry. 1985. *The Myth of Free Trade: Patterns of Protectionism since 1945.* Oxford and London: Basil Blackwell and The Economist Publications.

Smith, Adam. 1776. *Wealth of Nations.* New York: Modern Library, 1937.

Solomon, Steven. 1995. *The Confidence Game: How Unelected Central Bankers Are Governing the Changed Global Economy.* New York, NY: Simon & Schuster.

Stabile, Donald R., and Jeffrey A. Cantor. 1991. *The Public Debt of the United States: An Historical Perspective, 1775–1990.* New York: Praeger.

Starr, Martin K., ed. 1988. *Global Competitiveness: Getting the U.S. Back on Track.* New York: W.W. Norton.

Stein, Herbert. 1990. *The Fiscal Revolution in America.* Rev. ed. Washington, DC: AEI Press.

Suro, Roberto. 1996. *Watching America's Door: The Immigration Backlash and the New Policy Debate.* New York: Twentieth Century Fund Press.

Tanzi, Vito. 1995. *Taxation in an Integrating World.* Washington, DC: Brookings Institution.

Templeton, Paul, ed. 1993. *The European Currency Crisis.* Cambridge: Probus.

Thomas, Rich. 1997. "Why the United States Is Doomed to Deficits and U.S. Workers to Sweat." *Jobs and Capital* 6, no. 2 (Spring 1997): 14–21.

Thurow, Lester L. 1992. *Head to Head: The Coming Economic Battle Among Japan, Europe, and America.* New York: William Morrow.

———. 1996. *The Future of Capitalism: How Today's Economic Forces Shape Tomorrow's World.* New York: William Morrow.

Tolchin, Martin, et al. 1993. *Buying Into America: How Foreign Money Is Changing the Face of Our Nation.* Washington, DC: Farragut.

Tsuru, Shigeto. 1995. *Japan's Capitalism: Creative Defeat and Beyond.* Cambridge: Cambridge University Press.

Tyson, Laura D'Andrea, 1993. *Who's Bashing Whom? Trade Conflict in High-Technology Industries.* Washington, DC: Institute for International Economics.

Van Wolferen, Karel. 1989. *The Enigma of Japanese Power: People and Politics in a Stateless Nation.* New York: Alfred A. Knopf.

Vargish, George. 1988. *What's Made in the USA?* New Brunswick, NJ: Transaction Books.

———. 1992. *Where Have All The Jobs Gone?* Highland City, FL: Rainbow Press.

Viorst, Milton. 1997. "Algeria's Long Night." *Foreign Affairs* 76, no. 6 (November–December): 86–99.

Volcker, Paul A., and Toyoo Gyohten. 1992. *Changing Fortunes: The World's Money and the Threat to American Leadership.* New York: Times Books, Random House.

Walker, Martin. 1996. *The President We Deserve: Bill Clinton, His Rise, Falls, and Comebacks.* New York: Crown.

Wallach, Lori. 1997. "Who Needs Fast Track?" Opinion, *Journal of Commerce,* September 19, 1997.

Wei, Jia. 1994. *Chinese Foreign Investment Laws and Policies: Evolution and Transformation.* Westport, CT: Greenwood Press, Quorum Books.

Winham, Gilbert R. 1986. *International Trade and the Tokyo Round Negotiation.* Princeton: Princeton University Press.

Witt, Matt, and Steve Trossman. 1997. "NAFTA, Round Two." *Working USA* (September–October).

Wolman, William, and Anne Colamosca. 1997. *The Judas Economy: The Triumph of Capital, and the Betrayal of Work.* Reading, MA: Addison-Wesley.

Wood, Christopher. 1992. *The Bubble Economy: Japan's Extraordinary Speculative Boom of the 80s and the Dramatic Bust of the 90s.* New York: Atlantic Monthly Press.

Woodward, Bob. 1994. *The Agenda: Inside the Clinton White House.* New York: Simon & Schuster.

Yamamura, Kozo. 1982. *Policy and Trade Issues of the Japanese Economy: American and Japanese Perspectives.* Seattle: University of Washington Press.

Zysman, John, and Laura D'Andrea Tyson, eds. 1983. *American Industry in International Competition: Government Policies and Corporate Strategies.* Ithaca: Cornell University Press.

Index

About the Authors

All three authors have extensive trade backgrounds. **William A. Lovett** is a lawyer (J.D. New York University) and economist (M.A. Harvard, Ph.D. Michigan State University). He worked in the Antitrust Division, U.S. Department of Justice (1962) and the Federal Trade Commission (1963–69) as a lawyer and industrial organization economist. Since 1969 Lovett has taught at Tulane Law School; there he is presently Joseph Merrick Jones Professor of Law and Economics, and Director, International Law, Trade, and Finance Program. His principal work has been economic regulation, antitrust, financial institutions, and international trade–finance. He has lectured or taught abroad in Britain, Ireland, Sweden, Finland, France, Germany, Netherlands, Switzerland, Italy, Greece, Japan, China, Korea, Taiwan, Thailand, Singapore, the Philippines, Canada, and Jamaica. Lovett's books on economic and trade policy include: *Inflation and Politics: Fiscal, Monetary, and Wage–Price Discipline* (1982); *Banking and Financial Institutions Law* (four editions, 1984–97); *Competitive Industrial Policies and the World Bazaar,* Staff Report, U.S. House of Representatives (1984); *World Trade Rivalry: Trade Equity and Competing Industrial Policies* (1987); and *U.S. Shipping Policies and the World Market* (1996). In June 1994 Lovett was a lead witness on GATT 1994 and the WTO before the U.S. House Ways and Means Committee in one of the few Congressional hearings on this matter.

Alfred E. Eckes Jr., has an M.A. from the Fletcher School of Law and Diplomacy, and a Ph.D. in history from the University of Texas. He wrote his dissertation on the Bretton Woods international monetary system. His academic work has been mainly in contemporary economic and diplomatic history at Ohio State University (1969–79) and as Ohio Eminent Research Professor in Contemporary History at Ohio University (1990–present). From 1979 to 1981 he served as Executive Director of the U.S. House of Representatives Republican Conference and was appointed as a Commissioner of the U.S. International Trade Commission (1981–90), serving as

Chairman between 1982 and 1984. Eckes has published three books on U.S. trade policy, *A Search for Solvency: Bretton Woods and the International Monetary System, 1941–1971* (1975); *The U.S. and the Global Struggle for Minerals* (1979); and *Opening America's Market: U.S. Foreign Trade Policy Since 1776* (1995). This last is now a leading work on the history of U.S. trade policy.

Richard L. Brinkman began his work in biology (B.A. Rutgers, 1953), but switched to economics (B.A. Rutgers, 1954; Ph.D. Rutgers, 1965). His dissertation was on the European Common Market. Brinkman also earned an M.A. from the Fletcher School of Law and Diplomacy. An outstanding teacher at Portland State University since 1965, Brinkman's specialties have been international economics, economic history, economic development, and cultural economics. He has taught and lectured extensively abroad, including Germany, Japan, China, South Africa, Canada, and Scandinavia. Brinkman's work emphasizes institutionalism and social economics, stressing the incompleteness of neoclassical economic models for international trade. He has been active in the Association for Evolutionary Economics (AFEE) and the Association for Social Economics (ASE), and has authored seventy-five articles and papers for professional journals and meetings, together with a book, *Cultural Economics* (1981).

All three authors support expanding world trade, capital flows, and technology transfers. We believe the "global economy" is well established with many blessings for humanity. But a naïve dichotomy between *complete free trade* (not really used by many countries) and *general protectionism* clouds understanding. The world reality is an asymmetrical network of trading relations, with the United States being the most open major market, while the majority of the world is more restricted (including Japan, China, Russia, and most developing countries.) We insist that recent U.S. trade policy erred in neglecting reciprocity interests and in failing to maintain overall U.S. trade balance. Chronic U.S. current account and trade deficits were neither necessary nor desirable in promoting a healthy growth for world trade and broader economic development. Now the time has come for U.S. trade policies to support a more realistic, balanced, and sustainable pattern of world trade growth. This is urgent, not only for Americans, but for the whole world.